To freda

Italy? It Seemed Like a Good Idea at the Time

On behalf of Farha
with love & best wishes

HAPPY BIRTHDAY FREDA

Happy reading
Simon Gogg

First published in Australia in 2008 by
New Holland Publishers (Australia) Pty Ltd
Sydney * Auckland * London * Cape Town

1/66 Gibbes Street, Chatswood NSW 2067
218 Lake Road, Northcoate, Auckland New Zealand
86 Edgeware Road, London W2 2EA United Kingdom
80 McKenzie Street, Cape Town 8001 South Africa

A record of this title is available from the National Library of Australia.
ISBN 9781741106954

Publisher: Fiona Schultz
Publishing Manager: Lliane Clarke
Production Manager: Linda Bottari
Design: Tania Gomes
Proofreader: Christine Chua
Printer: Ligare Book Printers, Sydney, Australia
Cover photograph: Getty Images

10 9 8 7 6 5 4 3 2 1

Disclaimer

No research materials were harmed during the making of this book.

The Website of the Book

Go to simoncapp.com to see all the photos from the book. While you're there you can test your knowledge on the Readers' Quiz, download some of Ivana's recipes, try your hand at the fun and games, explore the useful links, listen in to Radio Italia, post a message, have a look through the Extras and...other stuff.

Italy? It Seemed Like a Good Idea at the Time

OR

Come Imparai A Non Preoccuparmi E Ad Amare Il Latte Macchiato
(How I Learned to Stop Worrying and Love the Latte Macchiato)

SIMON CAPP

NEW HOLLAND

Acknowledgements

It's been great fun retelling this story to the computer and along the way reliving all the fabulous (and not-so-fabulous) experiences of our time in Italy. To think that others might one day get to read these chapters and share in the experiences makes me feel proud and humble, and also extremely grateful to all those involved in the process of transforming my words from a sad little text file into the chunky tome you now hold in your hands.

In particular I should like to give thanks to: My long-suffering project editor Lliane Clarke, and the team at New Holland; my astute literary agent Margaret Connolly, without whom this book would never have seen the light of day; the mighty Tim Richards, whose service went beyond the call of duty (i.e. he didn't get paid properly); Alessandra Argese, Charlie Caldas, Carolyn Cuming, Michelle Giacobello, Susie Kennewell and Euan Mitchell, for advice and contributions; Marius and Christine, for being so endlessly helpful and informative; and Ivana and Raffaello and the extended family—*grazie per tutto.*

And of course I am indebted to my wonderful wife Eleni, for your love and support and encouragement throughout, and to my children Ruby and Felix, for coming along for the ride.

While I'm at it may I also take this opportunity to thank those friends and family who suffered through a year's worth of interminably long emails that formed the basis of this book, as well as anyone anywhere who has ever bought a book about living in Italy, travelling to Italy or eating pizza, thus helping to sustain the literary juggernaut bandwagon onto which I have unashamedly jumped.

Simon Capp
March 2008

Glossary

Fancy Italian words

agritourismo: farm-stay accommodation
avvocato: lawyer (not to be confused with avocado)
bar: café and pub all rolled into one
biscottate: dry biscuits used to support small mountains of Nutella
campanile: bell-tower
campanilismo: love for one's bell-tower (= local pride)
centesimi: cents (in the new-fangled Euro currency)
cornetto/i: croissant/s
crostata: huge lake of jam or Nutella with pastry underneath
gasolio: heating oil
latté macchiato: equivalent to an Australian caffé latte
mentalità: something that Umbrians have
pane salato: salted (ie proper) bread
pomorola: all-purpose tomato base
presepio/i: nativity scene/s
sandwich: small roll
sbandieratori: performers in the synchronised flag-waving ceremony
scuola materna: kindergarten
vasca: lap (of the main street)

Acronyms

HGV: Hulking Great Volvo
SWGTD: Signora Who Gets Things Done

Official nomenclature

Comune: local council
Carabinieri: local police
Questura: immigration police
Polizia Stradale: highway police
Guardia di Finanza: Finance Police
Codice Fiscale: tax file number

Contents

Prologue

'You told me…' he intones slowly '...that you were staying for a whole year.'

'But that was before the fridge,' I protest, 'and the television, and the kitchen chairs and the heating oil and all the rest. We've had enough of this. We're moving out.'

Strangely, the wizened old prune isn't surprised to hear this. No doubt he thinks that I'm bluffing, and that once we've sorted out the latest dispute we'll be grateful as always for his magnanimity in providing a roof over our heads. Time to crank it up a notch.

'And by the way you owe us over 300 Euros,' I venture boldly, brandishing my sheet of calculations.

There's that thin, watery smile again. Clearly we won't be getting our money back without a struggle.

Patiently I go through the sums, trying not to be unnerved by the stony silence. When he finally ventures to speak, it is to reject the figures outright and counter instead that it is we who owe *him* money. The temerity of the man! There's no point in carrying on; it will only escalate into yet another heated argument, another throbbing headache.

This is not how things were meant to turn out. Curse you Valfabbrica, unlovely isolated backwater peopled with narrow-minded greedy opportunistic tourism hacks. I see now that the whole thing was a mistake, an ill-advised and misguided attempt to be adventurous. We should never have trusted that travel agent. We should never have kept trying so hard, for so long, to make it work out.

We should never have left home.

Too late now though; nothing for it but to cut my losses and get out. Though not without one last salvo: 'Don't forget you owe me money!'

'I'm not paying you a cent,' he retorts.

'Righto then, let's sort this out with the Carabinieri,' and I storm out.

He's still shouting at me, 'Go ahead then, call in the Carabinieri!' as I slam the door, nice and hard. I can picture the smile on his face; he'd be in there chuckling away to himself, convinced that once again I'm too feeble to see it through.

But not this time.

A new phase in the Italian Odyssey is about to begin.

1
Arriving

Valfabbrica is not a pretty town. In fact it's hardly a town at all, more a series of drab post-war buildings strung along the main road through the valley, which doubles as the trunk route between Perugia and Ancona and carries a steady stream of trucks and trailers all day long. The name Valfabbrica means Valley of the Factories, and the founding fathers clearly took this to heart, for in addition to the official industrial zone throbbing and churning away on the outskirts of town there are several more factories belching smoke right in the centre for good measure.

Being the administrative base for the local region, Valfabbrica boasts a modern council complex and school building, hideous 70s-era monstrosities featuring cutting-edge design aesthetics that suggest the civic authorities had only just discovered the exciting visual and structural possibilities of concrete. Most of the houses and shops along the main road date from the same period and display a similar fascination with concrete.

Meanwhile, the Medieval Bit is confined to a few squares of houses squashed together uncomfortably in the shadow of the factories. At one end is a potentially interesting old edifice that may be a clock tower, although we cannot tell because it is under reconstruction and will not be open until next year.

There's no central piazza, only a small spot with a fountain to one side of the road which is roundly ignored by the locals. The actual centre of town is the sharp ninety-degree turn in the road right in front of the butcher's shop where the trucks have to slow down virtually to a halt, spitting and hissing at the absurd inconvenience of it all, before gearing back up noisily and speeding off into the hills.

In terms of places to eat, Valfabbrica boasts a handful of scruffy cafés, a couple of bakeries and a lone pizzeria which (at the moment at least) doubles as the only restaurant for miles around. No wonder we could never find this place in the guide books—far from being the beautiful undiscovered hamlet that we were imagining, it has nothing whatsoever to recommend it to the tourist. Or to your average Italian citizen if you ask me.

How on earth did we end up here?

It seemed like a good idea at the time: a year in Italy, land of pizza, piazzas and palazzos. It could have been anywhere really. I work as a translator; my job is to turn inscrutable Japanese documents into less inscrutable English documents. Thanks to the internet, the ancient art of translation is now a truly global, borderless, twenty-first century profession. To my clients in Tokyo, I could just as well be across the street as at home in Melbourne. Most of them I have never met face to face. No matter; so long as they keep sending me Japanese documents and I keep sending back English ones, all parties are satisfied. So in theory, a translator should be able to work anywhere in the world that has an electricity supply and a phone line.

Several years ago it was decided that we as a family would put this very theory to the test by spending a year overseas. What prompts a mild-mannered family from suburban Melbourne to venture across the globe to a part of the world about which they know nothing? It's not as if we're inveterate travellers. I spent a year in London in my early twenties; Eleni and I spent five years in Tokyo in our late twenties. But that was when we were young; then we came back to Australia and the idea was to produce kids, settle down, stay put.

The temptation provided by an internet job, however, was too great. There was never any compelling reason for the Odyssey; it just sounded like fun, a sort of extended working holiday. The kind of thing that one does simply because one can, thanks to the wonders of modern technology. Indeed, we saw it as our moral duty to all of mankind to exploit this wonderful opportunity and report back,[1] even if it meant mercilessly uprooting our two children, Ruby and Felix, for the interim.

Nobody knows quite when or how the original germ of an idea came to be a serious proposition. The more we talked it over between ourselves and ran it past friends and family, the more inevitable and inescapable it became until, quite suddenly, we realised there was no turning back. It was now or never; take the plunge or regret it forever.

Having thus made the decision to sacrifice our comfortable suburban Australian lives in the name of research, the next step was to decide on a destination. Europe was the obvious choice. Many years back we had taken a holiday in Greece that included a short stopover in Rome; leading historians now believe this provided the inspiration for the Odyssey.

There was only one problem. My wife, the beautiful, dark and Aegean-inclined Eleni, was keen on the idea of a year on a tiny Greek island, whereas I'd had my heart set on Italy ever since the idea was first floated. This I attribute to three key defining life moments: being entranced by the magical lilting tones of Robert de Niro talking Italian in *Godfather II*; being captivated by the seaside Italian village depicted in *The Talented Mr. Ripley*; and being told that the pizza is much better in Italy. The four-day stopover in Rome only served to strengthen my convictions: the pizza really was better.

The task therefore was to convert Eleni to the cause. This I achieved using that time-honoured retina-driven multimedia tool: a list.

On the plus side for Greece:

- Nice cafés with backgammon tables
- Lovely ancient traditional cultural whitewashed houses
- Huge tasty doughnuts
- Access to Total yoghurt[2] throughout the country
- Prior in-country experience (well, three weeks)
- Cute cats everywhere

1 Hence this book.

2 The best yoghurt in the world. So thick you can stand a spoon up in it. Heavenly with honey.

On the negative side:

- No pizza or pasta
- No caffé lattes per se
- Question mark over telephone infrastructure
- Distinct possibility of becoming thoroughly fed up with taramasalata and fetta cheese after a couple of months
- Feral cats everywhere

The Greece versus Italy debate raged for some time but was eventually won by the Italy camp, with Eleni graciously conceding that a year of pizza and pasta would be in the best culinary interests of the family.

Now all we had to do was find a place to stay. This turned out to be a far trickier proposition. We initially considered a house swap but, oddly enough, were unable to track down any Italians interested in moving over to suburban Melbourne for a year. Next we tried contacting holiday home rental agents, but they could only offer super luxury Tuscan villas at super luxury prices. We even sounded out a few Italian universities, hoping that the homes of recently seconded professors might be available, but to no avail. And so it was that we came to rely on the expertise of a local travel agent in Melbourne, who knew a travel agent called Sandro in Italy, who said he had just the place for us, in a charming little village high in the Umbrian hills called Casa Castalda.

Sandro emailed across photos of the house he had in mind. It looked beautiful: bright and clean, with a sunny balcony and spacious garden for the children to run around in. Friends living in Italy drove down to check out Casa Castalda on our behalf and sent back a glowing reference, describing it as a delightful medieval village with plenty of old things and lovely views over the surrounding countryside. Even the name sounded like one of those Italian desserts from the local pizza shop. Perfect.

Late August was chosen as the departure date. With the Italian school year beginning in mid September, Ruby would have a couple of weeks to settle in before her cruel parents consigned her to the bewildering environment of a foreign kindergarten. It had been decided at an early stage that Ruby would be attending Italian kindergarten for the purposes of ethnological research. Happily she did not put up any resistance, though it must have been a daunting prospect for a five-year-old. Boisterous young Felix, meanwhile, would be staying at home—a different home, to be sure, but at less than two years of age he would be happy anywhere so long as his favourite Blankie was brought along.

In all the best formulaic Hollywood scripts, the setback known as the Second Turning Point does not occur until the protagonists have already embarked on the irreversible journey towards their goal.[3] Thus it was not until we had taken the vaccinations, updated the passports, completed the basic Italian course, organised the going-away party and arranged to lend out our home to cousins and our car to friends, that the Shock Horror email arrived…the deal at Casa Castalda had mysteriously fallen through. Not to worry, said Our Sandro, I have another option for you, this time a farmhouse on a hill in lovely Valfabbrica, surrounded by beautiful countryside and serviced by all local amenities.

Back to the map to find Valfabbrica: there it is nearby, marked with the smallest size dot (Casa Castalda didn't even rate a dot). Obviously just another delightful medieval village but slightly larger, thus promising a slightly higher quotient of piazzas, cafés and narrow laneways. Funny sounding name though: an ancient craft centre perhaps? The farmhouse interior didn't look quite as flash in the photos, but the views of the surrounding countryside were most impressive. Italian country lifestyle here we come!

There is only one problem, added Sandro a couple of emails later: the owner is a rather strange old retired teacher.

What could he mean? Creepy? Cantankerous? Axe-murderer? Eleni wasn't too perturbed, being confident that she could win him over with her charms, but I was sufficiently alarmed to fire off a Please Explain. After a flurried exchange of emails it was eventually established that the owner was actually a lovable old codger; the word 'strange' was merely a product of Sandro's limited English

3 Approximately 20 minutes before the final credits.

capabilities and should not be taken to imply any negative connotations whatsoever. Or something similarly placating.

In any case, time was fast running out and Sandro sounded like a reasonable enough person, so we put our faith in his judgment. After all, said we, rationalising madly, he's a travel agent and a local, he should know what he's talking about. Thus convinced, we packed far more than the luggage allowance and hopped on the plane armed only with return tickets and boundless optimism.

Here we are then, hot and tired after a gruelling 26-hour flight from the deepest Antipodes followed by a three-hour trip from Rome airport in a sweltering burst of late summer heat. We pile out of the car, glad to be on firm ground at last. I am expecting to be flooded with emotion—We've finally made it! All that planning has come to fruition! They said we'd never make it, they said we were crazy etc etc—but strangely there is nothing, as if packing the family off to a lonely hillside in Umbria for a year were just part of the rich and varied tapestry of life. Perhaps the emotion will come later.

What I do feel, however, is the full force of country charm in the warmth of the afternoon sun. This is indeed a marvellous spot up on the hill, surveying the broad valley of fields and houses and rolling hills in the distance. It will be lovely to wake up in the morning to this view. The massive old farmhouse, our home for the next year, is perched halfway up the hill a couple of kilometres from the centre of town. It is even more impressive up close than in the photos. We gaze around at the expansive garden, abandoned olive groves, overgrown farm tracks and various odd pieces of rusting farm machinery and old cars, marvelling at the potential for exploration adventures with Ruby and Felix.

But before we have time to admire the surrounds any further, the strange old retired teacher owner shuffles out to inspect his new tenants. Signor Morelli looks every one of his 76 years: tall, gaunt, and with the kind of weary, weathered features that suggest ingrained grumpiness, though not without the potential to muster a smile if pushed. I pigeonhole him as an Italian version of Walter Matthau.

Our landlord does not, it has to be said, look particularly pleased to see us. With barely a nod in our direction he launches into a tour of the facilities, Sandro scurrying alongside doing his best to interpret. The first comment that Sandro passes on—possibly unnecessarily—is that the landlord is grumbling about wanting more money. I ignore this: we've signed a contract with Sandro and paid six months' rent in advance—any further issues can be sorted out between the two of them. But thanks anyway for the hearty Italian country welcome, Signor Morelli. Maybe Sandro was right and the old codger is indeed a bit strange. His manners could certainly do with improvement.[4]

First we reach the laundry, an open-air hut which is still in the process of being concreted in preparation for the arrival of the washing machine. Eleni is mortified. What, no laundry? Thanks to an airline stuff-up with the luggage, we currently have only two small suitcases worth of clothes for the whole family. We desperately need a washing machine. It was, after all, stipulated in the contract. But don't worry, says Sandro, it will surely be finished within the next several days. And that seems to be that.

On now to the shed where you store your wood. Wood? I thought this place had heating? Of course it does, says Sandro quickly, but everyone here burns wood because the heating is so expensive. Gosh, that sounds a bit...*primitive*. Lighting a fire for cosy atmosphere is one thing; trying to keep your home warm by fire power is quite another. Still, we wanted the genuine Italian country experience, and this is clearly it.

The next stop is the underground oil tank, where we receive a lengthy explanation on how to measure the oil level. First you stick an old steel rod down to the bottom, then whip it out and measure the length of rod with oil on it using a folding ruler. Then you consult the calculations laid down in Morelli's ancient handwritten Book of Knowledge to determine the oil volume corresponding to the oil length on the rod. All rather quaint, but he's obviously been doing it this way since last century, so we'll let it pass.

4 Are you allowed to say that about old people?

Morelli is keen for us to give our formal consent to the oil volume thus calculated. Sure, we say, that looks right, whatever you say. The jet-lag has started to kick in and Ruby and Felix are understandably bored; is this really the time to be discussing oil measurement techniques? But then the significance of this ritual dawns on me: we are required to agree, and to be seen to agree, in the presence of witnesses, on the volume of oil in the tank at the exact moment of our arrival. Morelli is obviously not one to take such matters on trust.

Yet this is only half the story: now he wants to discuss payment for the oil. Surely this too is covered in the contract? Did we not spend months negotiating these details before we left? It seems not. Or rather that we may have, but without realising—silly us—that it was merely provisional haggling. After a lengthy discussion we agree that we will be paying three-quarters to his one-quarter. This seems to settle the matter; the lid is duly replaced on the oil tank and we are free to move on. Eleni and I exchange furtive glances: why is this Morelli character so preoccupied about money? Do we really look that shifty? Actually, in our current jet-lagged state we probably do.

In any case, the Moment of Truth has finally arrived—it's time to check out the inside of the old farmhouse. Hopefully it will be better than it looked in those photos.

And the truth is… it's a shabby, second-rate backpacker hostel. A complete shambles aspiring to be a home. The place doesn't appear to have been touched—or cleaned—since the early 1970s. It has all the typical elements of a cheap student hostel: grotty kitchen complete with back-breaking eighteenth-century sink; grimy stove with only one working gas ring; motley collection of Arcoroc glass plates, old aluminium pots and pans and cheap bendy cutlery; and the classic combined shower/toilet arrangement in the bathroom. (How are you supposed to keep the toilet paper dry?) Plus some truly inspired aesthetic touches, such as the brown-and-orange foam modular couches and the swirly rococo-style copper power point covers.

In short, it's a dump: solidly built, very spacious, located in a great spot on the hillside, but a dump nevertheless. Sandro tells us that it's a fantastic place, he'd love to live here himself—after renovating it first, of course. So it's good enough for gullible tourists but not for a real local, is that it, Sandro?

And by the way, I'd like to check that the phone line is connected and ready for use as promised.

There ensues a sharp exchange between Sandro and Morelli. Er, no, it isn't. That neatly coiled phone cord lying there on the floor is not actually connected to anything.

My heart sinks like a stone. The phone line was the most important prerequisite of the whole deal. Sandro knows this full well; at my insistence he even agreed to insert a special clause into the contract.[5] The plan was to begin working again within a few weeks of our triumphant arrival in Italy, but this is now looking unlikely. No phone line means no work; no work means no money; and no money means… well, less pizza for starters.

So what happened? When is a promise not a promise?

Sandro says that Morelli led him to believe that it was a working phone line; it never occurred to him to bring over a telephone and try it out. Fair enough, I suppose. Morelli, meanwhile, denies ever saying such a thing. Furthermore, he can't possibly entertain the prospect of sharing his existing telephone line with us due to privacy concerns—we will have to get a separate line connected.

But don't worry, comes the semi-automated response from Sandro, you can apply to Telecom Italia tomorrow, it's a very simple and convenient procedure.

Really? Is this the same Telecom Italia that I have heard so much about, the bureaucratic behemoth that takes months to get onto anything and that's only if you know someone on the inside? The Italian Odyssey, not to mention my career as a translator, is already starting to crumble before my eyes.

But there is no time to dwell on this setback any further, for here we go now with the heating lecture. Downstairs is a massive old boiler which looks like it dates back to the Industrial Revolution, and which is operated from a grubby plastic switch box in our kitchen upstairs. We are not to touch the temperature gauge on the switch box under any circumstances, only the on-off button. Righto. And

5 That increasingly worthless document.

the heating is all inter-connected, which means that when Morelli downstairs feels a bit chilly, we are to turn on the heating for him. Yes sir. (What if he wants the heating on but we don't—then who has to pay for it, eh? We could use this as a bargaining tool later on. See how Morelli's stinginess is already beginning to rub off on us.)

The bigger question though is: does the heating system actually work? A number of the rusting old panels look decidedly dysfunctional; some appear to be missing key parts. I won't be convinced until I see the system in action. But this will not be for several months yet: there is a special lever down at the boiler which releases the hot water into the system, and this shall only be operated at such time as Morelli designates that summer is officially over. Whenever that might be. Let's hope he starts feeling the cold before we do.

By this stage our heads are spinning from too many lectures; everything else will have to wait until tomorrow. Our thoughts turn to dinner. Can we possibly nick down to the town—such as it is—and get a few supplies? No, is the short answer. Absolutely everything is shut for miles around because it is Sunday.

Luckily we have an emergency supply of Weetbix on hand, and this becomes dinner. Tonight we will have to live with our failure as parents to provide the five main food groups; the children, meanwhile, are delighted at the opportunity to eat breakfast for dinner. We say our goodbyes and agree to meet up tomorrow to discuss procedural matters in more detail, then fall into bed exhausted.

Time for the post-mortem then: what do we think of the old farmhouse? Eleni, always the optimist, puts on a brave face. Let's give it a good clean, she says, make it nice and cosy. The views out the window are wonderful, the massive fireplace will be great in winter, before long we'll be settled in and used to its unique charms. Her comforting words are just what I need, because right now I'm acutely aware of my role in all of this. Why didn't I just agree to Greece instead?

In spite of the bravado, though, deep down inside Eleni shares my sense of disappointment. You know instinctively when you've found a home; I remember the feeling well from student days spent endlessly looking through sub-standard rental houses. This farmhouse isn't much of a home and, while we're at it, Valfabbrica isn't much of a town. And as for Morelli the miserly grouch…

But with no knowledge of the local area, let alone the rest of the country, and with severely limited language skills and two young children in tow, it seems we have little choice but to stay put for the time being. The contract does say that Sandro will help us to find alternative accommodation if necessary. Let's hope he's true to his word. Otherwise it could be a very different year to the one we had envisaged.

Day One of the Italian Odyssey, then, hasn't exactly gone to plan. Not that there was a plan, it's just that we were expecting…what exactly? For the entire township of Valfabbrica to erupt into wild applause on our arrival? For the neighbours to be knocking down our front door with gifts of homemade food and wine?

Well, at the very least, our landlord could have feigned a modicum of pleasure at meeting his new tenants. A smile and a handshake might have been nice.

Perhaps we will have to readjust our expectations of Italy. In any case, it's too late now—figuratively and literally. Time for the blissful sleep of the severely jet-lagged.

The next Moment of Truth comes the following morning, for this is when we take delivery of the car that will be our transport for the coming year. In another foolish act of blind faith in the inherent goodness of humankind, I have already paid for it in full, sight unseen, on the strength of a recommendation from some email acquaintances in Italy whom we've never even met.[6]

We know precious little about the car except that it is a Volvo 940—one of the classic cardboard-box models from the good old days before Volvos sold out and went all curvy—and we are desperately hoping that our faith has not been misplaced. Please let

6 I know what you're thinking, dear reader, and you can keep it to yourself thanks.

the car make up for the disappointment of the farmhouse...

John, the owner of the mystery vehicle, has agreed to meet up with us at the post office in Valfabbrica to hand it over, so at the appointed time we troop down the hill and along the main street carrying two large child seats. On the way there, a frightening possibility occurs to me: we will arrive at the post office to find no car, no John, no nothing, and will be left standing there looking sheepish with two child seats and two tired children. Then the Italian Odyssey would surely be complete—twelve months marooned in a dumpy old farmhouse halfway up a hill two kilometres out of a nondescript town with no phone or means of transport.

But no, there is John waiting at the agreed point; and what's more, the car looks to be in good condition. Relief floods over me (finally, an emotional flooding experience). We hop in and discover that it already has a built-in child seat—one of those little things you never think of checking before relocating overseas. Within the hour we have filled up with petrol and made our way to Città di Castello, where John switches to a hire car and hands over the keys. This is it: we are on our own and in control of a large station wagon with the steering wheel on the wrong side.

Not quite though—first we must have a celebratory coffee in the piazza in the centre of town. And at this point our plight in Valfabbrica is thrown into stark relief. For Città di Castello is a beautiful and impressive town in every way that Valfabbrica is not: full of old buildings, cobbled streets, interesting shops and cafés, and a large and gracious central piazza buzzing with pedestrian traffic, the whole lot enclosed within a set of well-preserved medieval castle walls. Over coffee we explain our predicament to John. It turns out that he knows a friend of a friend called Mario who rents out furnished apartments here in town. Our eyes light up: this would be a fantastic place to live! It's the fairytale solution! It probably has a working phone line too. We resolve to ring Mario as soon as possible and plan our escape.

The thought of driving home this afternoon suddenly brings me back to earth. The last time I drove on the right-hand side of the road was in Greece; we survived, but not without the usual tourist quota of hair-raising lane-switching incidents. At least we are lucky today in that the trip back to Valfabbrica is mostly on the freeway. Just remember to stay in the right lane unless overtaking, says John. Sounds like good advice to me.

At Valfabbrica, Morelli greets the arrival of our enormous Volvo with raised eyebrows. I can see his point—it is twice the size of his tiny Fiat. Sandro laughs openly: You bought a big heavy station wagon, with a petrol engine, and it's larger than two litres? You must be mad, he adds helpfully. I try to explain that back in Australia a car this size is nothing unusual; also that we had to buy it sight unseen from Australia because…well I can't remember really, for various reasons.

Perhaps we are mad after all: I have already learnt from John that diesel is the fuel of choice in Italy because it is considerably cheaper. And later I will find out that insurance premiums are virtually double for cars with engines larger than two litres. So, yes, I have to concede that probably no Italian in their right mind would buy a car like this. Especially with English number plates, just to add to its strangeness. But at least our big, expensive and laughable car is extremely safe—the perfect thing, in fact, for foreigners with children used to driving on the other side of the road. Let's see who comes off second best when we plough into your tiny Fiat then![7]

On Tuesday, emboldened by our successful and triumphant return from Città di Castello, we take the Perugia freeway down to the shopping centre at Collestrada about 20 minutes away. This shiny new mega-complex is home to the largest supermarket I have ever seen, roughly the size of a small Greek island, selling everything from sliced cheese to computers. I love exploring supermarkets in other countries: a familiar environment yet with new and exciting goodies on offer that demand to be purchased and eaten. This one presents a real challenge; it will take us months to work our way through everything here. I think we're up to it though.

Today we end up buying nearly half of the food section, since the lonely old farmhouse has no supplies whatsoever. Next door to the

7 Not deliberately of course.

supermarket is a home appliances centre, where a patient shop assistant manages to put up with my diabolical Italian for long enough to send me out the door with a new mobile phone card, which will provide us with at least some form of contact with the outside world.

By the time the shopping expedition finally comes to an end the children are monumentally bored. Ruby spots a climbing frame contraption in the car park outside the McDonald's and the Parental Committee agrees that the two of them deserve a bit of play time after their ordeal; but, says Eleni, we have a moral obligation to buy something if we want to use their equipment. Normally we would never set foot in McDonald's yet here we are, eating tasteless plastic ice-cream in a huge concrete car park right opposite the freeway entrance listening to the trucks hurtle by just metres away. Is this what we came half way across the world for?

To top it all off, a short while later as I am sitting inside the shopping centre later having a coffee and idly watching the huge television screen above, my senses are rudely assaulted by a series of trailers for low-rent Australian current affairs programs and reality TV shows. What is happening here? Surely this is the antithesis of the high culture that we ought to be wallowing in by now. Day Three of the Odyssey and our expectations have taken a very severe battering indeed.

The rest of the first week is spent on riveting procedural matters. Cecelia, Sandro's assistant in the office in Perugia, is already working on the phone line application; Telecom Italia has assured her that it will take only a couple of weeks. I register our names at the council offices and sign up Ruby at the local kindergarten with the help of Marta, a teenage relative of Sandro's who speaks passable English and has agreed to act as our interpreter. Our visa papers state that we must front up at the Questura immigration office within eight days of arriving or risk expulsion and bringing shame on the family name.

Marta's father Walter, the Deputy Mayor of Valfabbrica, kindly drives us in to Perugia in his hot Alfa Romeo with flashy red interior at speeds reaching up to 170 kilometres an hour. Presumably the local constabulary have learned to turn a blind eye to the Deputy Mayor's car. The applications are duly lodged and we hope that the authorities will be so kind as to allow us to stay.

Back at the farmhouse, Eleni sets to work briskly scrubbing down cupboards, light fittings and various other surfaces in an attempt to make the place a bit more homely, or at least slightly cleaner. Following a thorough inventory of the kitchen, we present Morelli with a list of pots and pans and other things that are conspicuously lacking; he is none too impressed at the prospect of outlaying more money on top of the laundry fit-out. Clearly the old miser has difficulty with the concept of maintaining a furnished rental property.

But before he has had a chance to protest further, a new character appears on the scene: a sturdy, no-nonsense signora who looks to be around sixty (Morelli's girlfriend perhaps?). She seems to have taken a liking to us, or at least sympathises with our predicament, for she whips the list away from him and announces that we shall have all the things for the kitchen *subito.*[8]

It turns out that she is responsible for managing the business side of the farmhouse, which is normally rented out by the week to tourists during the summer. We dub her the Signora Who Gets Things Done and make a mental note to get her phone number next time: she may prove an important ally in future.

Meanwhile Sandro, presumably racked with guilt for having failed to deliver a telephone line as promised, gets a computer-savvy friend of his to help me set up an Italian email address, and offers me use of the phone line in his spare room for connecting to the internet. Together with the recently Italianised mobile phone, this means that we are now in a position to re-establish contact with the outside world, and in particular with Clients who will provide Work which will bring Money to eat Pizza.

With great excitement I fire off several emails to distant Tokyo. Before long the channels of communication are re-established and

8 Hopefully this means 'right away'.

the work starts flowing in. Checking the emails entails packing up the computer and driving across to Sandro's house twice every day, but it is a tremendous relief to be connected nevertheless. The only thing lacking is a fax machine, but here again Sandro comes to the rescue: you can have faxes sent to my office in Perugia, he says, and I will bring them home at the end of the day. Not quite the ideal home office set-up but it will do for the moment, until we either get the phone on or move out.

Thus one of the major hurdles—re-establishing the home office—has been overcome, and not a moment too soon. I have been waking up regularly in the middle of the night wondering what on earth we have gotten ourselves into, and in particular whether I still have a career as a translator left.

For the time being it appears that I do, provided the bizarre email/fax/phone arrangement holds up. In hindsight we were overly optimistic to expect that everything would simply fall into place; as on any decent holiday, something was bound to go wrong. But then, if it weren't for optimism we might never have left Australia in the first place.

The other major excitement of the first week is my daring attempt to roll the Hulking Great Volvo off the side of the hill by parking it outside the farmhouse in Drive without the handbrake on. (In my defence I should point out that our car back home is a old manual with a handbrake that hasn't worked in years. I *always* park it in gear without the handbrake on.)

As I'm walking away, I notice out of the corner of my eye that the HGV is creeping, slowly but surely, down the gentle slope and towards the steep precipe adjoining the driveway. Luckily I haven't bothered to lock the door, so I can leap in and plant the foot on the brake. Except that power-assisted brakes don't work too well when the ignition is off.No time to fumble with the keys as the car gathers momentum—should I attempt a stunt tumble out the door or simply go down with the *Titanic*?[9] Just then I recall that the handbrake in this car actually works. The HGV is saved, though at the price of a few grey hairs.

9 In which case should I strap on my seat belt?

For weeks after this incident, I force myself to repeat *Park gear, handbrake on, Park gear, handbrake on* like a mantra every time I get out of the HGV. And resolve to fix the handbrake on the old car when we get home.

Gradually, life begins to assume some sort of order and we are able to relax a little and explore the surroundings. Our first priority is to check out the cafés in town. (For some reason, a café is called a *bar* in Italian. The bar serves alcohol as well as coffee, and is usually open until late into the evening, especially in summer or when the soccer is on.) Mario's bar is our favourite because it has the best jam-filled croissants; unfortunately it's right on the main road, so there's no such thing as a peaceful coffee in the morning sun.

Our next mission is to road-test the lone pizzeria, and it is declared to be good: they make excellent thin crust pizzas with minimal topping and, as an added bonus, are open well before 7.30 pm, which seems to be the standard opening time for Italian restaurants.[10] In no time at all we have ingratiated ourselves there and devised our own set menu of three large pizzas, a salad, half litre of red wine, sweets and coffee.

Other retail highlights in Valfabbrica include a couple of classic we-stock-everything country hardware stores, the ones where the longer you stay, the more you discover. We pick up a few odds and ends designed to make the farmhouse feel a bit more liveable, including the ultimate luxury item: an electric kettle. Because making cups of tea out of a saucepan is too much like camping.

Among the general stores, the Conad on the edge of town is our preferred choice because it is run by friendly young Italians with movie-star good looks. After all, if you have to buy milk and bread you may as well get it with a smile from a handsome young thing looking like a young Robert de Niro or Nicholas Cage. I like the clean-shaven one best, while Eleni prefers his younger brother with the goatee. All in the name of research of course. Before long we make

10 When on earth do Italian children go to bed then?

the important discovery that, despite being on a major truck route, Valfabbrica gets fresh milk delivered only twice weekly. Even Mario is producing coffees with evil UHT milk by about Thursday. The handsome young things at the Conad soon get used to us making off with the bulk of their fresh milk supplies on Tuesdays and Fridays.

Finding shops in Italy, or country Italy at least, can be quite a tricky business, because often there are no signs out the front, no displays in the windows—no obvious indication at all, in fact, that this is a place designed to help you part with your money. You have to venture inside, hoping that it's not the front room of somebody's house, in order to see what is on offer. So far we have managed to avoid blundering into a lounge room and tripping over the telly, but this remains a distinct possibility. We conclude that the lack of signage must be on account of regulations designed to keep the streetscapes uncluttered—a good idea in principle, perhaps, but it does put the visitor at a distinct disadvantage. Unless that's the whole point.

Our meanderings during the first week even extend as far as the Umbrian hillside town of Gubbio. We have selected Gubbio for our maiden visit on the strength of a vague recommendation by somebody or other, somewhere in the distant past.[11] Neither of us can quite remember why it was said to be worth the visit, but it's not really important anyway; the destination is little more than an excuse for a drive through the countryside.

As it turns out, Gubbio is a wonderful town, extremely medieval and built on the side of a hill, which means endless steep, narrow, cobbled stairways and laneways to explore. Judging by the number of buses it is clearly an important spot on the tourist trail too. Not quite sure why though; must remember to read the guide book before leaving next time.

Although we have only a couple of hours to spend in Gubbio, there is plenty to see, not least an ancient cable car contraption with tiny narrow birdcages that swing precariously to and fro on their way up the hill. Unfortunately it is already closed for the day. Just as well; I'll need time to build up courage for that one. Gubbio also boasts an enormous permanent Christmas tree light display built into the

11 Probably last month back in Australia. It all seems so long ago.

hillside, which is switched on in early December. The cable car takes you right up to the star at the top.

So it looks like we'll need to come back to Gubbio in a few months and do it properly. Including the tourist attractions.

Arriving back at the car, we discover that we have left one of the windows open the entire time. Are we subconsciously trying to get rid of the HGV? Of course not! In any case, no Italian robber in their right mind would bother stealing such a ridiculously large, petrol-driven car with foreign number plates. The HGV lives to ride another day.

In the evening, Cecelia rings to say that the good folk at Telecom Italia appear to have completely lost my application. She is most apologetic: Telecom Italia is like that, she says, you'll have to send in the application documents again. One whole precious week wasted. I duly fax off the documents again from the dingy little newsagency in town, doing my best not to dwell on bureaucratic incompetence. It could have been worse I suppose; at least our spot on the hillside has good mobile phone reception.

It's strange taking telephone calls from Japan while staring out the window at the countryside. Could there be any greater contrast than between the concrete canyons of Tokyo and the gently rolling hills of Umbria? Such are the wonders of modern technology, making our small planet ever smaller. When I was a child it was a thrill just to be able to talk with a holidaying relative on the other side of the world; today the thrill is being able to take your job to the other side of the world.

2

Acclimatising

We have decided to take advantage of the continuing good weather to explore the nearby countryside, sometimes for an hour or so after kindergarten but more often on the weekends in a bid to recreate the era of the family Sunday drive. (If indeed there ever was such an era; I'm taking my cultural cue from old tinted 1950s movies here, but it sounds plausible enough.)

The days are cooler but still pleasant; there's been hardly any rain and although the early mornings are sometimes cold and foggy, it is usually warm by midday. The late afternoon sun on the hills creates a striking palette of colours that has me spellbound.

The effect is truly magical, especially after rain, when the hills look as if they have been washed and scrubbed clean. According to a photographer friend, it is a well-known fact that the light in Umbria reflects off tiny droplets in the atmosphere, thereby creating unique shimmering hues. Or something like that.

The radio reception in the car is very patchy, no doubt on account of all the hills, and for some inexplicable reason the only cassette that we have brought from Australia is *The Best of the Seekers*. Being children, as they are, Ruby and Felix insist on hearing it over and over and over again. As a result, songs such as 'Georgie Girl' and 'Morningtown Ride' have long ceased to be pleasant chunks of nostalgia from our parents' generation. Now when I hear 'World of Our Own', it inevitably drags images of the hills and dales of deepest Umbria up from the depths of my consciousness.

Speaking of hills, it is quite amazing to see how, from any given vantage point, it is possible to see the hills forever rolling, overlapping one another, extending out to the horizon. Around here it seems that every second village is perched on top of a hill with commanding views. I don't understand how you can physically cram so many villages with spectacular views into the same area—surely the hills would start to block one another out sooner or later. As well as the villages, there are houses perched on top of smaller hills too. Presumably the hilltop locations were necessary for people to spot their enemies coming in ancient times. Strange how a predilection for warfare has left such a wonderful legacy for today's tourists. All they wanted was to maximise their defences; all we can think about are the bella vistas.

The tracks up in the hills are generally gravel or dirt, with no traffic to speak of—perfect for walking along with the children. We try to stop the car at a different bit of nowhere-in-particular each time, then hop out and explore the surrounds. In this way we discover all manner of hidden delights: a crumbling old church; a picturesque farm with the requisite quota of sheep and ducks; an austere graveyard enclosed within high stone walls; a working horse stud with an exercise yard; a set of luxury tourist apartments tucked away in a fold of the hills, complete with pool; fields of enormous poppies waving in the wind; a network of historic trails supposedly trodden by St. Francis of Assisi in years past; and countless interesting little towns and hamlets.

One day our aimless meanderings meet with spectacular success: we finally manage to track down a secret pizzeria in the middle of nowhere. Of course it has no signage, no indication at all of its hallowed status; we would never have known about it except that Marta once made an off-hand remark about a pizzeria 'somewhere at the top of your road' and we have been keeping an eye out for suspicious buildings ever since.

This building looks larger than a house and is located at the end of a dirt lane with about ten cars parked outside—highly suspicious. We troop down the lane and brazenly poke our heads inside. Bingo!

The mystery is solved. Tragically, the oven has been turned off for the day so we have to content ourselves with coffees and ice-creams. This being an extended Sunday lunch, there are still crowds of people inside finishing off the last remnants of dessert, with children running all around the place. It looks highly convivial and we resolve to have our own traditional cultural long lunch experience here sometime soon.

But why all the secrecy and lack of signage? Why does the pizzeria feel no need to advertise its presence? Presumably it's because the locals are already in the know. Although we wonder if there might not be some darker subtext about excluding out-of-towners. (Nyar, nyar, we found it anyway.)

Now that we have a second pizzeria option at our disposal, the world is an infinitely more diverse and interesting place. Not least because Ruby, until recently completely uninterested in pizza, has finally seen the light—enough to bring tears to her father's eyes.

Another time we set out in an attempt to find a village that somebody or other has told us about up over the other side of the valley, on the same basic pretext as the Gubbio trip. After several hours of fruitless searching and getting lost down muddy country lanes we wind up quite by accident in Casa Castalda, the tiny hamlet where our home was originally to have been. As it turns out, Casa Castalda would have been perfect—naturally it's set on top of a hill and boasts magnificent aspects of rolling hills in all directions, but it also has a handsome medieval town centre complete with archway entrance and lots of narrow winding cobbled laneways to get lost in, and even a wonderful park with play equipment for the children. Since I am not yet fixated with castle walls, the absence of fortifications in Casa Castalda is no problem; I very much want to live up here on top of the world, not down there in the squalid industrial valley with the factories and the smoke and the trucks.

So I embark on a fruitless quest to track down the house that could/should have been ours, hoping to recognise the exterior from the photos, hoping that the owner will be in, hoping that when he sees us in the flesh and realises what nice people we are he will take pity on us and reconsider… even though, deep down, I know that this is all perfectly futile. Particularly as I can't locate the house in the first place. But the injustice of it all niggles away at me. Why did he pull out of the deal at the last minute? What did we do wrong?

Later on we discover from Sandro that the owner's change of heart came about when he found out[1] that we had asked our friends to drive up to Casa Castalda to check it out but *without getting them to pay their respects to the rightful landlord first*. Either this guy is a tad flaky—why baulk on such a flimsy pretext?—or there is some ancient traditional cultural subtext to do with renting that we don't know about.

What is it with landlords around here anyway? They're all a bit weird if you ask me.

The answer, according to Sandro, is that they are used to dealing with rich German tourists hiring their homes for a few weeks at a time during the peak summer season; the idea of tying up their lucrative holiday properties at normal rental rates for an entire year is strange and frightening. Even though it actually generates more income for them in the long run. Even though Sandro has patiently pointed this out to them many times. Even though there are countless charming holiday homes in charming locations sitting there perfectly empty for nine months of the year…

The children seem to have adapted to our new life without problem. Felix has not started talking yet and is thus obliged to keep any issues he may have concerning the abrupt change of environment to himself. However in the absence of any dramas such as crying or waking in the middle of the night, we are assuming that he is happy enough.

Unfortunately he is still waking up far too early in the morning, whereas the rest of us have largely recovered from our jet-lag. The Parental Committee has solved this problem by taking advantage of one of the quaint characteristics of the farmhouse—lockable internal

1 From guess who? Thanks Sandro.

doors—to imprison Felix in his bedroom at night with a supply of toys for the morning. All goes swimmingly until one morning we discover an enormous Umbrian flying beast also locked in his room, doing a remarkable impression of a light aircraft as it buzzes aimlessly around the overhead light. How it got in is a mystery—as much to the beast as to us—and it seems to have been droning on for some time, judging from Felix's traumatised face. Then a few days later I discover a scorpion, no less, sitting happily on his bed. From this point on the door stays open and we start conducting spot checks for dangerous mountain beasts at random intervals during the evening.

Both children are enjoying the sense of space in the enormous living room, which measures something like 20 metres from end to end. The long wooden table is great for craft activities, the tatty old couches are perfect for jumping all over and there are plenty of spare sheets and blankets for making tents. And thanks to the toy section at Collestrada, we have acquired a plastic Baby Gaggia coffee maker with traditional whistling sound and real dribbling action to serve as the centre piece for endless culturally enriching activities.

The land around the farmhouse is ideal for exploration, featuring as it does countless old outhouses in various stages of construction, as well as pieces of rusting farm machinery, piles of wood and bricks and overgrown vehicle tracks. When we're not out gallivanting around the countryside in the HGV, we hack our way fearlessly through the undergrowth collecting kindling for the fire, or crawl over the tiny 1950s-vintage Fiat left rusting at the far end of the field, or wander down the track to watch Morelli's minions harvesting olives from his last remaining olive groves.

Eleni and I are amazed by the extent of Morelli's vast tracts of land. Why the penny-pinching when he's clearly not struggling? We conclude that it must be the legacy of war—that convenient catch-all for old people. I recall long ago visiting a friend's grandmother who, despite her obvious wealth, used to recycle Glad Wrap by carefully washing each piece and pegging it out to dry. Rather excessive, one would think.[2] Then again, I wouldn't put Glad Wrap recycling past Morelli either. I must check his kitchen one day.

2 Unless of course that's how she got wealthy in the first place.

Inside, the farmhouse is gradually starting to look lived in. In the kitchen, we have cleared the cupboards of unnecessary detritus such as whisky glasses and tacky German bare-breasted beer mugs and carefully installed our new Italian plasticware from the hardware shops. The magnanimous landlord, urged on no doubt by the Signora Who Gets Things Done, has agreed to call in the electrician to fix some shonky-looking light fittings and power points in which Felix has started to take an unhealthy interest.

Leonardo the electrician turns out to be yet another handsome young thing; we decide that he is an Italian version of Tom Cruise, though with better hair and no sneer. Leonardo is also extremely personable, and we soon establish a rapport despite the language limitations. Eleni and I resolve to go around the farmhouse finding appliances and fittings in need of repair—breaking them if need be—in order to get Leonardo around again and this time make him stay for a cup of tea. In Japan many years ago we took a photo of Eleni cuddling a life-size cardboard cut-out of Tom Cruise; the aim now is to get a corresponding shot with Leonardo. Not *too* cuddly though.

Meanwhile, the main bathroom/toilet has been infinitely improved by a makeshift shower curtain hanging from an extendable rod, which keeps the shower water down the shower end where it ought to be. Now there's no need to hang a box over the toilet paper before turning on the shower, and we can even put a bath mat down. What luxury! The curtain arrangement was purchased by the SWGTD, although with a proviso this time: *If you are staying for a year then we will buy these things for you*, she intones sternly. Of course we are in it for the long term, say we. We love it here.[3]

Ruby has settled happily enough into her kindergarten routine. When we go in to pick her up we generally find her drawing alongside the others, if not quite interacting with them. Sometimes we go to the park afterwards to have a play on the swings, and her friends will call out to her with a wonderful trilled *Rrroobbi!*

3 Fingers crossed behind back.

Rrroobbi!, causing her to come over all embarrassed. Ruby takes a while to warm to new people, so initial embarrassment is standard procedure.

But one day Ruby comes home with a birthday party invite from Anna at kindergarten, who lives down at the ritzy end of Valfabbrica where the houses are all large and new and well-appointed. (Including Sandro's enormous Italianate mansion.) It's our first ever authentic Italian gathering and we are excited but a bit nervous too. Must remember to use polite Italian. How big/expensive/showy should the birthday gift be? This is the rich end of town after all. Do guests bring along food/wine/both/neither? I attempt to consult some of the mothers from kindergarten but come away none the wiser. We'll just have to trust in our instincts.

It turns out there was nothing to fear; the party is much like any other. Except for the food: tray after tray of tempting tidbits, including endless rounds of home-made pizza appearing in steady succession throughout the afternoon. These are being churned out by the grandparents in the special pizza oven that lives outside in the front garden.

Anna's father Marco takes me down to have a look. I recognise the domed shape and front window immediately; I have spotted a number of these around town without appreciating their tremendous significance. The authentic Italian outdoor pizza oven is a massive and elaborate contraption when you consider that it only serves one purpose; but what an important purpose! We may have to take one home with us when we leave.

In another exciting development, we have taken delivery of two large boxes of second-hand English-language children's books, kindly donated by an English couple living near Umbertide, whose two teenage boys are now well beyond rubbish kiddie stories such as Pooh and Piglet walking endlessly around a tree getting scared of their own footprints. Two boxes will be more than enough to keep Ruby and Felix occupied for the year—an enormous relief given our dismal failure as parents to make any provision for English-language education during the Odyssey year.

Ruby's current favourite is a cassette book called *Barbie's Mountain Kidnap*, which recounts the gripping tale of how Barbie is kidnapped on a Swiss mountain only hours before she is due to appear at the World Pop and Rock Awards[4] with her imaginatively named band Barbie and the Rock Stars. The French and Swiss accents in this English production are atrocious, and we have great fun mimicking them as we drive along. 'Duzz...Barrbi...hyevv...enny...ennimiz?' asks the Swiss inspector called in to investigate the shocking kidnap. (Well, at least it makes a change from The Seekers.) But we are mightily affronted on behalf of all decent Barbie-loving Australians to find that the villain, disgruntled groupie Rex Blake, sports an Australian accent (also atrocious). Mercifully he makes no mention of throwing prawns on barbies.

Down at the home appliance centre in Collestrada one day I spot a mobile phone with built-in modem and computer cable. Imagine if I could access the internet from my mobile phone—there would be no need for a new phone line at all! It's time to replace the old phone anyway; this could be the perfect solution. With great excitement I take the shiny new phone home and plug it in, only to discover that it is far too slow to be of any real use. The technology clearly has several years to go yet. Never mind; at least it has some nice ring tones.

At the behest of Jane, a friend from London who has popped across to Europe for a couple of days, as the Brits are wont to do, we decide to do our cultural duty by paying a visit to Assisi, barely 20 kilometres away. But our woefully under-prepared mission is doomed to failure from the outset due to several base errors:

(a) going during the summer season

(b) going on a weekend, and

(c) arriving after nine in the morning.

The car parks at Assisi are all full to bursting and we are obliged to settle instead for nearby Foligno, which is perfectly nice (I gave the

4 'The most important pop and rock awards in the world.' Apart from the Eurovision Song Contest, obviously.

piazza three and a half stars) but obviously no Assisi. Although it does have plenty of parking. On the way back from Foligno, things get more interesting when we spot an ancient township clinging improbably to the side of a mountain and turn off to investigate.

This turns out to be beautiful Spello, around the same vintage as Assisi and every bit as impressive—unless of course you're keen to see churches and frescoes and cultural things in Assisi.. Having decided fairly early on in the piece that we're not too interested in paintings, coloured windows or small tile chips—we're here for the coffee and pizza, the unsigned mystery shops, the arches and laneways and cobbled streets and medieval buildings, the long lunches and the rolling hills—and thus liberated from these cultural imperatives, we are free to not visit Assisi at all if we don't feel like it.

Appreciated in this context, Spello is immensely enjoyable, especially the lovely outdoor café about halfway up the main drag on the right-hand side where you can sit for hours and admire the regulation sweeping vistas. Highly recommended when the Assisi car parks are full.

While still in the travelling mood, we decide to go on the inaugural Sunday drive to the coast around Ancona for a crash course in European beach culture.

After getting lost in the wilds of industrial Ancona, we negotiate our way south and stumble across a picturesque beach nestling in a small enclosed bay, accessible only via a steep track down from the forested area above. Small yet uncrowded, with warm sand and sparkling blue sea, it is much like the beaches we are used to in Australia. For some inexplicable reason—a subconscious sense of touristic duty to explore and discover?—we then decide to pack up camp and try a second beach.

Which turns out to be the total opposite of the first: a typical European beach experience with thousands of matching deck chairs and umbrellas lined up in neat little grid formations on their own privatised squares of sand, flanked by a string of restaurants, bars, kiosks and shower blocks. All taking up valuable public beach space if you ask me.

Then again, I suppose it might be quite a pleasant way to enjoy the beach once you got used to it. For a start, it's much more openly sociable—there's no use trying to set up camp away from the madding crowds because there's no room, so you may as well join in instead. And the thought of ready access to pizza, cakes and coffee all day long is extremely tempting. But no: the notion of having to pay for beach space is outrageous and unAustralian. We'll be going back to that first beach next time.

On the way back we stop to fill up with petrol. Studying the receipt I realise that Sandro was right: the HGV is going to cost a fortune to run, given the price of petrol in this country. Maybe we should switch to a tiny diesel Fiat after all. Why, you could buy three or four pizzas per tank with the money you saved.

It turns out that Sandro has a friend, or possibly a relative, in the second-hand car trade. Naturally. So a couple of days later I take the car down to his car yard to see how much I can get for it. Eleni and I are already attracted to the idea of a long-term lease on a shiny new Peugot or Renault, which would be more fuel-efficient and thus cost less over the course of a year. All we have to do is get rid of the Volvo first. Sandro's friend/relative is out today, so his cousin/brother/business associate looks over the car, takes down all the details and promises to get back to me.

He never does. One can only assume that the HGV is not even worth the cost of a phone call. Sandro and Morelli were right to laugh at us after all. We'll just have to hang onto our petrol-hungry monster for the time being. From this point on I make a concerted effort to conserve petrol by driving slowly and gently like an old granny in a Fiat, with one eye glued permanently to the petrol gauge—not such a clever idea on narrow winding mountain roads.

It has been very therapeutic having Jane to stay, providing us with an outsider's perspective as well as a sympathetic ear. For despite all the frustrations and disappointments, it cannot be denied that sitting in the garden enjoying the late afternoon sun with the children, drawing pictures, kicking a ball, writing letters, having a drink or two, bringing out a hastily arranged dinner and admiring the sunset over the hills as evening falls, is nothing short of magical. At times like this, the hassles with the house, car and phone line all melt quietly into the background.

A couple of days later I am sitting at my makeshift office—a plastic garden table in a corner of the bedroom covered with a tatty old tablecloth discovered in a drawer—when Cecilia rings with a Telecom Italia update. They have decided that I need an additional document for my application—something called a Codice Fiscale, the equivalent of a tax file number. I must go into Perugia, three-quarters of an hour away on the freeway, and apply for one of these, then submit a new application for the phone line. Back to square one, then. But we had been meaning to go into Perugia anyway, so it is the ideal excuse.

Perugia is a fantastic old city, positively pre-medieval in its oldness, full of winding laneways, steep inclines and narrow archways as well as the odd graceful boulevard and countless open squares and piazzas. There are grand churches and palazzos, as well as tiny streets and houses and shops and restaurants. There are sweeping views from the bars that sit atop the city walls, as well as cramped residential laneways strung with washing through which you can barely make out the sky above. The overall impression is of a chaos of styles, as if the city has been progressively rebuilt at different times to suit different needs, resulting in a wonderful hodge-podge of streets and alleyways that are perfect for poking around. I doubt that there would be a single straight road in the place, with the possible exception of the main boulevard—and even that's got a bit of a kink in it down one end.

But above all, despite the appearance of chaos and irregularity, Perugia is very much a living, working, down-to-earth city. We give thanks to Telecom Italia for bringing us here today and vow to return as soon as possible.

Unfortunately, our mission of the moment—to obtain a Codice Fiscale—takes us outside the Old Bit of Perugia into the exceedingly ugly Rest of Perugia, which is full of freeways, office buildings and sensible wide roads. Due to a combination of bad luck and bad planning, we arrive at the Finance Ministry office at a couple of minutes past one o'clock. The sign says that it is open again from three to five. Two hours to kill until the office reopens. Excellent.

We decide to head over to the University for Foreigners, where Eleni wants to enquire about taking an intensive Italian course. The university zone is a particularly lively part of town, where the streets are full of genuine card-carrying Young People as opposed to well-heeled tourists, and more down-to-earth bars and shops. I notice a bank right inside the university building and decide to try my luck at setting up an account while Eleni is in at the university office. Incredibly, the nice man behind the counter has opened an account for me in less than 20 minutes, even keeping the children entertained at the same time with a steady supply of caramels. (In stark contrast to the pathetic local bank manager at Valfabbrica, who last week spent half an hour prattling on about the difficulties of foreign currency and bank transfers and credit card accounts before ultimately deciding that it was all too hard and sending Sandro and I on our way.)

We've been having so much fun exploring the back alleys of the university zone that we've almost forgotten our afternoon appointment at the Finance Ministry. Back we go, managing to arrive before five, only to find that the office is still closed. Re-reading the sign, I discover that the office reopens from three to five *on Tuesdays and Thursdays only*. Grrrr.[5] Yet another delay with the phone line application. Never mind; it's another excuse to come back to Perugia.

On the way home we are caught up in a massive traffic jam caused by an accident in one of the freeway tunnels. Having spent so much time horsing around Perugia, we've left our departure a bit late and now with this delay on the freeway we won't be home in time to cook dinner. With a heavy heart I reach for the mobile: we have no option but to order take-away pizza from the secret pizzeria in the middle of nowhere that we discovered so successfully the other day.

5 Meaning: next time read the sign properly, you idiot.

Sensibly, we'd copied down their phone number for just this sort of eventuality, and within ten minutes of arriving at the pizzeria we are back in the farmhouse happily munching away. The perfect ending to a day of successful dealings with Italian bureaucracy.

Today's family Sunday drive takes us up north. Equipped with sandwiches and a slightly dodgy orange creation—our first attempt to bake a cake in the creaking old farmhouse oven—we are heading for the tiny village of Citerna, just this side of the border with Tuscany, to meet Marius and Christine, fellow Australians who relocated to Italy permanently a couple of years ago. Marius and Christine have been extremely helpful with our preparations over the last year—indeed, it was they who drove down to check out Casa Castalda on our behalf and they who found us the car—and we count them as our friends and mentors in Italy. But we have never actually met.

Our purely cyberspatial relationship began about a year ago, when I came across a feature article written by Christine for a Melbourne newspaper describing their experiences in Citerna. The article grabbed my attention, as we'd only recently made our own decision to relocate. Even better, there was an email address at the end, so I duly sent off a request for information, advice—anything—about moving to Italy. This chance encounter eventually grew into an ongoing email exchange, as a result of which, to cut a long story short, we are now making our way up a narrow winding mountain road to their home.

As we admire the exterior walls of Citerna, pass through the portal and creep along the cobbled main street under the arches, it soon becomes clear that this is a gem of a hillside town. As one would expect, it is perched on top of a hill with the regulation commanding views in all directions, but because the hill on which it sits falls away sharply on all sides, the original township of Citerna, plastered neatly over the top of the plateau like icing on a cupcake, has been effectively quarantined from any hint of modern development. Add years of painstaking and sympathetic renovation following extensive war and earthquake damage and you end up with a pretty well perfectly preserved medieval hillside village, like an open-air museum. I am once again overcome with envy and longing.

The lounge room window at the rear of Marius and Christine's house sits on the very edge of the precipice and provides a commanding view over a vast flat valley covered in patchwork fields—the Valtiberina, or Tiber Valley. Marius points out some of the main towns: straight ahead is Sansepolcro, with the Buitoni pasta factory; every September they hold a week-long festival with cross-bow competitions and flag-waving performances. Next to it is San Giustino, which has a huge castle complete with an outdoor maze. Up on the hill is Anghiari, where the famous Battle of Anghiari was fought with neighbouring Sansepolcro in the 1400s (possibly over sovereignty of the pasta factory); it also has an excellent pizza-by-the-slice joint on the central piazza. And over there you can see Pistrino, and Fighille, and San Leo… My eyes start to glaze over: it all sounds so intriguing and exciting, yet so remote and unattainable. As if we've got any chance of finding a place to live around here. We're going to be stuck down in our piazza-challenged valley of the factories for the rest of the year, listening to the throbbing and churning of the machinery and dreaming of quiet cobbled streets and coffees made with fresh milk.

As we wind our way down the hill on the way home, our thoughts turn to Sandro the gormless travel agent. Sandro earns his living catering to the expectations of tourists: how could he possibly have thought that we would be happy in Valfabbrica when there are so many wonderful alternatives on offer? He must be blind to the obvious shortcomings of his home town. (The fact that he lives in a sparkling new home built by his father-in-law, complete with fully functional kitchen, may have something to do with it.)

It is true, as Sandro has often pointed out, that Valfabbrica is well positioned, close to important landmarks such as Assisi, Spoleto and Perugia. It is also true that the scenery is spectacular—the number of holiday villas and apartments dotted throughout the area is testimony to its appeal. But still: Valfabbrica itself is the pits, characterless and joyless, the kind of place you would visit only long enough to do some shopping before heading straight back up to your luxury villa to admire the rolling hills. Better still, you would bypass it entirely and shop at Collestrada, notwithstanding the very real possibility of being assailed by an Australian current affairs presenter.

While musing on this point, we find ourselves passing the Buitoni factory on the outskirts of Sansepolcro, and we realise that the modern, industrial landscape here is not particularly attractive either. Nor even the slightest bit medieval. Perhaps Valfabbrica is not so unusual in its dreariness; perhaps the wonderful towns we've seen so far—Spello, Città di Castello, Citerna—are exceptions to the norm. Perhaps when all is said and done we would be better off down among the rolling hills, despite the faults and foibles of the farmhouse.

I feel mightily confused. Why did we come here? What were we expecting? Will we ever be satisfied? A great sense of weariness envelopes me. Just remember to stay in the right lane unless overtaking…

It is early afternoon and we are about to head off to pick up Ruby from kindergarten when a client rings with a rush job: if they fax it over right away can I have it finished by tomorrow? Unfortunately Sandro is out of the office all day, which means that we will have to go in to Perugia to pick up the fax ourselves. Much as we love Perugia, an hour and a half's round trip is an unwanted distraction at this time of the day.

Never mind: we will try to make the trip a little more interesting by taking the scenic route rather than barrelling down the freeway as we would normally do. It turns out that the scenic route is much more enjoyable and takes no longer than the freeway anyway. As well as passing through countless little villages and hamlets, it offers views right across the valley as far as Assisi. It also yields several unexpected treasures: a second-hand junk shop, where we pick up a few more homely things for the farmhouse; a Chinese supermarket, where we buy various odds and ends not available in the normal supermarkets; and a tasty pizza-by-the-slice place just near Sandro's office.

The views on the return trip after sundown are especially beautiful, with Assisi lit up like a fairy castle in the distance. At a small town further down the road we encounter preparations for the village festival: streamers and banners, tents and stalls, tables and cooking equipment with the tantalising promise of tasty local goodies.

As yet there is no food on offer, since the start of festivities is still several hours away, but it looks like loads of fun: down-to-earth local folk culture, the very thing that we have come half way round the world to see. We'll just have to come back tomorrow night. [*Sadly they never did make it back. Ed.*] So all in all the unwanted fax hassle has turned out to be a highly worthwhile experience.

The next day, after I have successfully completed the rush job and sent it off courtesy of Sandro's phone line, Cecilia rings to say that Telecom Italia have decided that I need yet another document for my application: a copy of the Permission to Stay forms issued to us by the Questura in Perugia. (Yes! They said we could stay.) Whatever, sighs Our Hero wearily, before rewriting the date on the application form for the third time and trooping down to the newsagency to fax it off again. The lady there is used to me now.

Meanwhile, the tripartite discussions between myself, Sandro and Morelli drag on and on; though we meet almost daily, progress is excruciatingly slow. To add to the workload, there have been a few mysterious incidents at the farmhouse which remain unexplained due to the combination of poor language skills on our part and supremely gifted obfuscation on Morelli's part. I have attempted to impose some order on proceedings by listing these on a piece of paper, from which I now read.

Agenda Item One: Why did you come into the kitchen the other day and make off with all the chairs?

A crisp exchange between Morelli and Sandro: it turns out that they are special chairs given to him by his parents and he can't possibly leave them with us. (So why were they in the kitchen in the first place?) The problem, I continue smoothly, is that the chairs you have provided in exchange are rickety old things, so low to the ground that the children can't reach the table any more.

Then you should buy some cushions at the local market, comes the response.

Um, OK then.

And on to the next agenda item, which concerns the heating system, steadily shaping up as the single most annoying aspect of life in the farmhouse. It is too unreliable, making the morning shower a tense and unpredictable experience. We have complained to Morelli repeatedly; his answer is to harangue us further for not adhering to the instructions prescribed in his increasingly confused and rambling Heating System lectures. Exasperated at our continuing intransigence, he has resorted to taping over the Switch-That-Must-Not-Be-Touched (OK I admit it: we did try it once or twice under extreme duress during cold shower incidents), and has called in handsome Leonardo several times to repair various bits and pieces down in the ancient boiler room, but all to no avail.

These issues will all need to be addressed in the fullness of time, but for today, in the interests of clarity and impact, I will have to keep this agenda item nice and simple or we'll be arguing for hours on end.

Agenda Item Two: Why is it that sometimes the boiler doesn't come on when we flick the switch in the kitchen?

That'll be because of the new timer control I had fitted the other day, is the response. It's been set to turn the boiler on only at certain times of day, he adds with a triumphant smile.

Thanks for letting us know, landlord. I'll bet he changes the hours around every now and then just to keep us guessing, the old bastard. And then sits in his apartment downstairs listening out for the groans of anguish and disappointment first thing in the morning.

But Morelli is unrepentant; in fact he has an Agenda Item of his own.

Morelli's Agenda Item: Why do you keep moving the furniture around all the time?

That's not true, I protest, we have hardly changed a thing.[6] You are welcome to come and have a look any time. Morelli however is not convinced; he hears scraping noises often, he says, especially in the mornings.

In a flash the answer comes to me: Morelli's lounge room is directly under Felix's bedroom. Felix has been pushing things around the floor in the mornings as he plays alone in his prison, waiting for the rest of the household to come to the party. This is the source of the scraping noises.

For the moment Morelli is appeased, but in the course of today's confrontations, I sense that we have reached a new level of misunderstanding. Morelli is becoming increasingly irritated with Sandro and quite possibly with us as well. This adds a new and dangerous element to our predicament: what if Morelli were to suddenly spit the dummy, much like his predecessor in Casa Castalda? Never mind our rights as tenants; I wouldn't put it past him to abruptly change the locks one day and turf our bags out the window onto the driveway below. Another interesting possibility to ponder as I lay awake at night wondering how this is all going to turn out.

6 And anyway, since when is rearranging the furniture an offence?

3

Shenanigans

Eleni has started her intensive Italian course at Perugia. She has been allocated 9am classes every day, with an 8am class on Fridays for good measure. This entails getting out of bed at 6.30 in the morning and 6am on Fridays, which would be enough to put any normal person off the entire idea, but to her credit she has managed to make it down to the bus stop on time every day. And by happy coincidence, the University for Foreigners is located within walking distance of Sandro's office, which means that if I have a fax coming from Japan, Eleni can collect it before catching the bus home. In this way, I can have faxes home delivered within hours, as opposed to waiting until the evening. Now *that's* efficiency.

But this morning tragedy has struck: Eleni has missed the bus by a matter of seconds. While the children and I are eating our breakfast she appears, breathless and disgruntled, at the back door, having slogged it all the way back up the hill. Never mind: let us turn the situation to our advantage. We shall all sally forth to kindergarten earlier than usual and pop in to Mario's bar for a family coffee before depositing Eleni on the next bus.

On our way down the main street, we notice the Carabinieri executing a swift U-turn in the street as if to pursue us. Hearts thumping: what have we done wrong? Are they going to deport us? But no, the smiling Carabinieri man has come to return Eleni's student card, which she dropped on the street in her haste earlier in the morning. The Valfabbrica approval rating goes up a notch.

On to Mario's then, conveniently located right opposite the bus stop, for a morning cappuccino. We have long since given up on the caffé latte, our warm brown beverage of choice in Australia. If our experiences thus far are anything to go by, the caffé latte in Italy varies wildly in terms of strength and temperature due to a woeful lack of consensus among Italians on what the thing actually is. Every bar has a different idea on how to make a caffé latte; some even use cold milk. Ugh!

At one stage I tried providing my own definition when ordering, stressing the key concepts *hot* and *strong*, but a couple of decidedly frosty reactions from behind the bar put an end to that. So, after enduring a succession of weak, tepid milky coffees, we officially abandoned our pursuit of the caffé latte altogether and reverted to the safer and more consistent cappuccino, which brought on a wave of nostalgia for 1980s Australia when coffee in a glass was unheard of and a cappuccino was the only known alternative to Nescafe.

Today Mario isn't behind the counter; instead it is Manuella, his wife, whom we recognise from kindergarten, since her five-year-old daughter Chiara is in the same class as Ruby. Where is Mario this morning? He is still asleep—early morning is the wife's shift. Alternating shifts seem to be norm in family-run bars such as this; when, we wonder, do they get to have time together as a family?

Seeing as Manuella is an extremely agreeable type, I wonder aloud to Eleni, perhaps we could try ordering a hot, strong caffé latte, just this once...No, we do not want to offend her. Best to stick with nostalgia for the moment.

On Tuesdays Eleni has a two-hour class at 4 pm as well as the regular morning class. Rather than spending the entire day poking around the shops in Perugia, she has selflessly decided that she will catch the bus back at lunchtime to be with the family. We will then escort her into Perugia for the afternoon class, and while Mother is studying, Father and the children will spend a couple of hours engaged in narrow alleyway adventures in the endlessly interesting university precinct, stopping for coffees and gelatos on the way.

This Tuesday, however, the fun will have to wait—we must return to the dreaded Finance Ministry and apply for a Codice Fiscale. Ruby and Felix are not impressed with this prospect, nor am I looking forward to spending hours waiting around in the gloomy corridors of the Ministry trying to keep the two of them amused. Imagine my surprise then when the entire procedure is over in about 20 minutes. I stare down at the piece of official paper in my hand in disbelief. Surely it can't be that simple? Perhaps I should check with the enquiry counter just in case. No, best not to tempt fate. The three of us get our coffees and gelatos after all, thanks once again to the startling efficiency of Italian bureaucracy.

In the second week of Eleni's course, the Tuesday afternoon class coincides with the annual chocolate festival in Perugia, so we make a special effort to get in early. Initially I had dismissed the Chocolate Festival as a cynical tourism and marketing exercise, but after sampling some of the goodies on offer I've undergone a complete conversion; I now view it as an excellent initiative by civic-minded municipal authorities providing ordinary citizens with direct access to high-quality chocolate produce from around the world. In other words, we have all gorged ourselves silly. The children are most impressed with the Lindt train that does a loop around the piazza and finishes with free chocolates for all, as well as the (nominally) life-size Fiat sports car made entirely from chocolate, apart from the metal steering wheel and gearstick thrust rudely into the chocolate floor.

Upon our return from Perugia we find the Signora Who Gets Things Done doggedly mowing the lawn under the supervision of Signor Morelli. He spots us and looks up long enough to mumble 'oh my hernia, my hernia' in a feeble voice. There's something oddly familiar about that voice…Yes! It's Doctor Smith from *Lost in Space* with the classic line 'oh the pain, the pain...' Morelli is actually Zachary Smith, not Walter Matthau at all.[1]

1 The allegory extends further: I see us as the fearless brave Robinson Family, transplanted abruptly to the Alpha Centauri of deepest Umbria, with Sandroa as a hairy space monster in a cheap gorilla suit. And the HGV as the robot of course, getting all the choice one-liners.

Eleni suggests that I take over pushing the lawnmower. The poor Signora shouldn't have to do it; and besides, it will earn us brownie points for later. Fair enough then. As it turns out, the mower is self-propelled and a breeze to operate since you simply trail behind while it pulls itself along. (Strange that we don't have these in Australia, land of large back gardens that require constant mowing. Particularly ours.) Trimming the lawn with one of these is hardly hernia-aggravating stuff, and I am sorely tempted to put Morelli back behind the wheel—a life-threatening experience would probably do him the world of good.

Unbeknownst to His Grumpiness, we have been secretly exploring other accommodation options. Mario's apartment in Città di Castello, which we saw fairly early on, was spectacularly renovated and located right on the wonderful central piazza, but sadly far too expensive, and not, as it turns out, equipped with the all-important phone line. Meanwhile, Sandro has done the noble thing and located alternatives close to Valfabbrica. The first is a newly refurbished apartment belonging to a 'close relative',[2] located in a quiet, picturesque hamlet up the mountain on the other side of the valley. It is very small and, oddly enough given the picturesque setting, has virtually no windows. Too much like living in a box: we have to turn it down.

The next one, which Sandro discovered by chance after overhearing a conversation in his local bar, is a wonderfully spacious 1950s apartment with not two but three bedrooms and a proper working phone line into the bargain. The catch this time is that the apartment faces directly onto the main road, where the trucks rumble past all day long. Although we have been continually downgrading our expectations of Italy since arrival, the thought of a year of constant traffic noise is too much for our touristic sensibilities. Sorry Sandro, can't do this one either.

What shall I do about the phone line application then, he asks innocently. The *what*?

2 Probably his second cousin's sister-in-law.

It turns out that Sandro kindly took it upon himself to cancel the application when we asked him to look for some other houses, reasoning that we would have no need for a new phone line at Morelli's if we were planning to move out. With a supreme effort I manage to maintain my rage—for Pete's sake I said *if* not *when*, I want to shout at him. Another two weeks wasted. Back to the dingy newsagency. New date on the application. Try to ignore the bemused look from the lady at the counter.

We ask Sandro to consider accommodation options further afield—as in, not in Valfabbrica at all. You're a travel agent, we say, you must have the necessary contacts. Well, I guess I could ask around, he ventures cautiously, but I don't know, it might be hard to find something so late in the year...

He sounds decidedly evasive. Have we inadvertently done something wrong, we wonder; one of those cross-cultural blunders perhaps, that you only find out about much later?

It turns out that the problem runs deeper than that: Sandro's whole attitude has changed. He clearly feels he has done his moral and contractual duty by finding us a couple of alternative homes and is not obliged to provide any further help. He has even started to drop hints about the cost of the internet calls from his house, the cost of receiving faxes at his office, the amount of time taken up by the endless discussions with Morelli.

I promise to compensate him handsomely; it is vital that we keep Sandro onside, not only to help smooth our dealings with Morelli but also because at this stage he still represents our best chance of finding alternative accommodation.

But it is already too late. Sandro drops his bombshell: he wants to wash his hands of the whole deal. Let's annul the contract and I'll give you back the advance rent you paid me, he says; from now on you can deal with Morelli directly. After all, you've learned some Italian, you should be able to negotiate with him by yourself. (This last comment is most flattering but quite untrue. Never mind: nothing like being thrown in at the deep end to really push your language development.)

There seems little point in trying to convince Sandro to change his mind; he has clearly had enough of Morelli, and I can't say I blame him. At least he has promised to refund our money. Minus an overly generous commission for himself, as it turns out, although I don't bother challenging it because I'm just happy that we haven't been completely fleeced of all our cash and keen not to upset our now delicately balanced relationship any further.

But wait, there's more: another few hundred Euros for an unnamed mystery person (*I can't tell you who*, he says darkly). This is surely none other than Carla, Ruby's kindergarten teacher and a longstanding friend of Morelli. It seems that some time ago Morelli asked Carla to help him find some extra income in the form of tenants for the farmhouse, and Carla duly obliged by putting him in touch with Sandro who was at that time casting around for alternatives after the Casa Castalda home fell through.

Talk about small-town relationships: Carla is Sandro's close relative, being married to Walter, speeding Deputy Mayor of Valfabbrica and cousin of Sandro.[3] She is also the mother of Marta, our one-time interpreter. We see Carla every morning and occasionally discuss kindergarten matters together, so we feel as if we know her quite well. Now we find out she is to be paid handsomely for her role in getting us into this mess. Doesn't she feel bad about the way it's turned out? Couldn't she at least have a quiet word to Morelli on our behalf? But this is clearly not the way you do things around here.

How the hell *do* you do things around here then? I'm fed up with all these interfamilial connections and internecine relationships and pay-offs and favours and lack of moral obligation and unhelpfulness and obfuscation, not to mention the language barrier and the potential for cross-cultural misunderstanding.

Even Sandro thinks that Carla, and by extension Walter, both have a moral obligation to intervene on our behalf; they on the other hand clearly feel nothing of the sort. Apparently one evening Sandro went around to their house to discuss the Morelli situation and Walter barely took his eyes off the television the whole time. How rude is that! (Especially to such a close relative.)

3 Is there anyone in Valfabbrica that Sandro isn't related to? Maybe that's the root of the problem right there.

Our prospects for moving out are now more remote than ever, and we resign ourselves to the inevitable. Thus far our suitcases have languished on the floor only half unpacked, but now, reluctantly, we start taking out all the clothes and putting them away in the cupboards. Much as one doesn't want to admit defeat, one has to be realistic: barring a minor miracle, this is where we're staying for the next year.

I'm starting to hate the morning routine of delivering Ruby to that stark noisy concrete kindergarten day after day, a false smile plastered over my face: Yes, we're loving it here in Valfabbrica. Still settling in of course. *The minute we find a new place we're outta here.* Ruby's having a great time at kindergarten. *It's a wonder she still has any hearing left.* Such beautiful countryside. *Shame about the town.*

I just hope Ruby doesn't see any of this. At least Felix is still too small to understand. Will the children forgive me for dragging them into a strange and unfriendly environment on false pretences? And as for Eleni, she can't be expected to remain kind and supportive and understanding for ever. When this happens, I'll need to summon all my mental reserves just to maintain an even keel.

It could have been worse I suppose; at least it's a nice quiet spot up here on the hill. And there has in fact been one positive development: after weeks of constant badgering by the combined forces of myself and Leonardo the Handsome, Morelli has finally relented and allowed me to use his phone line twice daily to send and receive e-mails.

His change of heart has come at just the right time: with Sandro feeling less magnanimous these days it is as well that I won't have to bother him any more. And what a luxury to not have to pack up the computer and drive across town every day!

On the other hand, this leaves me dependent on Morelli's goodwill to keep my translation career afloat until such time as the good people at Telecom Italia deign to connect us to the outside world. What would happen, for instance, if I had to send off a job while Morelli was out and couldn't get to the phone? Or if I offended him somehow, causing him to renege altogether on the deal? I don't fancy carrying the computer down to the town and shuffling from doorway to doorway pleading for spare bandwidth like some sort of cyber-beggar.

Meanwhile, it is an enormous relief to have finally put an end to those interminable meetings. Morelli had taken an obvious dislike to Sandro and seemed to revel in wilful obstruction, and I realise in hindsight that having Sandro as a middleman was actually hindering rather than facilitating the flow of communication. In the course of a single session with Morelli and the SWGTD we manage to reach agreement on the deposit, bills and monthly rent, which the landlord has been trying to bump up ever since our arrival; the need to purchase heating oil and wood for the coming winter; the state of the kitchen; and a new list of things required around the house.

With the money repaid by Sandro I am in a position to give Morelli the deposit and a whole month's rent in advance—the prospect of a big dollop of cash ought to cheer him up. We are startled to discover that Morelli has received not one Eurocent of the advance rent that we sent from Australia, nor any of the additional 250 Euros Sandro charged us for refurbishment of the outdoor laundry. This goes a long way towards explaining the animosity between the two, particularly given the old man's predilection with money; after hearing this we almost feel sorry for him.[4]

Buoyed by this new atmosphere of harmony and understanding, we allow ourselves to speculate that there may be a glimmer of hope that the situation could improve and things could work out after all. As proof of good character and willingness to engage constructively, I waste no time in presenting Morelli with his first payment in cold hard cash. (It never occurs to me to ask for a receipt.)

The events of the very next day, however, will change the landscape entirely, making me wish that I'd held onto my money for just 24 hours longer, making me realise that Sandro was, once again, quite possibly right after all.

It all begins when the fridge breaks down. Morelli calls in Leonardo, who examines the fridge at length and pronounces that it is beyond repair and must be replaced. Upon hearing this, Morelli

4 Almost.

refuses outright to entertain the idea of buying a replacement. The fridge broke down, he argues, because you put too much food in it.[5] How would he know what's in our fridge anyway? Has he been sneaking up here while we are out? Better start putting hairs across the doors.

Surely, I protest, recovering my wits after realising that he is not joking, this is a *furnished apartment*; that means that when something breaks down, you as landlord are supposed to replace it. Besides, you'll need a new fridge for the tourists that come next year after we've left. But Morelli is having none of it. He knows that he has us over a barrel, since with two small children we can't survive long without a refrigerator. Unfortunately it is not yet winter, or we could put everything in a box outside the back door.

After a while he offers a generous compromise of a 50:50 split, but now it's our turn to refuse point blank. It's outrageous, we splutter; we have rights too you know. Not that we have the slightest idea how to exercise them, with no recourse to Sandro and no contract. Does anyone know the Italian for 'Tourism Complaints Centre'?

With impeccable timing, the Signora Who Gets Things Done suddenly turns up—she must have a sixth sense—and Eleni demonstrates how upset we feel about this shabby treatment by promptly bursting into tears. (In truth Eleni is exhausted after a week of early morning starts but we're not about to point that out.) The SWGTD consoles Eleni as expected and promises that we shall have a new fridge soon, although she fails to say exactly when. Eleni and I are tempted to nail her down on a date—how will we keep the milk cold in the meantime?—but decide against pressing the SWGTD further and switch to grateful mode. Best not to push our luck since she is an important ally and must be kept onside at all costs.

Now it is Leonardo's turn to spring to our aid, the champion. Let's go and find a fridge, he says; hop in my car. What does he mean? Surely you don't 'find' fridges, you buy them. Does the Italian word for *find* have some special connotation to do with fridges perhaps, or have I misunderstood him?[6]

5 Seriously.
6 Always a possibility.

But no, we really are going on a fridge hunt. Near the edge of town on the road to our place, although I have never noticed it before, is a sort of industrial garbage dump where, according to Leonardo, you can often find a perfectly good fridge for free. Hard to believe on first appearances, but we set to work nevertheless picking over the most promising candidates: this one looks to be in good working order but doesn't have any shelves; this one is fitted out inside but missing some vital electrical part according to Leonardo; most of the others on offer are obviously broken or filthy.

Suddenly I am gripped by an uncontrollable desire to laugh out loud: who would have thought that within a month of arriving in the land of culture and coffee that I would find myself spending a Saturday afternoon at the tip picking over discarded white goods?

Weekends were meant to be for bracing walks through the hills with the family reciting Sound of Music ditties, lazy coffees in the piazza watching the world go by, long lunches in the bosom of hearty locals keen to shower us with gifts of home-made preserves...OK, so maybe our original ideas about Italy were based on ridiculously romantic notions—stereotypes even—but still, not this, surely.

Leonardo shakes me out of my reverie: There are no good fridges here today, he says, but I've got a bar fridge which you're welcome to borrow. Off we trot to Leonardo's amazing junk shed, where he proudly shows off the vintage car that he is restoring together with his father. And presents me with a tiny but eminently usable refrigerator. It even has a couple of tiny shelves.

We carry it back and plonk it on top of the dead fridge like a modern art sculpture, then with bated breath plug it in. It clicks, it whirs, it works! Eleni and I are now in super-grateful mode, but what can we offer Leonardo in return? Back in Australia, a home-made cake would be the order of the day, but the old farmhouse oven cannot be entrusted with baking tasks. We resolve to buy him a bottle of Australian wine on the next shopping trip to Collestrada.

Needless to say, the fridge incident completely overturns our good resolutions towards Morelli and intensifies the confusion about whether we could put up with him for a whole year. The urgency level goes up a notch when, with impeccable timing, the hardworking and efficient team at Telecom Italia ring to say that Men will be around within a week or so to start installing the new phone line.

We don't know whether to be pleased or scared. They have charged us an enormous amount to have the phone connected; if we cancel now, we should be able to get the money refunded, but if we let them connect the phone we're virtually committing ourselves to the farmhouse simply because it would be such a tragic waste of money in the event that we did subsequently move out. And, more importantly, because the Miser King would get the benefit of a lovely new phone line at absolutely no cost to himself.

Meanwhile, in another interesting development on the fridge front, we learn that the SWGTD is simply going to pay for our half of the new fridge herself rather than attempting to convince Morelli of the error of his ways, as we had assumed. Furthermore, we are not to breathe a word about this arrangement to Morelli, presumably for fear of upsetting him further. (He has wised up to our cosy relationship with the SWGTD and told us in no uncertain terms not to go behind his back in future.)

This latest turn of events means that the evil landlord will conclude that he got his own way on the fridge after all, thus setting an alarming precedent for the future. What if—when, more like—the crappy old washing machine in the outhouse breaks down? *You put too many clothes in it.* The ancient boiler? *You take too many showers.* The last remaining gas ring on the stove? *You cook too much.* It doesn't bear thinking about.

Only one thing to take our minds off the dilemma: a nice Sunday drive with the family. Today we are heading to Bevagna, having read a highly positive reference in our guidebook.[7] A 'gem of medieval town planning' boasting 'the most well-proportioned piazza in all of Italy,' we are assured. Bevagna is indeed a beautiful city set on the flat plains among vast expanse of picturesque farmlands, complete with gentling winding cobbled streets, castle

7 See, I've done my homework this time.

walls and even a moat. The piazza is certainly lovely, flanked by fine churches and palazzos, although whether it is the finest in Italy I could not say. At this stage my vote is still going to Città di Castello. No prizes for guessing which town gets the gong for Worst Piazza in Italy.

While we are enjoying a coffee in said piazza, I spy the tourist information office opposite and it occurs to me to ask them about permanent accommodation in Bevagna. Not your average tourist query it is true, but there's no harm in trying.

Why yes, I may be able to help you, says the man at the tourist information office.

He dashes out and reappears five minutes later bearing a telephone number scrawled on a scrap of paper. We are elated. Bevagna would be a great place to live! How clever we are to deal direct with the locals! We ring the number and arrange to meet the owner the very next day.

With hearts in mouths we head back to Bevagna on Monday to meet up with Paulo, a spiffy looking bescarfed young man who gets down to business immediately, informing us that the house is almost right on the piazza and has a rooftop balcony. A view over the best piazza in Italy! It just gets better and better.

Without further ado we set off. Thirty seconds' walk from the piazza, in through the door leading off the lovely cobbled main thoroughfare, up a flight of stairs and… oh dear.

Bloody hell.

We stare in horror at a cold, stark, sparsely furnished apartment that appears to have been abandoned for several months, if not years. There is a pile of dirty dishes in the kitchen and broken bottles in the fireplace. There is a pigeons' nest right outside the kitchen window and a mountain of droppings on the sill. The bedrooms look like prison cells—high windows, grubby walls, dirty floors, nothing but droopy old chain-mail beds and dilapidated wardrobes in the way of furniture. The lounge room has no television or couches, the kitchen has no table. The place is a dive; it's uninhabitable. It actually makes Morelli's farmhouse look cosy.

Unbelievably, Paulo launches straight into negotiations. Surely he doesn't think we're interested in this hovel. Bevagna or no, it's insulting. Especially when his starting offer for the rent is 50 per cent more than what we're currently paying. Tellingly, his own apartment, to which he now leads us, is in immaculate condition and lavishly furnished. I can see a pattern emerging here: well-heeled local tries to set up gullible foreign family in sub-standard accommodation. Another one to put down to experience. Unfortunately this episode will forever sully our image of the beautiful city of Bevagna. We won't be back.

After the disappointment of the day we decide to flop down in front of the television for the first time, eager for a dose of Italian popular culture. (For language practice of course, as recommended by Eleni's university instructor.)

With great anticipation we switch it on and … the screen remains resolutely blank. The television is out of order. Naturally.

In light of the fridge incident, it hardly seems worth bringing the matter up with Morelli; he'd probably say that we stared at it too hard. Nor with the SWGTD, who has recently had a massive argument with Morelli over said fridge incident and as a result is no longer on speaking terms with him, ever, which means we have lost our only remaining ally in the great struggle. We have won the fridge but lost the war—truly a pyrrhic[8] victory. It seems that from now on, if we want anything fixed in the farmhouse we'll just have to do it ourselves. Time for another trip to the junkyard with Leonardo.

8 Just had to get this word in; it's got that triple-letter high score look about it.

4

Brinkmanship

Eleni is discovering some of the peripheral benefits of an intensive Italian course—inside information gleaned through conversations with other students and plenty of free time between classes for shopping. This turns out to be a potent combination. Every day she returns with stories of new clothing outlets, gelati shops, fresh pasta shops, even a specialty food store selling exotic foreign goodies such as soy sauce and coconut milk and curry paste. The classmates are a veritable font of important knowledge, and we are now well informed about what's on around town in Perugia, where to see films in English and where to find the best pizza.[1] Not to be outdone, Eleni has also been exploring on her own and has unearthed, among other things, an 87-centesimi shop (the equivalent of a $2 shop) selling a wealth of handy plastic items for around the casa.

Then one day in late October during the last week of her course, Eleni arrives home in a state of high excitement. I've been talking to my student friends about their apartments, she says, and they pay less than us and have normal decent landlords. I've found out where the rental agencies are in Perugia; let's go and find a new place ourselves. We're sure to find something better than here.

She's right: we've put up with more than enough from horrible old Morelli. It's time to draw a line in the sand, to teach him a lesson, to take the bit between the teeth and grab the horse by the

1 Capri Pizzeria, according to our sources.

mouth and throw the baby out with the bathwater and... But first of all we'd better cancel the phone line application before it's too late; Telecom Italia is due any day now.

On the way back into Perugia for the afternoon class I speak to an excitable young operator at the Telecom Italia call centre and somehow manage to negotiate the cancellation. After all the dithering of the last couple of months, it comes as something of a relief to have finally taken a stand and made a decision. Now we are in control of our own destiny instead of always being dependent on others (usually Sandro) to help us out. We are excited and brimming with confidence. Perugia, after all, is set up for foreigners, particularly around the university, so we'll have no trouble dealing with real estate agencies. Why, it'll be just like the old days looking for student housing.[2] Just imagine living in Perugia! We can be genuine chocolately Perugians ourselves!

The next morning is fine and sunny here on our patch of the hill. Things are looking up: the phone line has been successfully cancelled, the weather is beautiful, tomorrow we are heading into Perugia to start preparing for our new life. Eleni has left for university several hours ago, Ruby has been deposited at kindergarten for the day and Felix and I are enjoying a quiet moment in the garden when who should arrive but...the Cable Guy from Telecom Italia!

Is this some sort of joke? All those weeks of endless waiting, of jumping up hopefully from my desk at the sound of every passing truck, and he finally turns up the day after we cancel.

Furthermore, this poses a nasty dilemma—I could, I suppose, take this opportunity to reconsider our rash decision of yesterday; to Just Say Yes and get the telephone connected and restore some much-needed stability to our confused lives. Is this some sort of sign? Should I pass up our last chance to settle down?

2 Notwithstanding the two-year-old in the pram.

Were we serious about all that line in the sand stuff yesterday? Gulp. Yes we were.

While Cable Guy is still dismounting from his truck, I approach cautiously and quietly—best to keep Morelli out of this if at all possible—and, with a conspiratorial air, hiss at him to go away because we don't want the phone any more. Cable Guy is completely nonplussed by this. I attempt to explain further but suddenly here is Morelli, who has overheard the truck arriving and is now bearing down on Cable Guy, telling him to ignore me and shepherding him over to one side. Time to assert my rights then.

Ahem, I say in a loud and confident voice, we actually cancelled the phone line application yesterday. Didn't they tell you at the office then?

Morelli stops dead in his tracks. This is indeed a moment to savour: the small but pathetic satisfaction of being able to show the old codger who's in control.

Alas, it lasts for but a fleeting instant. Morelli quickly regains his composure and switches to incredulous mode: I thought you were desperate for this phone line, he splutters. What about all your internet and faxing and email business then?

Meanwhile Cable Guy stares at us both in disbelief like we're some sort of cheap cabaret act. I'm starting to feel acutely uncomfortable. So much for being in control: what can I say now? Should I spill the beans and tell the evil landlord the real reason why we don't want the phone line? No, that would be foolish in the extreme.[3]

In a sudden flash of inspiration I recall the failed mobile office experiment and hastily concoct an excellent excuse, if I do say so myself, about being able to connect to the internet using my new mobile phone, so I don't actually need a new phone line after all, thanks very much anyway, and isn't modern technology amazing, and how odd that you weren't told about the cancellation and I'm so sorry that you've come all this way this morning and...Cable Guy has heard enough crazy foreign rambling. He climbs back in his Cable Truck, no doubt rapt because he gets to take the rest of the

3 Though immensely satisfying.

day off, and trundles away down the road. Morelli gives me a withering look before stumping back into his apartment and peace returns to the hillside once more.

The next week is spent slogging around a succession of real estate agents in Perugia with young Felix. As expected, he finds the whole process exceedingly boring, and I dare say he can probably sense our growing sense of frustration as each one in turn fails to yield the anticipated cheap rental housing solution. Either it's the wrong time of year, or there's nothing suitable for children, or there are no car spaces available, or the cheap places are all reserved for incoming students—for some reason our particular needs are too difficult to accommodate, except at the luxury end of the market. At one point we half-heartedly make an appointment to view a house that is well out of our price range, only to cancel it a couple of hours later after thinking it through properly. It's no use: living in Perugia is clearly not the answer either.

Depression settles over us like a thick fog. Could we sink any lower? Could we make our lives any more difficult? We tried to take the initiative, but we've ended up shooting ourselves in the collective foot. We're still stuck in the farmhouse, the same as two months ago, but with no Sandro and no SWGTD to help us out any more. And we're still without a phone, the same as two months ago. Two months! I can hardly believe that we've spent this long stuffing around without making any progress.[4] Our prospects are hopeless: this is turning into the year of disappointment and unfulfilled dreams. Most embarrassingly of all, we'll have to ring Telecom Italia and reapply for the phone line yet again, and this time they'll probably take extra-long to get around to it just to pay us back for sending away their Cable Guy…

Shortly after our arrival, I went through a period of waking up regularly in the middle of the night wondering what on earth we were doing on the other side of the world away from all that we

4 Unless finally getting all the Telecom Italia documents in order counts as progress.

knew and loved. Happily this died down once we got settled in and the provisional home office was set up. After the disappointment of Perugia, however, the nightly waking has returned, and with an added note of urgency this time. Because the general sense of dislocation has been replaced with a more definite goal—to escape. Yet we have little idea how to go about it and only a string of failures to show for our efforts. The sense of helplessness, of stupidity, is profound. How optimistic we were, how naïve! Instead of being in a position to savour all that Italy has to offer, we will spend the year enduring constant battles with our recalcitrant landlord just trying to maintain a normal day-to-day existence.

It could be worse, says Eleni—at least you have an office of sorts; Ruby and Felix are settled and happy; we have a car and a roof over our heads; we are all in good health. *And* there are two pizzerias close by. She's right of course. But as a card-carrying grass-is-greener type, I can't help wallowing in righteous indignation thinking of how much better it could have been, of how some other family somewhere is right now enjoying the Italian Odyssey that we were meant to have. And probably making a reality TV show about it too.

One afternoon an email arrives from Marius in Citerna: I thought you might like to try a couple of real estate agents up our way, he writes. The phone numbers are sitting right there on the screen, taunting me to have another try at finding a new home: go on, just one more time, it's easy. Well that's all very tempting, but I think I'm at the thanks-but-no-thanks stage now. What if they show us a house like that one in Bevagna?

I don't think I could cope with getting my hopes up again only to have them comprehensively dashed. Again. But Eleni, optimistic as always, insists that we give it a go; if we don't, she points out, we'll be forever saying 'what if' and cursing ourselves.

Incredibly, within fifteen minutes I have managed to arrange appointments to inspect one property in Anghiari next Monday and three more in the general area of Sansepolcro on Wednesday, all of them for about the same rent as we are currently paying. We stare at one another goggle-eyed. Anghiari and Sansepolcro—the very towns we saw from Marius and Christine's balcony that time, pining on about how wonderful it would be to live in the area. Perhaps it was meant to be! Thank heavens for wifely wisdom.

After what seems like an eternity, Monday finally comes around. Ruby is unceremoniously deposited at kindergarten and we are off up the highway once more, first to Citerna to pick up Marius and Christine who are coming along for the ride, and then onto the real estate agent at Anghiari.

Anghiari is yet another magnificent medieval township built on a hill, but with one important qualification: it's a bloody steep hill. The main street plunges straight down through town at a vertigo-inducing, have-you-checked-the-brakes-recently type of angle before bottoming out abruptly on the flat plain of the Tiber Valley. The perfectly flat central piazza juts out from the slope on a massive retaining wall like the bow of the *Titanic*, while the older section of town sits on top of towering vertical cliffs which must have given their ancient enemies pause for thought.[5] Viewed from the flat plain, Anghiari looks for all the world like a storybook fairytale castle poised on the hillside, the effect bizarrely offset by a tapestry of colourful twenty-first century washing hanging out of medieval stone windows.

The house we are looking at today turns out to be some distance away from all of this—in the middle of a field, in fact, at the bottom of the hill. It is a clean though unremarkable third floor apartment, and comes with retired landlords downstairs and the promise of endless fresh produce from their massive vegetable garden out the back. Now *that* sounds more like the Italian Experience. There's even a phone line!

Eleni, however, is not convinced.

And I in turn am horrified. Surely you couldn't possibly turn your nose up at this opportunity to get out of the Valfabbrica farmhouse, I plead; this place looks OK, it'll do won't it? But she is concerned about safety and also the isolation factor. It is true that the

5 Before being doused with boiling oil, presumably.

combination of a boisterous two-year-old and a third-storey balcony is sub-optimal; also that being a couple of kilometres from the centre of Anghiari would place us in much the same situation as we are now—on our own in the middle of the countryside with a steep walk into town. A very, very steep uphill walk, too, B2. Not to mention having to traipse up and down three flights of stairs several times a day, as Eleni wisely points out.

And finally, there's something about the husband that she doesn't like. This at least is understandable—the Morelli experience has instilled in us a deep suspicion of elderly male Italian landlords.

Sigh. Alright then. Personally I would be happy to take any offer at this stage, but it is agreed that we will wait until Wednesday and see what the other places are like. At least we have the consolation prize of lunch today with Marius and Christine at the pizza-by-the-slice place on the piazza.

On the way back from Anghiari we pass through the outskirts of Sansepolcro and are reminded that it is not a particularly pretty place. Panic attack: what if the Sansepolcro houses on Wednesday are all terrible and by the time we ring back for the Anghiari house it's been taken? Ah, the joys of searching for rental housing; it's been years since I went through all this.

Just then inspiration strikes and I decide to ring the real estate agency at Sansepolcro—could we possibly see the three houses today, seeing as we're in the area? This would save us another trip up the highway and half a tank of petrol; plus we would be able to make an immediate decision on the Anghiari flat. And there is another, even more compelling reason: tomorrow the gasolio (heating oil) man is coming to fill up the tank at the farmhouse.

Morelli has been on at me for several weeks about the need to purchase more gasolio for the ancient boiler downstairs, what with the level being so low (as determined using the ancient traditional dipstick method) and winter steadily approaching. I had successfully stalled for some time while we looked at other houses, but eventually gave in and had to arrange for the man to come on Tuesday. For his own inscrutable reasons Morelli insisted that I arrange the delivery and payment in my own name and refused even to dial up the gasolio company on my behalf.

But *if* we could see the Sansepolcro houses today, and *if* one of them were deemed acceptable, and *if* they let us have it, then we could not only make good our escape but avoid paying for the gasolio altogether. Which would be immensely satisfying. Such a bold, daring plan; tragically, however, the real estate agency is unable to accommodate us today.

When the gasolio man arrives on Tuesday I make a last-ditch effort to convince Morelli to buy the gasolio in his own name rather than mine, which quickly develops into a heated[6] exchange. Eventually Morelli throws down the gauntlet: Have it your way then, he barks, let's have no gasolio this winter, it doesn't bother me. Once again he has the upper hand: I have noticed, when down in his flat checking my emails, that he lights a fire almost every day; also I strongly suspect that he isn't the showering type. A crusty old ex-olive-farmer like Morelli probably could survive the winter without hot showers and central heating; we city slickers, on the other hand, most definitely could not.

Fair enough, say I, trying a new tack, how about you pay for it by cheque today and I'll pay you back in cash? No dice: for some reason Morelli is determined to distance himself from the purchasing process. At this point the gasolio man takes me aside for a quiet word.

Look, he says, you'll never get anywhere with that miserly old sod. Why don't I just fill the tank and write you out an invoice, then you two can sort it out and pay at the office later in the week? This is what ends up happening, although I know exactly who will be footing the bill because Morelli has got his way and it is my name on the invoice.

Morelli wastes no time in capitalising on his gasolio victory by hassling me again for the rent. It is already two weeks late and I cannot stall him with lame excuses any longer. Besides, I can't be bothered. Because I have given up. On everything. The gasolio episode has left me drained. Morelli is a stingy rotten madman and

6 No pun intended.

we are stuck with him. Why didn't we just take the Anghiari house and be done with it? Anything would be better than here. There have been too many ups and downs over the last two months, mainly downs. I feel utterly defeated. I don't care about anything any more, all I want is some peace and stability. It is in this spirit of resignation that I plod down the road once more to resubmit our phone line application to the dreaded Telecom Italia.

Wednesday morning finds me feeling gloomier still. I don't want to drive up to Sansepolcro and go through it all again. I bombard Eleni with excuses: we've just paid for all that heating oil and reapplied to Telecom Italia, Ruby is happy enough at kindergarten, let's just call it quits, settle down, no more of this emotional roller-coaster business...

Right then the phone rings. It is my sister back in Australia. At the sound of a familiar voice from long ago, I unexpectedly burst into floods of tears. The endless shenanigans with Morelli, Sandro, Telecom Italia and house-hunting have worn me down. Bloody farmhouse, bloody Valfabbrica, bloody Italy: I hate it here. Why the hell didn't we just stay at home? At least Australia is relaxed and comfortable, whereas here everything's such a goddamn struggle and I'm trying to be a breadwinner on a crappy plastic garden table with no phone line in a scorpion-infested house with a grotty kitchen that you can't even bake a cake in and there's no piazza in town and they make coffees with UHT milk for Chrissakes and we're never going to get out of this mess and it's all *wrong*, this is *not* how it was meant to be.

What, I would like to know, is the point of it all? Sure the countryside is wonderful, but that won't count for much in winter; sure there are lots of wonderful things to see, but you have to drive for half a day to get there; sure we've been able to spend more time together as a family, just the four of us, but I realise now that we need more, we need some social contact with others. It's too lonely and isolated up here on the hill. We'd be better off back at home among family and friends. Except that we can't go back—our house is already rented out for the year, and besides, I couldn't face having to explain over and over again how we tried and failed to live the dream.

Cheer up, soothes Eleni. Don't worry if this place is a dump, we'll simply use it as a base to go exploring through Italy and beyond, we'll have a great year regardless. Her kind words have the desired effect. She's right of course: it's time to shut up and get on with it. And right now, getting on with it means honouring our 10am appointment in Sansepolcro.

We arrive with minutes to spare. Unlike the industrial back blocks we were driving through on Monday, the road into the town centre turns out to be a pleasant tree-lined boulevard that finishes up next to what looks suspiciously like a castle wall. This could be promising.

I leave the family in the car and start pelting down the main street, searching for the real estate agency. Despite my haste I can see that this main street is a rather good one: traffic-free, lined with grand old buildings and full of contented townsfolk going about their business. Now I can see bars with tables and chairs out on the street, now a bakery, a grocery store, a fruit shop, a florist; now I am running past smart clothes and shoe shops, music shops, even an old theatre. The further I go the better it gets, and by the time I finally reach the agency, on the other side of a beautiful wide open piazza lined with yet more bars and shops, I am already sold. So much for the no more ups and downs: I desperately want to live in Sansepolcro.

Here we go again, then. Up the stairs and into the real estate agency, which is located in part of a stately old palazzo overlooking the piazza. Today's real estate agent is a sprightly old gent who looks to be in his sixties, very dapper in a fur-lined coat and pork pie hat. We introduce ourselves and, using the broken Italian of a recently depressed but now suddenly excited foreigner recovering from a short sprint through town, I attempt to explain that the family is waiting in the car park out the front. Raffaello (for that is his name) counters with something equally unfathomable: one of the houses we're going to look at is mine, he says. Of course it's yours, I'm thinking—you're the real estate agent, they're all yours. Perhaps the Italian word for *mine* has some special real estate connotation; either that or I have misunderstood him completely.[7] In any case we're off on the house-hunting roller-coaster once more.

House Number One is out in the country several kilometres from Sansepolcro and has no central heating, only fireplaces. It appears to have been shut up for some time. My idyllic farmhouse tourist sensibilities are momentarily aroused but Eleni sensibly points out that we would simply be swapping one draughty isolated farmhouse for another. Next please. House Number Two is an apartment on the fifth floor and is immediately struck out of contention; no point in even getting out of the car. Sorry Raffaello.

Finally we arrive at House Number Three, which turns out to be an apartment on the bottom floor of Raffaello's own home (so I understood him correctly after all). At the moment the apartment is being tidied out by two middle-aged women, a well-groomed, motherly type and a bustling matron in an apron; they are Ivana, Raffaello's wife, and Vittoria the Home Help. Raffaello must have told Ivana that the children are still in the car for she is over there in a flash, cooing over them and making admiring comments. The children take this all in their stride with great magnanimity; they are used to Italians now.

Amazingly enough, the apartment is quite acceptable. Much smaller than the old farmhouse, certainly, but clean and modern. (We're no longer interested in medieval homes—lovely to look at, not to live in.) It comes with a proper enclosed shower, heating system (fully independent of the landlord!), new stove and washing machine, even a dishwasher—what luxury. *And* there appears to be a phone line—look, there is the socket on the wall.

But does it really work? I press Raffaello. Can you use a phone with it?

Raffaello stares at me for a long moment. This here is a phone socket, he explains slowly: you get it switched on at the exchange, you plug in a phone, you have conversations.

It doesn't seem worth running through the whole saga of the fake

7 Always a possibility.

phone cord at the Lonely Farmhouse at this point. Let us once again place our faith in our good friends at Telecom Italia, in human nature in general, and in the Patron Saint of Telecommunications and all other relevant gods and stars and planets just in case.

Out the back of the apartment is a large garden area, which Ivana says we are welcome to use during the summer. And Raffaello will lend us his spare television so we can catch up on the popular culture we have been missing. In short, we could live here. The apartment is good, Sansepolcro is fabulous (Eleni takes my word for it) and we have warmed to the landlords already. We'll take it.

Raffaello breaks out a celebratory beer, even though it is still mid-morning. What was that about suspicious elderly Italian landlords? Raffaello is nothing of the sort. And Ivana has welcomed us like long-lost relatives. There is an undeniable warmth and generosity to these two.

We start chatting, and the conversation inevitably moves to our current abode in Valfabbrica and the difficulties with Morelli. Ivana makes some comment that we can't decipher other than the word 'mentalità', but the look on her face says it all: she can't abide the dirty rotten Umbrians and their disgraceful mentality.[8] Before long we are all getting along famously. Finally, after two-and-a-half long months, we have landed on our feet. I feel like crying all over again, with relief this time.

To say we are excited would be an understatement: we are positively giddy with joy. We have arranged to go back up to Sansepolcro on Friday to sign the contract, and then move in on Saturday morning. Now all that remains is to pack our things and attend to a few procedural matters such as paying the gasolio bill and picking up the mobile phone from the repair shop down at Perugia (it has started playing up already—what is it with telecommunications technology in this country?). And we must farewell our

8 Sansepolcro is part of Tuscany; barely two kilometres north of the border with Umbria, yet worlds away in respect of history, culture and mentalità. Or so Tuscans will tell you. Mind you, at this point in time, given our experiences down south, we're inclined to agree.

friends in town: Mario and Manuella at the bar; the nice lady (name unknown) in the hardware store next to the pizzeria; the young girl Angelica in the bakery who adores Felix and always slips him a treat when we pop in; the four young dudes in the Conad minimart on the edge of town; and Ruby's other kindergarten teacher, Antonietta. Although sad to see us leave, they are all highly sympathetic when we explain how we have been driven to despair by Morelli's intransigence. There is some small satisfaction in knowing that he isn't that popular down in the township.

We will have to load the car in the dead of night so that Morelli doesn't get wind of what is going on. I still need to use his phone line for the next two days, so we can't afford to have him offside quite yet. Incredibly, there is a back stairway leading from our lounge room straight down to the garage, providing the perfect escape route for clandestine removal operations.

He won't hear a thing—unless he suddenly feels the urge to make an unexpected late-night trip to his car, in which case our cover will be blown in spectacular fashion. Please may the television be especially engrossing tonight! Meanwhile, our friends have promised to keep the secret for the next two days. Let's hope there aren't any double agents amongst them; one can never be too careful in a small country town.

The children throw themselves into the task with aplomb. Books and toys back in their boxes, tear the couches apart to see what's fallen down behind, search all nooks and crannies. Clothes back in suitcases. Food into boxes. Sort out our kitchen things—quite a few by now—from those that stay behind. Should we clean the farmhouse before we leave? To hell with that say I, but Eleni insists on doing the right thing: We don't want to lower ourselves to his level do we? Grumble grumble, alright then. Just so long as Morelli can't hear all the commotion from downstairs. What if he thinks his furniture is being moved around and comes up to check? Tremble tremble whimper whimper. Even though we are now theoretically beyond his grasp, fear of Morelli is still strong.

And I'm starting to get last-minute nerves, too. What if something goes wrong in the last 48 hours? We haven't actually signed a contract yet, anything could happen—they could ring up and say they've thought better of the whole thing. Then again, we did share a beer—that's tantamount to a statement of intent isn't it? What if they weren't genuinely friendly people after all, what if it was false pretences?... Shut up and keep packing.

Finally everything is ready. On Thursday night after the children (and hopefully the landlord) have gone to sleep, we start sneaking boxes and bags down the back stairs and into the Hulking Great Volvo, which has been backed up tightly into the garage in order to camouflage its contents as much as possible. Soon the car is packed to the rafters, and that's only half of it. There is only just enough room for two adults and one child—sadly, Ruby will have to spend the day at kindergarten tomorrow.

Friday morning and we're off, guiding our heavily loaded vehicle carefully through the back streets of town so as not to arouse suspicion. Who knows where Morelli's spies might be lurking?

In Sansepolcro we park in the same spot and with great fanfare I lead Eleni and Felix along the main street, the one I ran down on Wednesday, the day the world changed for the better. Today we're nice and early, with time to spare for our first ever coffee in Sansepolcro. We stop in at a suitably upmarket bar in the corner of an impressive palazzo that features massive old wooden doors out the front and soaring vaulted ceilings inside. Now *this* is how a café/bar/whatever should be.

Immediately we are struck by the range of cakes and panini on offer. Unlike the scruffy bars in Valfabbrica with their measly offerings of two or three tired old rolls and a few limp croissants, this place has a glistening array of panini, baguettes and rolls with a bewildering selection of fillings, as well as all manner of cakes, doughnuts and pastries. Just as well we're here for the rest of the year—it's going to take us a while to get through them all.

After the coffee it's a leisurely stroll along the main street, up past the lovely piazza and into the real estate agency to sign the lease. Today we meet Raffaello's daughter Cristina, who comes across as a stylish blonde thirty-something high-powered real estate woman of the twenty-first century. It soon becomes clear that it is Cristina who is in charge of the family business these days, with Raffaello relegated to minor duties.[9] And Cristina is feeling slightly put out, because until this morning she was fully intending to move into the downstairs apartment next June while awaiting the completion of her new house.

But we have clearly made a strong impression on her parents because the next thing we know, Raffaello is doing his best to convince Cristina to live upstairs with them so that we can stay on until August. There ensues a fantastic father-daughter argument in high-speed Italian complete with much hand waving and rolling of eyes on Cristina's part until it is finally resolved that, OK, we can stay for as long as we like. It has been such a wonderful performance that I'm looking forward to coming in every month to pay the rent just so I can see them in action again.

Back in Valfabbrica after disgorging our first carload into the new apartment, we pick up Ruby from kindergarten and head to the farmhouse for the very last time. Now comes the moment we've all been waiting for: the chance to stick it up Morelli. I've drawn the short straw on this one, having been unable to convince Eleni to come along for moral support.

How is it that Daddy always lands the nasty jobs? I hope the landlord doesn't get too angry. At least he can't do anything to us now. Unless he turns out to be an axe-murderer after all, Shining-style. Are we safe in our beds tonight?

The confrontation turns out to be not too confrontational after all. Morelli listens impassively and refuses point blank to reimburse any of our gasolio money.

Happily, I still owe him the rent for this month and haven't paid the water or electricity bills, so we are only out of pocket to the tune of around 300 Euros.

It could have been worse; the gasolio bill was nearly 600 Euros. Why on earth did Morelli insist that I purchase the gasolio in my name—was it just sheer bloody-mindedness or did he suspect something? Deliberately or otherwise, the crafty old bugger has forced us to choose between paying the bill up front and trying to

9 Such as dealing with odd foreign families.

extract some change from him later, or leaving it unpaid and hoping that his lawyers and/or the gasolio company don't come looking for us. We've chosen the safe but expensive option.

The landlord and I end up raising our voices at one another, but that's nothing new. I threaten to take the issue up with the Carabinieri (local constabulary), having heard from someone that Morelli's failure to issue me with receipts is in breach of the tax laws or some such. Morelli is completely unfazed by this lame attempt to call his bluff. With nothing further left to argue, I storm off and leave him to it.

The dead of night sees us once again stealing down the back stairs with bags and boxes and suitcases. We still have to be stealthy because I suspect that Morelli still doesn't think we mean it. If he sees what we are up to he could get a nasty surprise, and one doesn't want to surprise a potential axe-murderer. Eventually the job is done and the car is groaning under the weight—this is the last load, we've burned our bridges. There's barely space enough for the poor children to squeeze in. Hopefully they won't mind; we'll tell them it's an adventure.

Which it is, really, for both adults and children alike. All the excitement of the original move two and a half months ago, now with extra added herbs and spices. Who could have envisaged that so soon after our triumphant arrival we would be plotting a midnight escape from the clutches of a crazed homicidal maniac?[10] Tomorrow heralds the start of a new phase in the Italian Odyssey, the chance to make amends for the last couple of months. And we are looking forward to it immensely.

Saturday morning. The Great Escape. Freedom. The New World. Here we go. This is it.[11] Eleni has expelled the three of us while she attends to a last-minute spot of cleaning, although in my opinion the farmhouse is already in much better condition than when we arrived. The children and I bring the car out of its hiding place in

10 Poetic licence; we're actually leaving in the morning.
11 I'm so excited I can only think in short sentences.

the garage and wriggle into our seats, ready for a quick getaway. But Eleni does not arrive for some time. Ruby is getting increasingly agitated; no doubt she can sense the tension and drama of the moment. Where can Mummy be? What can be taking so long? Even the Barbie tape is not enough to pacify her.

Suddenly Morelli's car hoves into view. He is on his way out somewhere when he spies the three of us sitting expectantly in the heavily-loaded car and comes to an abrupt halt. For a long, drawn-out minute he sits there motionless, surveying the scene, taking in the implications. Finally he has worked out that we really do mean it.

Meanwhile I am struggling to maintain my best stolid stony-face expression. Though it would be immensely satisfying to smile, laugh in his face even, I am still gripped by fear of Morelli and what he might do if provoked. Come at us with a piece of rusting farm machinery perhaps?

Fortunately, Morelli makes no attempt to get out of his car or engage in combat. After an eternity he moves off slowly, crunching along the gravel driveway and down into town. How I'd love to know what's going through his mind right now. No: on second thoughts, I couldn't care less.

This time we barrel straight on through the middle of Valfabbrica, flaunting our bags and boxes to all. Eleni wants to say one last goodbye to Angelica in the bakery, so we park brazenly in the main street, oblivious to the ramifications.

This turns out to be a major tactical error: no sooner have we pulled up than an official from the comune (local council) spots the unmistakeably foreign HGV and strides over to accost me about an unpaid parking fine.

With a jolt, I recall the parking ticket which appeared one day on the windscreen many moons ago; the parking ticket which we ignored at the time on the basis of our long-standing suspicion that the crusty old parking inspector was booking only those vehicles he didn't recognise while giving his friends and relatives the freedom of the city; the parking ticket which, in the recent flurry of excitement, we have conveniently forgotten about altogether.

So near and yet so far: even now, the good city of Valfabbrica refuses to let us depart in peace. Will we ever escape its clutches? Time to switch to Plan B; employing my best Dumb Foreigner persona, I try to pretend that the man from the comune is interested in buying our car. Comune man is singularly unimpressed by this charade, but eventually gives up and stomps off anyway. Phew. Given that the HGV has UK number plates, surely they won't be bothered to try and track us down for the price of a measly parking ticket. Surely not.

In any case it no longer matters; Eleni has returned from the bakery and Valfabbrica is now officially history. For we are free, free to begin our new lives, to start experiencing the Italian Odyssey as it was meant to be, as it was written in the script concocted in our heads long, long ago in a land far, far away. Goodbye Valfabbrica, goodbye parking inspector, goodbye Morelli, goodbye Sandro and Carla and Walter, goodbye and good riddance to you all.

The view in the rear-vision mirror is, I very much hope, the last I will ever, ever, *ever* see of this place.

5

Euphoria

The promised land, we have found to our delight, is full of good things to eat. Our first few weeks in Sansepolcro have been spent in a delirious orgy of consumption, fuelled by positive ions and natural endorphins and healing energy flow and the overwhelming relief of having made good our escape. It is only now that we understand the real underlying motivation behind the Italian Odyssey—food. The realisation of this most fundamental objective, hitherto only vaguely expressed, combined with the unbridled joy of waking up in the morning and *not* being in Valfabbrica, has unleashed a feeding frenzy of embarrassing proportions.

The very first thing we did was to check out the bars. The early favourite was the wonderfully named Happy Bar (*Appy Bar* in the local lingo), which ticked all the right boxes: child-friendly name, feel-good husband and wife team behind the counter, central location right on the piazza, good selection of panini and even, if you arrive early enough, doughnuts. Many of our early formative experiences of Sansepolcro are based in and around Happy Bar.

It wasn't long before we became restless and began to stray further afield—to the grand old bar next door to the theatre, the dark mysterious one opposite the bakery, the one that looks like an English tea-room further up on the left. And of course to the bar we now know as Appennini,[1] the sacred site wherein we consumed our first ever coffee in Sansepolcro and which is consequently of

1 Officially: Bar Degli Appennini.

tremendous sentimental value. It turns out that Appennini is by no means the only place to offer an impressive array of rolls and cakes; every bar in town is burgeoning with delectables, not just the trusty staples such as cheese and tomato panini and cornetti[2] with marmalade inside, but also the various little specialties that are unique to each. Clearly there is much research to be done.

Also on the piazza is a wonderful gelato shop offering not only the second-best hazelnut gelato in the world but also frozen yoghurt with your choice of toppings. (Eleni's current favourite: fresh raspberries and chocolate sauce.) Just metres away down a suitably narrow cobbled laneway is a wonderful pasticceria selling handmade biscuits, cakes and chocolates. For those who crave additional sugar intake, the bakery on the main street also supplies ancient traditional cultural Nutella-filled crostata tarts in addition to sixteen variations of hard crusty bread.

Barely a minute's walk from our front door is the fabulous SMA supermarket, which sports a delicatessen section groaning with all manner of oily delicacies as well as fresh pasta and—yes!—pizza slices. And right outside the huge arched gate that leads into the Old Bit is Sale e Pepe, our local take-away shop where you can pick up a two-course meal of pasta primo and meat secondo carefully packed into separate hermetically-sealed containers.

Then there are the restaurants, from humble trattoria types to swanky upmarket affairs; the laid-back wine bars; the bustling street market every Tuesday and Friday with its fruit and veg stalls and fresh produce vans; the take-away roll shop on the main street; and no end of titbits to be found lurking down the back of the various alimentari and other food stores dotted around town. And for the ultimate cheap and cheerful family dinner, our favourite pizza-by-the-slice place on the piazza at Anghiari is only ten minutes away by car. If all these can be tracked down by newcomers in a matter of weeks, then who knows what other culinary delights lie in store?

But enough about food already.

Sansepolcro itself is sensational: the perfect incarnation of the country Italian town that we had been fantasising about back in

2 Italy Fact: A croissant is called a *cornetto*. Not to be confused with the familiar ice-cream that appears during summer, known as a cornetto-without-italics.

Australia—proving that our idyllic notions of Italian country life weren't so far off the mark after all. It has a long central thoroughfare for wandering, narrow laneways for exploring, a big central piazza for eating gelato and practicing soccer, a veritable plethora of shops and cafés, mountains looming away in the distance, olive fields all around, and medieval things absolutely everywhere you turn.

The real estate agency, for instance, is located in part of an enormous palazzo that lines one side of the piazza and was built, according to Raffaello, in the third century (thirteenth century actually; for some reason 'third' and 'thirteenth' are used interchangeably in spoken Italian, a nuance which I will not pick up on until much later, much to the amusement of friends and family: 'They weren't building massive ornate palazzos in the third century after Christ you idiot!' But what's a thousand years here or there, I say, when everything is so fabulously old anyway.)

The castle walls around Sansepolcro survive almost in their entirety and form a neat enclosure delineating the symmetrically-proportioned old quarter. There are two gates into the city, Porta Romana at the southern end (our end) and Porta Fiorentina at the front end.

There are also several slightly less salubrious entrances to the city from the various car parks around the perimeter,[3] some of them hacked through rudely at points where the walls have fallen into disrepair.

Our apartment is located five minutes' walk from Porta Romana. A couple of minutes later you arrive in the piazza; a few more and you are walking out the Porta Fiorentina entrance. Thus the attractive medieval part of Sansepolcro is barely five minutes from end to end: big enough to hide countless little surprises, but compact enough so that you can never get lost. Furthermore, the square castle wall layout houses a perfectly straight grid of streets inside,[4] a layout which is instantly appealing to our Melbourne sensibilities.

Beyond the walls lie the outer suburbs, full of new houses and shopping centres, as well as no less than three industrial zones. Apparently this is evidence of a miserable failure of town planning;

3 Italy fact: Moats around medieval walled cities are filled in and used as car parks.
4 Notwithstanding the odd lovingly medieval bend in the main thoroughfare.

a town this size ought to have one Industrial Zone, maybe two, but certainly not three.

Although we are technically located in a suburb, there are a few crumbling old stone houses mixed in amongst the newness, leftovers from the days not so long ago when the area was all open farmland and the boldest and bravest farmers lived outside the comfort of the walls. (Presumably when the enemy arrived they had to abandon their fields and homes and rush inside the city and slam the gate shut.) Oddly, none of the new buildings in the suburbs appears to be more than about fifty years old, suggesting some sort of post-medieval, pre-post-war construction twilight zone during which no-one could be bothered to build anything.

Our position at the southern end of Sansepolcro is perfect for country walks to burn off pizza calories. Heading east towards the hills or west into the vineyards, one can be out in the fields in five minutes, gazing up at the mountains and checking out the state of the crops. And while the mountain ranges may be close by, Sansepolcro itself is located squarely on the river plain and is completely, gloriously flat and non-threatening—once again, instantly appealing to Melburnians.

Much as we enjoy visiting steep medieval hillside cities such as Gubbio and Perugia, you wouldn't want to live there, trying to negotiate steps and slopes with the shopping and the pram on a daily basis. The entire Old Bit of Sansepolcro has, at far as we can tell, just the one set of steps. Here's that number again: ONE. Plus we have a second-hand child's bicycle lined up that will enable us to get extra mileage out of young Ruby on outings with the pram. Flat is good.

And finally, our new abode is located in Tuscany, no less, which always looks good on the CV: if Umbria is the new Tuscany, then we can say we've lived in both the new one and the old one.

So: we've arrived, we've found our feet. Sansepolcro is paradise—so many things to see and eat. Our apartment is fully functional, complete with agreeable landlord and landlady. It even has a phone line. Finally, after two and a half months, I can settle down and start working and we can all get on with enjoying the Italian Odyssey as per the script.

Telecom Italia, it seems, has other ideas.

On our very first day in Sansepolcro—indeed, barely an hour after unloading the groaning HGV—I headed on down the road to re-establish hostilities with my favourite corporate behemoth by sending them yet more money and asking very nicely if they wouldn't mind turning the phone on at our new abode sometime soon, pretty please. An altogether much less arduous procedure this time around—none of this digging up the roadside and laying new cable; all they had to do was flick the switch at the exchange and connect us to the outside world. Simple! Or so one would think.

That was two weeks ago, and it comes as no surprise that we have not heard from them since. I have been begging Laura, the young girl from the real estate agency who has been assigned to assist us on procedural matters, to give them few hurry-up calls in the forlorn hope that a real Italian speaker might have better luck than a common foreigner. Also on the basis of that old chestnut about the squeaky wheel getting the grease (brought to you courtesy of my father), which I interpret here to mean the more complaints the better. However Laura is as resigned as Cecelia was before her. Telecom Italia is like that, she says; there's no use ringing them to complain, you just have to wait.

Well I know all about waiting for Telecom Italia.

Half of my time in Italy thus far seems to have been spent on hold to their call centre; that irritating jingle with the corny drum roll at the beginning is indelibly etched into my auditory cortex. Sometimes, while waiting half an eternity for an operator, I see visions of myself as a senile old man in a nursing home, confined to bed, unable to recognise my own children, incapable of lucid speech yet reciting the Telecom Italia jingle from dawn to dusk (including the corny drum roll through gritted gums), driving the staff around the bend until finally they go on strike and refuse point blank to tend to me any longer. Hopefully there will be decent euthanasia legislation in place by then.[5]

At least we still have the trusty old mobile phone, although tragically the reception at our end of town is so poor that when it rings I have to rush outside into the garden in order to sustain a normal conversation—the sturdy stone walls of our apartment are too much of a challenge for its feeble antiquated antenna. There is a solution, of course: switch to the other mobile phone company, which provides superior reception. And which one would that be? You guessed it: the one with the drum roll.

I can't bring myself to do it. The fresh outdoor air will do me good anyway.

Despite fully intending to never again set foot in the Town-That-Must-Not-Be-Named,[6] it is not to be.

Sandro rings me one day not too long after the great escape. Apparently Morelli is furious; he has been in touch with Carla and Walter, Sandro, his lawyer and anybody else he can find, ranting and raving about the injustice of it all and threatening various forms of legal action. Sandro, clearly rattled, says he'll have his day in court with Morelli, if only to get him back for all that he's put him through.

Sandro and I agree half-heartedly that the legal threats are likely to be mainly bravado; Morelli is already up to his ears in protracted legal wrangling with his ex-wife,[7] and this should be enough to discourage him from going after poor defenceless Australians.

Nevertheless, Sandro wants me to be ready to testify if need be. We all hope that it will not come to this, although I must admit that testifying against Morelli would be immensely satisfying. (So long as we win.) But unfortunately it does mean that I will have to make the pilgrimage back to Valfabbrica in order to brief a local legal advocate on the situation.

5 Clause 12a: In the event that I start reciting the Telecom Italia jingle please disconnect all forms of life support immediately.

6 OK then: Valfabbrica.

7 No wonder she left him, says Eleni.

It feels strange heading back to my old nemesis. Despite having only recently fled the place, I have already consigned it firmly to history. Returning today is therefore almost an exercise in nostalgia. It feels like such a long time ago: months, years even. I wonder if everything will look the same.

As I trundle cautiously down the main street I am assailed by a horrible thought: what if the council man spots the HGV (again) and finally decides to throw the book at us for that unpaid parking ticket? Perhaps this final visit will prove to be our undoing, with the parking ticket triggering an escalating chain of legal processes leading ultimately to revocation of our visas and heart-rending scenes of enforced deportation at Rome airport, the children screaming as the Carabinieri bundle us onto the plane, the roaring of the jets, the mad cackling of a victorious Morelli rising above the din…

Reality intrudes on the daydream: I have arrived at the office of the legal advocate (called avvocato in Italian—impossible not to think of tropical green fruit). He turns out to be an extremely agreeable young chap, highly sympathetic about the gasolio debt and the other outrageous shenanigans which the poor Australians were forced to endure for two and a half months.

How about I fire off a stiff letter to Morelli's lawyers demanding compensation for your expenses? offers the avvocato. You probably won't get any money out of him but at least it demonstrates that we mean business.

This kind offer unexpectedly unleashes a well-spring of self-righteous anger in me, and I resolve there and then to revisit the old farmhouse and reclaim the half tonne of firewood we purchased only last month, which with any luck will still be lying neatly stacked in the outlying shed. But suddenly I'm subsumed with fear: while the thought of Morelli appropriating our lovely firewood may be repugnant, the prospect of an ugly hillside confrontation is infinitely more terrifying.

How I wish the idea hadn't come into my head in the first place. Meek and pathetic is so much easier than angry and self-righteous. There's no getting out of it, though. I must go back up to the Lonely

Farmhouse and face the evil that lurks there, if only to reclaim a tiny shred of pride from the whole sorry mess. Up the hill and along the driveway, heart thumping fit to burst. Drive straight to the shed and spend the next half an hour frantically shovelling wood into the HGV: big logs, small logs, even some of Morelli's very own neatly bundled kindling. (The usual social norms no longer apply; Morelli deserves to be stolen from.)

I've been sneaking furtive glances over my shoulder every now and then but there's still no sign of the recently ex-landlord. He must be out at the moment. Seeing his lawyers, perhaps. Getting our deportation orders drafted. But at least we've got our wood back.

Or most of it, anyway: the HGV is already packed to the rafters and a small portion will have to be left behind. It pains me to think of Morelli laying his grubby mitts on anything of ours. Perhaps I should roll the remaining logs down the hill just so he can't have them? No, best not to waste any time: hurry up and get out now while the coast is still clear. At least he'll get a good shock when he discovers that the bulk of his free wood supply has abruptly disappeared.

Thank heavens for the HGV, with seats that fold down to create an enormous interior, the perfect thing for stacking wood. Just as well we bought such a ridiculously large petrol-hungry vehicle—you never know when you might need to move house, or relocate half a forest for that matter.

Down the driveway and away through town again. This time it really is for ever. Or is it? Strange how Valfabbrica still manages to maintain a hold on us. I have a nasty feeling that we'll be dragged back here again sometime.

On the way back to sunny Sansepolcro—alone again, naturally—I have time to pause and reflect anew on the role of Sandro the trusty travel agent in this fiasco. It would appear, with the benefit of hindsight, that Sandro has a bad habit of rubbing people up the wrong way. There were always too many unexplained questions. Why did the Casa Castalda home-owner, supposedly an old friend of many years' standing, suddenly spit the dummy? Why was Morelli already antagonistic the moment we arrived? Why did Carla and Walter, supposedly close and trusted relatives, become so reticent?

It seems that the process of dealing with Sandro and his new venture in agritourismo (the blanket term for farm-stay or long-term accommodation) became too much for these people to bear. For we now know that, in addition to his suspect interpersonal skills, Sandro has no prior experience whatsoever with agritourismo. His normal business involves short-term package tours, flights and hotels, the usual stuff; he has never before attempted to place foreigners in a furnished home for a year. And one suspects that after this experience he never will again.

Thus we were the guinea pigs. When the initial enquiry came from the travel agent in Melbourne, Sandro obviously decided he'd give this agritourismo caper a go by asking around among his friends and relatives in Valfabbrica in the hope that something would come up.

Sure enough, something did come up: an old chum had a house available in Casa Castalda. All Sandro had to do was to email some photos over to Australia and write up a standard contract, then slap a handsome margin on the monthly rent and sit back and wait for the money to roll in. Soon he got word back that the Australians were keen. It was all too easy. Sandro would have been pleased with his new business venture.

When the old chum suddenly refused to deal with Sandro any longer, our hero, bewildered but undaunted, simply asked around some more. This time, it was cousin Carla who came through with the lonely farmhouse option. It wasn't as nice-looking as the first place, but it would do. The Australians didn't sound quite so keen and were asking for more photos of the interior, but Sandro was able to fob them off—a less than perfect command of English can come in handy sometimes. And sure enough, they paid up in advance and turned up anyway. Money for jam, really.

And even though the whole exercise failed miserably and Sandro will no doubt be sticking to what he knows best from now on, he still managed to emerge with a most generous commission. In stark contrast to Morelli, who was left with an empty house plus an expensive unwanted outdoor laundry, and doubtless lost face down in the village as well. And as for the Australians… well, they're tourists, they'll see it as all part of the experience.

Sandro thus managed to be both gormless and cunning at the same time. Or was it simply beginner's luck? It must be said that he did us an enormous favour—unwittingly, one presumes—by choosing to annul the contract. For if we had fled the farmhouse while still under a contractual obligation, we would have been exposed to the possibility of legal action, just to add to the spice of the Italian Odyssey. And my defence would have been simple but stunning: there was never a phone line as stipulated in the contract, so there.

Also we must acknowledge the important supporting role played by Telecom Italia, who did a magnificent job in procrastinating for over two months while we attempted to search for new premises. As Eleni says, it was meant to be. For if the Cable Guy had come around any earlier we might have ended up getting the phone on and settling down and then we would have been stuck in the farmhouse with Morelli for the entire year and… it doesn't bear thinking about.

It's always easy to be wise in hindsight, especially in pure dollar terms. Thus, according to my calculations, if we add up all the expenses associated with finding our first home in Italy—including the commission to the travel agent in Melbourne, the hefty pay out to Sandro, the dodgy outdoor laundry surcharge, the thankyou money to Carla (thanks for nothing, by the way), plus the commission to the real estate agency in Sansepolcro for our new home, not to mention fuel costs associated with two months of criss-crossing Umbria and Tuscany in the HGV, much less the emotional cost of the anticipation and excitement, the disappointment and frustration, the anguish and hand-wringing, the tears and bedwetting[8]—it would have been cheaper if Eleni or I had simply bought a return ticket to Italy a few

8 Not really.

months beforehand and done a thorough reconnaissance. Or even if the entire family had spent the first month camped in a hotel while house-hunting in the traditional manner.

But it wouldn't have been half the fun, would it?

Winter has finally arrived in Sansepolcro. Up until a couple of weeks ago it was unseasonably warm, and we were out wandering the streets late in the evening (actually only about eight or nine o'clock, but ground-breakingly late for these parents), treating ourselves to coffees and ice-creams and soaking up the authentic traditional cultural Italian country town atmosphere, but alas no more. Not that there's anything wrong with winter—I'm on record as being a lover of cold weather—but we were just starting to get into the swing of the late-night strolling thing. Never mind; we shall simply have to take it up again in spring.

The nice lady in the bakery on the main street, where we have already ingratiated ourselves and are busily working through the hundreds of varieties of bread on offer,[9] assures us that it doesn't get much colder than this. Which is just as well because, despite the fortifications of the Sansepolcro food, our Melbourne bodies are not quite used to this brand of cold. Moreover the scruffy insubstantial coats we have brought with us are clearly not up to the task; we need some of those heavily quilted full-length numbers that are starting to appear around town.

As a result of the plummeting temperatures and almost constant rain, stepping outside the front door to have a telephone conversation is no longer a pleasant fresh air experience. We are still obliged to use the pathetic old mobile phone, since the shiny new one came back from the repair shop in Perugia in no better condition than before. The good news is that there is an agency right here in Sansepolcro which can forward the phone on to Perugia for us, thus sparing us the indignity of having to drive down to Perugia on the freeway past the turn-off to Valfabbrica.

9 Including cute little rolls called, inexplicably, *sandwiches*. Clearly something got lost in translation.

Still no word from our friends at Telecom Italia. Every day—often several times a day—I pick up the receiver forlornly and listen for a dial tone, hoping against hope that some brand of telecommunications magic might have somehow brought it to life. Alas, there is only the depressing, unrelenting silence. Like a car broken down on a remote highway, our telephone is nothing but a useless lump of plastic.

In light of the continuing stalemate in my battle with the behemoth, Raffaello has kindly allowed me to use the back garden extension of his home phone, handily located inside an old shed concealed behind a row of trees. Only it isn't a shed at all—it's a fully fitted-out kitchen, complete with fridge, stove, even a dishwasher. Raffaello and Ivana must be quite well off, because this is actually their second kitchen. Apparently they spend the entire summer cooking and eating meals in the large outdoor gazebo, disappearing indoors only to go to sleep.

The phone in the second kitchen is a major improvement on the previous email arrangement at Morelli's farmhouse, because the garden shed is always open and I don't have to beg for permission every time I use the phone. I have been taking advantage of this new luxury by trooping out to the shed with the trusty laptop up to three or four times a day.

Until recently, that is; the deteriorating weather has transformed the simple task of checking the emails into a major performance that involves dressing up in hundreds of layers, wrapping the computer up against the rain and negotiating a minefield of muddy puddles. There's nothing like rain and cold to really focus the mind, and I find myself once again cursing Telecom Italia bitterly for their intransigence, or incompetence, or quite possibly both.

In the end, unwilling to pester Laura any further, I decide to ring them myself. Nervously I run through the pre-call essentials:

(1) Phone battery charged (in case of long wait)—CHECK
(2) Rain holding off—CHECK
(3) Key words and phrases committed to memory—CHECK
(4) Hat, beanie, scarf, coat—CHECK

And we're off. Happily, the wait is not too long and today's call centre operator speaks half-reasonable English—certainly much better than my Italian—which relieves me of the need to trot out the pre-rehearsed lines. Startlingly, we manage to establish that Telecom Italia are under the impression that they have already connected the phone as of last Friday. This leads to the following surreal exchange:

Telecom Italia: What? You're calling from your mobile phone?
Me: Yes.
TI: That can't be right. It says here that your phone line is on.
Me: But it's not. That's why I'm calling from my mobile phone.
TI: Have you tried your home phone line?
Me: (*struggling to maintain composure*) Yes, but it doesn't work. That's why I'm calling you from my mobile phone.
TI: Strange. It says here that it should be working.
Me: (*suppresses anguished moan*)
TI: Can you wait for a moment please.
Hold music resumes. Our hero waits, shivering in the cold… etc etc

This must be a positive development, I suppose: it signifies that the hardworking beavers at Telecom Italia are actually doing something, or that they think they are. Unfortunately, they haven't quite got it right, whatever it is that they're doing; but full marks for effort, guys. Meanwhile, I'll just have to continue ploughing through the rain to the garden shed three times per day until you can WORK OUT HOW TO CONNECT A SIMPLE PHONE LINE YOU CRETINS.

I feel better now.

Today is Saturday and we are off on a family mini-trip to Arezzo, the nearest decent-sized town to Sansepolcro, to buy some winter gear at the street market. In the last week before Christmas we are taking the overnight train to Vienna; apparently they are having a cold snap over there with temperatures down as low as minus five (hurrah!), so we desperately need to acquire some decent coats, scarves and beanies.

The street market at Arezzo is absolutely enormous, putting the Sansepolcro one to shame. (Mind you, Arezzo is about five times the size.) After working our way along endless stalls selling the street market staples—shoes, clothes, kitchenware, books, and fruit and veg—we strike pay dirt in the form of a second-hand clothing stall, which has some slightly shabby but very cheap coats that will do nicely for the Vienna trip. And even a vivid red dress that will make a good play costume for Ruby, who is starting to feel the pinch of not having any decent dress-up clothes: there's a limit to how much fun you can have with oversized parent T-shirts.

About a third of the way along the street market we admit defeat—we're never going to make it all the way with the children—and retire to the nearest bar for coffees and doughnuts. Half an hour later, suitably refortified after the gruelling morning's work, we make our way into the centre of Arezzo, which turns out to be some distance away—thank heavens for the energy-giving qualities of doughnuts.

Old Arezzo, as featured in the Roberto Benigni film *Life is Beautiful*, is an absolute delight—magnificently preserved in all its crumbling glory, gently sloping though not too steep, and with a full complement of narrow winding lanes and stately shopping boulevards. And the main piazza is extremely handsome; I've got a bad case of piazza envy.

Today, the piazza has been taken over by some sort of German festa, complete with genuine oom-pah band—eight strapping young sheepish-looking uber-lads decked out in matching lederhosen and frilly shirts—plus a variety of stalls selling strange spicy sausages and apple strudel and various other things presumably Germanic. With apologies to those older Italians who still remember the war, it seems to be very successful, judging from the milling crowds in the piazza. Although it'd be interesting to see what the Italians put on at the reciprocal festa next year in Germany.

On the way back to the car Ruby spots an ice-skating rink in the middle of a park, set up as a temporary arrangement during the winter months. Ruby is keen to begin her ice-skating career immediately but as usual is vetoed by her cruel parents; it is too late in the day after all the excitement and adventure. We placate her with promises to return one day soon. After all, Arezzo is only 45 minutes away and winter has only just begun. There is plenty of time yet. [*Would you believe they never made it back? Ed.*]

Let 12 December be known henceforth as one of the great anniversaries of modern history, a giant leap forward for all mankind. It is a day for celebration, for inviting all one's friends and relatives around for drinks, for tears of joy and laughter and partying all day and late into the night, a day for letting off fireworks and driving around town madly beeping the horn and frightening dogs and small children, a day to get drunk and disorderly and be thrown in the police cells for the night—because today is the day that Telecom Italia has deigned to connect us to the real world. The man from Telecom Italia is right here in our home; he is down on the floor busily examining the phone socket; he is testing it with his tester. Now he is inviting us to try out the phone for ourselves.

IT WORKS. I CAN HEAR THE DIAL TONE.

Mamma Mia![10]

Telecom Italia Man is thanked politely and escorted to the door. Back inside, there is no unseemly whooping or breaking open of bottles of champagne; we take it all in our stride, grizzled old veterans of countless Telecom Italia campaigns that we are. First things first: let's try picking up the receiver by ourselves. Cautiously, gently, easy does it now—our new phone line may be feeling somewhat sore after its recent initiation into the real world of telecommunications. Incredible: the dial tone is still there. Now for the next big test—a real phone call. To the Telecom Italia call centre, of course, so I can bask in the delicious irony of not having

10 Note linguistic authenticity.

anything to complain about for once. (Besides, it's a free call.) Yes, there goes the corny drum roll. The phone really really works!

Now the fun begins. Over the next few hours we subject the phone line to gruelling endurance trials of progressively escalating difficulty, starting with a call to Ivana and Raffaello upstairs, then to Marius and Christine in the neighbouring province, followed by—why not?—an *international* call to relatives in Australia, moving on to excited emails to clients, friends and family with the new telephone number, and finally surfing the internet like real citizens of the twenty-first century.

After three and a half frustrating months, the last piece of the puzzle is finally in place. The Loneliness of the Long-Distance Translator phase is over. Now we can bask in the absolute luxury of checking emails and using the internet at any time from the convenience of our very own lounge room. Not to mention taking calls inside the house. It's time now to settle down and enjoy the Italian Odyssey in style.

Except that we're leaving the country tomorrow.

6
Pizza Paradise

The overnight train for Vienna departs this evening. The weather has been kind to us today and our bags are already half packed; there remains only to spend a leisurely day at home finishing them off before climbing onto the bus for Arezzo. From Arezzo we will take the local train to Florence, where we will board the sleeper at 10 pm.

During breakfast there is a knock at the front door. It is Raffaello the landlord, still in his dressing gown. He sounds rather agitated and keeps mentioning something called a *sciopero.*

What could this be? A quick flick through the dictionary…oh Christ: sciopero means strike. Yes, stroik, stroik, he says excitedly. Raffaello has just heard on the news that all the trains and buses are on strike today.

A strike! Surely not…our first big trans-European family holiday, doomed from the outset. Perhaps we could drive into Florence and leave the car there for the duration. That's assuming that the overnight train has not been hit by the strike too. How do we check? Who does one ring?

Fortunately, our helpful landlady Ivana comes to the rescue. Also in her dressing gown, having barely finished breakfast herself, she rings the local bus company and establishes that:

(a) The trains are in fact running; and

(b) There is a single solitary bus at lunchtime that will take us to Arezzo. (By law the bus companies must provide at least one bus at certain times of day even during a strike. Just the thing for stranded tourists.)

We all breath a collective sigh of relief until the realisation hits that our bus leaves six hours earlier than planned. Cue frantic packing session. Mind you, this family positively thrives under such conditions. Was it not highly efficient packing that got us out of the lonely farmhouse in Valfabbrica? In a relatively short space of time, all things considered, the bags are ready and stacked neatly at the front door.

Ivana has kindly offered to see us to the bus stop a few minutes' walk away. We are just heading out the door when the mobile phone rings; it is my sister Elizabeth calling from Australia to say hello. She wonders why our new phone number has been engaged for hours. Surely we haven't been talking on the phone all morning? Why no, we haven't used it at all. With mounting dread I take the receiver in my trembling hand and hold it to my ear to hear… total silence. The line is dead. In the space of less than 24 hours, our fabulous new telephone has once again been reduced to a lump of plastic.

I might have known.

But right now there is no time to stand outside the front door waiting on hold to the call centre for hours; the midday bus is due to depart any minute. Once again, Ivana saves the day by offering to report the line fault during our absence. Thus reassured, we manage to make our way onto the magic bus and thence to Florence without incident.

Given that we have six hours to kill, the only logical thing to do is to haul the children around on a whistle-stop tour of Florence covering regulation sights such as the duomo, the bridge with the shops on it and the famous museum, placating them with regular pizza and gelato stops along the way. Florence is a massive city in comparison to provincial Sansepolcro, and the intensity of human and vehicle traffic is actually rather unnerving. By evening we have all had enough, and it is rather comforting to be able to finally pile onto the train and be whisked away into the night.

Ruby is the first to wake in the morning—well before six o'clock, with that special knack our children have of waking up extra early on holidays—and alerts us to the winter wonderland outside. We are rolling through a picture-postcard landscape of Austrian mountains blanketed in snow, studded here and there with impossibly cute little farmhouses. In my sleep-deprived state I am tempted to believe that the train window is actually a giant plasma screen showing a European landscapes travelogue. But no, it is very real, and very beautiful. This one definitely goes in my Top Five Ways to be Woken Up Early.

A couple of hours of bleary-eyed window-gazing later and we are pulling up in the centre of Vienna. Here to meet us is Sonoko, an old colleague of Eleni's from the Tokyo days, who has been living in Vienna for the last eight years and working as a tour guide for the endless succession of Japanese music aficionados making the pilgrimage. Stepping out of the station after a fortifying coffee, we discover to our delight that it is still snowing, which means that we have to run around sticking our tongues out and marvelling at the sight of it on our clothes. All highly embarrassing for Sonoko, but a major novelty for the Melburnians.[1]

The main purpose of the trip, apart from renewing acquaintances with old friends, is to check out the Christmas markets, and this we do with gusto. The entire city of Vienna is very much in festive spirit, and Christmas markets are to be found around almost every corner: trees littered with lights, stalls festooned with decorations, huge crowds everywhere (including a great many Italians, we are told) and lots of cakes and doughnuts and goodies on offer. It is all tremendous fun.

Best of all, the Christmas markets sell a hot spicy red wine concoction called Gluwein which you drink together with your friends gathered around hearty fires that burn away in large metal drums dotted all over the place—wonderful on a freezing cold night.

In the space of one week we manage to take in five or six Christmas markets, both at night and during the day; eat out at a Japanese restaurant and a Turkish restaurant; give the children their

1 I still have trouble coming to terms with people from colder climes who consider snow to be little more than a wintertime nuisance.

first bath in four months (so much more fun than showers); and do a fair bit of exploration, occasionally without even trying, such as the day we hopped on the wrong bus and found ourselves winding through the centre of town until we were eventually tipped out at Stephensplatz.

There is even time for a day trip out to the Vienna woods for a quick get-to-know-you session with the local snow, followed by a visit to the cutesy village of Grinzing where legend has it that Beethoven once spent some time. Although I suspect he probably just stopped for a caffé latte on his way to somewhere else and unwittingly spawned an entire tourist industry. Apparently Austria and Germany are full of plaques claiming to have had Beethoven as a resident, permanent, temporary or otherwise. Surely he couldn't have done that much travel, what with having so many symphonies to compose and being deaf and all.

The highlight of Grinzing for me is when a car actually stops for us at the pedestrian crossing—unthinkable in Italy where, if our experience is anything to go by, the roads are littered with faded pedestrian crossings of which nobody takes the slightest notice. Once I nearly caused a pile-up on the main road in Sansepolcro by slowing down for an elderly woman on a crossing; here in Grinzing, by way of contrast, we've managed to hold up the traffic by failing to notice that all the cars are stopped and waiting politely. Which just goes to show that the great land of Europe, which appears largely homogenous when viewed from afar—namely Australia—is in fact full of important cultural differences.

At the end of our week in Vienna, we give ourselves an eight out of ten for sightseeing and a nine for child care: both children have survived the freezing temperatures without catching colds, mainly because we had them trussed up like mini Michelin men in about eight layers of clothing before allowing them to step outside.

The return leg to Sansepolcro is a model of Italian transportation efficiency: the sleeper delivers us right on time to Florence, where the local train is waiting to take us to Arezzo, where the bus is waiting to take us to Sansepolcro. We arrive triumphantly at our front door at the very civilised hour of ten in the morning. Sigh. How nice it is to be back home again in our apartment.

And I wonder to myself: how is it that this little town which we have known for barely four weeks already seems like home? What makes us feel that we belong, if only in a small way? It could be the lingering euphoria from the Escape; it could be the cheery atmosphere in town; it surely has something to do with the welcoming embrace of the friendly landlords upstairs. Nor should the psychosomatic impact of the improved food supply in Sansepolcro be underestimated. Whatever the reasons, we are still, one month later, deliriously happy in our new environment.

At this point my happy reverie is interrupted by the return of a niggling memory. It's been gnawing away at me all week, but I haven't been in a position to do anything about it. Now that we're back home, though, I'm going to have to deal with the situation. Conquer my fears and stare them down.

So, here goes. With heart in mouth, I gently pick up the telephone, fearing the worst, and hold it to my ear. And… the dial tone is back! The phone is working! The efficient teamsters at Telecom Italia have repaired the line fault in our absence. Life is complete once again.

A couple of days before Christmas, during a quiet stroll into town through light drizzle, Ruby spies a man disappearing into the church just near Sale e Pepe, the take-away shop on the edge of town. To date the front door of this particular church has always been firmly shut, so we decide to follow the man inside for no reason other than today it is not shut. And through this simple act of curiosity we unwittingly stumble upon the wonderful yuletide tradition known as the presepio.

My dictionary says that presepio means 'crib', but the editors obviously don't get out and about enough—as everybody knows, a presepio is actually an ancient traditional cultural nativity scene depicting anything from the standard collection of biblical figures to a full-blown miniature version of the local town and surrounding countryside (in which case the biblical figures are relegated to minor supporting roles and hidden up the back somewhere).

The presepio in the church near Sale e Pepe is rather excellent in my opinion, even allowing for possible local bias.[2] It measures roughly ten metres by four metres in size—enormous, in other words—and features models of the entire town of Sansepolcro and surrounding fields and farms, as well as the nearby Appennini mountain range and a variety of local landmarks. Notwithstanding the slightly uninspiring light show, in all other respects our local presepio is exquisitely executed, comprising what we now know to be the standard features of any decent presepio:

- One or more rivers with trickling water and ideally a waterfall
- Models of people involved in sturdy medieval activities such as chopping wood, baking bread, sewing, sharpening knives, etc
- Models of beasts involved in sturdy bestial activities such as ploughing the fields, threshing hay, grinding wheat, etc
- Fields and garden beds made from genuine local earth, grass and moss
- Tiny lights in the buildings
- An overhead light show with several distinct phases (day and night at the very least, plus morning and afternoon where funding permits)
- Backdrop of sky, cotton wool clouds etc, plus stars at night if possible.

In addition to the above, the Sansepolcro presepio boasts *real mechanised models*. This last point is most significant; there is an important distinction to be made between the mechanised models of people and beasts and the plain figurines. Put simply, once you've been spoiled by a few top-dollar presepi with real live-action drama,

2 The Italians have a wonderful term for this: campanalismo, meaning affinity with one's local bell tower, and by extension dislike of everyone else, including the people in the next town. *Especially* the people in the next town when you live on the border with Umbria.

the cheaper ones that remain resolutely still throughout just don't cut it any more. A stationary presepio would need to have several waterfalls (waterwheels offer a low-cost solution for introducing movement) or a spectacular light show of some sort in order to extract a gold coin in the donation box from this critic. Or a worthy cause; often the presepio is put on by a local charity or volunteer group, which alters the criteria slightly.

Around Christmas time, PRESEPIO signs start springing up all around town and in the countryside too, giving the impression that there is a presepio lurking around virtually every corner. And there virtually is, although not all presepi are created equal. Some, it has to be said, are not worth turning the corner for, but there are enough spectacular or impressive ones to make it worthwhile. And as our spontaneous church-going experience demonstrates, you never know until you step inside.

Apparently the presepio down at the Vatican in Rome is truly spectacular. But that's because the Vatican boffins have had plenty of time to perfect their presepio technology—rumour has it that the man in the Popemobile has been a mechanised model for some years now. And anyway, you'd have to battle through the madding crowds for hours just to catch a glimpse of the showy Vatican presepio. Give me a dusty unused church on the edge of Sansepolcro any day.

Mechanised or not, large or small, well-lit or otherwise, the presepio as a social phenomenon is indeed a wonderful thing: the attention to detail, the level of expertise and the obvious dedication that goes into producing these things year after year is quite astonishing. They are true works of art; they appeal to adults and children alike; they raise money for the local church or worthy cause. What's not to like?

The requisite boxes of presents having been parcelled off to distant family members many months ago, Christmas Day is a wonderfully low-key affair. Are we feeling lonely and depressed away from the bosoms of our respective families at this time? Well, no, actually; it's rather nice to have just the four of us for a change. We play a tape of Frank Sinatra crooning Christmas carols (cleverly spotted by Eleni at the newsagents) and eat celebratory pancakes in accordance with an ancient traditional cultural custom that we have just thought up. And in doing so we make the following exciting discovery: marscapone cheese is as good as double cream when you put it in pancakes with jam.

And when we've finished gorging ourselves, why, we go for a stroll into the centre of town, just for a change.[3] Where we are astonished to find several of the bars open for business, on Christmas Day in a staunchly Catholic nation no less. So naturally we zoom straight in for the obligatory coffee and doughnut. (Because you can.)

Then we kick the soccer ball about idly in the piazza, where many others are likewise out for a post-gorging stroll. Following the lead of the local Youth, and inspired by Ruby's new-found love of soccer, we now always take the mini soccer ball with us on walks into town and kick it around the piazza a bit in a pathetic attempt to blend in; though I suspect our obvious lack of basic footwork skills gives us away immediately. Apart from being a suitably fresh-air-and-exercise type of thing to do, it's also rather sociable, since people strolling by will often collect a stray ball and tap it back over with a smile. As opposed to cursing at nearly being tripped up, which they have every right to do.

The other day though a terrifying thing happened—a young boy of about ten joined in. We should start a proper game, he said, despite the fact that there were just three of us. My Italian skills don't extend to asking how to configure a match with just three players so we settled for goal-kicking practice. Naturally he was far too good for all of us and consistently shot the ball through the nominal goalposts (jacket on the left, bag on the right). This had the effect of unsettling Ruby the goalkeeper no end. Just as she was becoming thoroughly dispirited and looking fit to burst into tears with the next goal, our young star was summoned home for dinner by his mamma offstage. Equilibrium was restored, and not a moment too soon.

3 Warning: heavily ironic statement. These days we do little else but stroll into town and back out again, sometimes several times in the one day.

Having now made presepio-spotting our mission for the festive season, New Year's Eve finds us braving the rain to go and see a presepio recommended by Raffaello down near Città di Castello. It is supposed to be located at a monastery up on a hill a short distance out of town, but we are having no luck finding it. After a number of false starts we eventually decide to seek directions from a friendly local who, it turns out, just happens to have a close relative[4] in Melbourne—perhaps we know him? It seems heartless to point out that Melbourne is a city of several million people, but we chat amicably for a while and are eventually rewarded with some concrete directions.

With the assistance of our new friend we locate the monastery on the hill. There is no sign of human life, so we take the opportunity to snoop around a bit—in the name of research of course. The monastery is a most impressive old building with lovely internal gardens, though the presepio itself is only passable—not enough moving parts for my liking. However, in line with the journey-of-discovery theory, whereby the destination is considered no more than the means to an end, today's trip is adjudged highly worthwhile: we have managed to (a) chat with a local, (b) peek inside an impressive monastery and (c) check out some of the lovely countryside around Città di Castello, albeit without really intending to.

After the monastery we repair to the central piazza in Città di Castello, our second favourite piazza in the whole world[5] where we discover a wonderful exhibition on presepio-making. This is almost better than the real thing, since it shows how a presepio is constructed. There is a fascinating section devoted to showing how those tiny mechanised models work, which for me only serves to reinforce the distinction between the mechanised presepio and its poorer unpowered cousin.

At the tourist office at Città di Castello we hear about a New Year's Eve celebration tonight in the piazza. It would be great to see, but we are put off by the rain and the lack of babysitter. (And apathy.) Instead, we celebrate by staying in and watching a video. Eventually though my New Year's conscience gets the better of me

4 Probably a second cousin twice removed.

5 No prizes for guessing our favourite; that's campanalismo for you.

and I decide to nick into the centre of town to see what's happening locally.

Although the rain has now eased off, Sansepolcro appears completely dead, with the notable exception of a group of Youths letting off crackingly-loud penny bangers in the piazza. The combination of a total absence of human activity and sporadic explosions echoing off the walls reminds me of 70s-era television reports from war-ravaged Eastern Europe; all we need now to complete the picture is for former Australian *60 Minutes* reporter George Negus to burst out from behind the gelato shop in a brown vinyl jacket with massive lapels to deliver an on-the-spot report.

I wonder idly if this is what it was like when the war came to Sansepolcro, and whether the sound of penny bangers in the piazza still gives older citizens the shudders. I must check with Raffaello sometime. In any case there is clearly little to see here in town, so I start to make my way back home to the nice cosy fireside.

Suddenly all hell breaks out: the clock has just struck midnight, and firework displays begin to burst forth in all directions. Here in blow-your-fingers-off Italy you're still allowed to buy your own fireworks, and either they are reasonably cheap or people are prepared to fork out for decent fireworks on this one night, because it is a truly marvellous spectacle. Unlike the fireworks shows we're used to in Australia, which take place in a single designated location for safety reasons, this one is going on in all directions, as every household strives to outdo the Borghesis down the road. It's hard to know which way to look.

I arrive home to find Eleni standing out the front checking out the firework action as well. Together we watch in silent amazement until, after about twenty minutes, the show gradually starts to wind down, to be replaced once again by sporadic gunfire courtesy of the Youths in the piazza. We retire inside for the post mortem: not the most exciting and adventurous New Year's Eve ever, certainly, but the fireworks were most impressive. And at least we managed to stay up past midnight—a definite improvement on previous years.

A few days later, still in dazed holiday mode, we decide to take the HGV for a spin up into the nearby hills. Today's nominal destination, as per the journey-of-discovery theory, is a convent called Montecasale, about which we know nothing except that it scores a Point of Interest symbol on our map and features prominently in the local presepio.

On this occasion it is the destination itself which takes the points: Montecasale is a very handsome monastery with a lovely little collection of church buildings perched all alone high up in the mountains. It comes with the requisite sense of history, having been founded/visited/mentioned idly in conversation during the twelfth century by none other than St. Francis of Assisi, he who trudged through Valfabbrica (right past the lonely farmhouse in fact) on his way from Assisi to somewhere or other in Tuscany. Just our luck to be saddled with an enduring historical connection to Valfabbrica.

At the Montecasale church we boldly attempt our time-honoured technique of following a stranger into a church, only to stumble in on a genuine church service with real live-action people engaged in real live worship. Our sense of embarrassment is acute; but luckily no-one glares angrily and we manage to escape without causing a commotion.

Shaken by this blatant transgression of protocol, we switch to Plan B—a walk in the country. Raffaello upstairs has told us that we should follow the signs to something called the Sasso Spicco, and this we now do, dutiful tenants that we are. But the recent rainfalls have made the steep downhill path rather slippery and treacherous, and after a great deal of stumbling and cursing and soul searching we are reluctantly obliged to abandon the adventure without reaching any kind of discernible destination.

Back at the top of the track there is a sign directing us to the presepio. So there is one after all! The Montecasale presepio is located in a small darkened hut further up the hill, nowhere near the church into which we blundered so rudely. The hut has been expertly covered with blackout cloths over the windows and doors, giving it a nice sense of atmosphere, especially during the starry night phase of the light show. I decide to give it the award for Best Depiction of a Night-Time Scene in a Presepio. And the trip is deemed to have been a thoroughly worthwhile day out.

Several days later, I come across a pamphlet on Montecasale describing the Sasso Spicco as a stunning natural amphitheatre with 60-metre waterfall. Tantalisingly, we could hear delicious watery sounds the entire time along the track but never seemed to be getting any closer. We will have to go back again when the weather is a bit drier. [*Would you believe they never made it back there either—all of 15 minutes away by car. Ed.*]

New Year's Day is a glorious winter's day in Sansepolcro, the type of weather which has been all too rare of late. For the past three weeks it seems to have rained almost continuously, including Christmas Day and New Year's Eve, but today the sun bursts out and it is so warm we have been able to throw open all the windows and air out the house. In fact it is altogether far too nice to be inside. We resolve to go on a picnic in the mountains in order to acquaint ourselves a bit better with the area.

Today we will be tackling the snaky mountain road that works its way up and over the Appennini mountain range, over to Urbino in the neighbouring province of Le Marches and eventually through to the Adriatic coast.

Before long we find ourselves very high up indeed, and Eleni is terrified that we are about to plummet down the cliff face at any moment. Certainly, the scenery is so tempting that it is easy to imagine being distracted from the road at the wrong point and heading straight through one of the flimsy barriers. Happily, we manage to stay on the bitumen and eventually find a spot that provides a bird's eye view of Sansepolcro and the neighbouring town of San Guistino, both of which sit in a flat plain hemmed in by the Appennini mountain range on this side and some other mountains over on the far side.

It is glorious to be up here in the hills on such a beautiful day. How lucky we are to have the mountains so close by. How lucky, indeed, to live in Sansepolcro. Surely there can be no finer place to sample the delights that Italy has to offer.

When we get back down to safe flat ground again, Ruby and Eleni trundle off to see the new *Harry Potter* movie, which starts at the local medieval cinema today. The film is dubbed in Italian, as is all film and television here (except for the occasional musical; we once saw the *Rocky Horror Picture Show* in English on the television but that was an exception). Ruby has been comprehensively swept up in the Harry Potter phenomenon and knows all the stories backwards so I imagine she will be able to follow the film, if not the subtle nuances in the dialogue ('Harry! Watch out! Another monster/evil spirit/nasty teacher/school bully behind you!' 'For God's sake Ron, is that the only face you can do?').

I would like to have gone too, because I am keen to experience the ambience of the old theatre with a film in progress. However, Felix has inconsiderately chosen this moment to take his afternoon nap, so I am obliged instead to settle for a cup of tea and a slice of one of those huge cakes that appear at Christmas time in circular boxes with a little carry handle. In a previous life we might have cheerily referred to these collectively as Panettone, but as a result of intensive cultural retraining we now know of a sub-genre called the Pandoro. The main distinction between the Panettone and the Pandoro appears to be that the Panettone has bits of fruit peel in it while the Pandoro doesn't, which to my mind renders the Pandoro essentially a massive fluffy orange cake. This is a no doubt a most insensitive and culturally inappropriate observation.

Sitting back with my tea and orange cake, I reflect idly on the fact that today we have been in Italy four months to the day, officially one-third of the Odyssey.

Each month has had a different flavour: September was spent settling in and discovering our new surroundings; October was Perugia month—we were in there almost every other day; November was defined by the audacious escape from Valfabbrica and the giddying welcome to Sansepolcro; and December was taken up with the Vienna trip and Christmas.

And now life is set to change again: with Ruby starting at scuola materna (kindergarten for five- to six-year-olds) next week the apartment will suddenly be a good deal quieter. It took over a month to find her a kindergarten, due mainly to a combination of intransigence on the part of Ruby (who understandably didn't fancy the thought of having to having to learn a whole new set of names and faces) and chronic lethargy on the part of her parents. Meanwhile, owing to the inclement weather over the past month we have been cooped up inside much of the time and the two children have been, shall we say, getting on one another's nerves a little.

Late in December the Parental Committee finally decided something had to be done and leapt swiftly[6] into action. We established that Sansepolcro has two kindergartens which Ruby could attend. Initially I was initially under the impression that there was a third right in the centre of town, having watched young children and parents streaming through the piazza and down a side alley in the mornings from my vantage point at Appy Bar. I was already dreaming of an early morning routine of kindergarten drop-off followed by a coffee and cornetto at the bar, when it was pointed out to me that unfortunately my preferred option was not a kindergarten at all but a primary school.

Ruby was duly escorted to an interview at a lovely little kindergarten recommended by none other than Ivana upstairs. Tragically it is well outside of town and near to no bars whatsoever, in a tiny little hamlet five kilometres up the road called Gragnano. This is, incidentally, close to the first place that we looked at with Raffaello—House Number One, the isolated old farmhouse with no heating.

Despite the lack of nearby coffee vendors, the Gragnano kindergarten is very appealing: housed in a quaint medieval[7] building with a commanding view over the countryside, small and non-threatening with only around 30 children in total, and run by a couple of highly accommodating teachers. What's more, Ruby herself has pronounced it to be acceptable.

6 -ish.

7 Later found out to have been built in the 1960s. From medieval stone, though.

The other kindergarten option, though barely two minutes' walk from our front door on the far side of the fabulous SMA supermarket, is a very large and modern[8] affair which our delicate little princess dismissed immediately as altogether too scary. And I think she has made the right choice.

There was a short period of high tension while we waited to see if the Gragnano kindergarten could accommodate Ruby—the class was technically full, but the teachers hoped to be able to squeeze her in after checking with il Direttore. Eventually the call came in, shortly before Christmas, and it was agreed that Ruby would start in the new year.

Having rounded up the requisite kindergarten goods, including the regulation tri-fold pencil-case and the regulation backpack, taking care to avoid the hideously expensive cheap plastic versions plastered with Disney characters, we await with great anticipation the start of the new year. Indeed, for the last couple of weeks we have been scheming about all the things we can do with our new-found freedom, the new places we can go for lunch, the day trips which will be so much easier with one child rather than two… poor Ruby, we do love her really.

It is not until after the festive season that I begin to appreciate the ritual of wishing the compliments of the season to one and all. Back in Australia I am used to saying Merry Christmas pretty much only to friends and family, whereas in Italy the friendliness net is cast much wider. It is not only the people behind the counter at the bar and the bakery and others with whom we come into contact on a regular basis, but even people we have never met and probably never will again (such as our bus driver on the return trip from Vienna) who wish us the compliments of the season without fail. And we of course return the greeting; in fact there is so much goodwill flying around the place that a permanent warm rosy feeling endures for the entire period leading up to the big day.

8 Built in the 1970s. From concrete.

Then it starts all over again shortly thereafter with the Happy New Year salutations, both before and after the event. The first few days of the New Year in particular are spent furiously delivering salutations and kisses on both cheeks to friends and family, including—startlingly at first to the author—much uninhibited kissing from male friends and acquaintances. But why not! The Italians are altogether more tactile in displaying affection, and there can be no doubt that this is a good thing.

There is also another holiday on January 6 where, assuming I have got this correct, an old witch called Befana comes down the chimney (which Italian Santa sensibly doesn't bother with) and distributes yet more presents to good children as well as lumps of coal to naughty ones.[9] Italian children thus score two sets of presents in the space of a fortnight. This sounds a bit excessive, and I strongly suspect that Befana was dreamt up by the same retail industry marketing gurus that brought us Father's Day. In any case, being foreigners we can feign ignorance on the gift aspect of Befana if challenged by Ruby or Felix.

It's just as well that you don't have to wish everyone the compliments of the Befana too or the entire nation would have compassion fatigue by 7 January.

And it turns out that 7 January marks yet another important cultural tradition in Italy: the beginning of the mighty post-Befana sales. The Italians have the good sense to delay the post-Christmas sales for a couple of weeks, a far more civilised arrangement than the Boxing Day commotion that we are used to in Australia because it allows plenty of time to recover from indigestion. Who has the energy to go bargain-hunting at nine in the morning the day after Christmas?

Quite by chance we pop into our favourite Coop supermarket on January 7 for a quick stock-up only to find ourselves swamped by vast milling crowds in the clothing section. To our astonishment, almost everything has been reduced to half price. There is no time to waste: immediately we leap into the fray and before long have picked out several bargains for the children as well as some decent thick winter

9 'I wonder where I can get hold of some coal round here, hahaha.'
Pathetic Parent Jokes, p. 337.

coats for the adults (including a very fetching number with a fluffy collar for Eleni) at never-to-be-repeated-until-next-Jan-7 prices.

At last we can hold our heads high as we parade down the main street, mixing it with the locals in their quilted full-length garments. We are still coming to terms with the importance of dressing well in Sansepolcro. The scruffy look does not go down well; even casual has to be done properly and with a sense of style. And one certainly does not, for instance, walk through town in one's tracksuit pants on the way to a gym class. (One goes the long way around or takes the car.) You still have much to learn, grasshoppers. But at least, thanks be to Coop, we have managed to raise our winter dress standards to the required level and should be safe for the rest of the season.

With the festivities over, the remainder of the month is free to amble along without fuss. After all the rain of December, January brings beautiful blue skies and crisp winter air almost every day. Until recently the weather has been mild; in fact, when we got back from subzero Vienna, Sansepolcro seemed positively warm. But now there's snow on them thar hills, and down on the plains it's genuinely cold. Bitterly, breathtakingly cold; nose-numbingly, eye-wateringly cold; ye olde traditionalle European cold. (And of course, pop-into-the-bar-for-a-coffee cold.) Personally, I can't get enough of this kind of weather. And what's more, it has even snowed right here in town!

The first thing to say about the recent snowfall in Sansepolcro is: thank heavens we got a taste of it in Vienna last month or we might have seriously embarrassed ourselves. None of this running around with our tongues sticking out like we did in Vienna—here we've got our reputations to uphold.

We still managed to look foolish on the first day, though. A substantial overnight dump had left our little street all carpeted in white. As soon as I saw it I thought: better put the chains on so we don't slip all over the place and have an accident. Luckily Daddy had already done a practice run with the chains a couple of weeks prior and was able to slip them on in a jiffy.[10]

As soon as we turned out of our side street and onto the road it became blindingly obvious that all the proper roads, i.e. the ones with regular traffic, were quite clear of snow and not at all dangerous. Needless to say, nobody else had chains on. Boy did we feel like idiots in our absurdly huge Swedish vehicle puttering along at the maximum 40 km/h making gurra-gurra-gurra noises all the way to the supermarket. If the locals didn't think of us as blatant attention-seekers before, they surely do now.

Thanks to the improved weather we have been able to expand our strolling range around town without fear of rain. The exploration drive has already yielded excellent results in the form of an exciting new bakery discovery. La Spiga, as it is called, is hidden half underground and accessed by a low door set into the corner of a side street. As is so often the case, there is virtually no signage and no indication that it is a shop, so that stepping down inside to discover racks of freshly baked bread and cakes is something of a surreal experience, like opening the door into Dr. Who's Tardis.

It turns out that La Spiga makes a beautiful big white loaf which qualifies as the nearest approximation yet to the kind of bread we would buy at home. This loaf is known simply as pane salato, or bread with salt. I have never before thought of bread as a salty thing, but having tried it without (the standard recipe around here) I now realise how much you need the salt. Apparently an evil salt tax was introduced long long ago, as a result of which everyone started baking their bread without salt in the time-honoured tradition of tax evasion. Unfortunately nobody told them when the tax was abolished and the bread remains unsalted and tasteless to this very day.

Old habits die hard—as do old arteries—and we will find ourselves wedded to our pane salato over the coming months. Meanwhile, La Spiga also has hot doughnuts with custard inside on Tuesday and Friday mornings, as well as massive crostata tarts filled with Nutella. Not that we are interested in any of these, of course: they're entirely too delicious for our figures.

10 If half an hour of cursing and fumbling can be described as a jiffy.

In other wanderings we have located two pizza places and even, somewhat bizarrely, a Chinese restaurant. Although upon mature reflection I can see no reason why Italian people should not eat Asian food occasionally if the mood so takes them. Why should we expect them to be so relentlessly Italian all the time? Must be a tourist thing. And I suppose it might be rather nice for a change, on those occasions when one is sick of eating pizza.[11]

Meanwhile we have been making our presence felt at the cafés. Recently Felix has been waking up very early, at around six o'clock in the morning—there have even been a couple of 5.30 starts, the little tyke[12]—and I have taken on the self-appointed role of early morning caretaker while the rest of the household slumbers blissfully on. Hopefully this will earn me a few brownie points for later on. It's not such a bad thing actually, as Felix and I have developed a highly convivial routine of going out for a very early morning walk to have a coffee and cakie. A number of the bars are open from seven o'clock (including current Bar of the Month, the wonderfully named Bar Gerasmo—inspired by *Barbarella* perhaps?), and by the time we have managed to dress ourselves in all the layers required for a winter morning, the Gaggias are already steaming away in town.

Shortly before eight o'clock we witness the morning rush of high school students, mostly girls, coming in for their pre-school convivial: a coffee and a fag, and sometimes a bit of last-minute homework. They are fashionably dressed for school—there being no such thing as uniform here—and sport serious make-up for the day.[13] Before long they are all lighting up and getting into the gossip.

The teenage smoking question is certainly an interesting one. Though Italians in general appear fairly relaxed about smoking, I wonder what the parents would think. Not that the girls themselves make any effort to conceal their smoking habits. Far from it, in fact: short of standing in the middle of the piazza, the bar would have to be the most open and public forum in town. I imagine that a few of their parents will be stopping in here for a coffee themselves later on.

Would the parents quiz the man behind the bar on what their daughters had been up to? Surely not.

11 I'm referring of course to Eleni; I *never* get sick of eating pizza.
12 Terminology varies depending on time of morning.
13 Plenty of product in there, as Eleni says.

Would Fabrizio let on even if they did? Surely not. Perhaps special diplomatic privileges apply within the bar, a form of *Don't look, Don't ask* policy.

I desperately want to know the answers to these and other cultural conundrums of Italian life. Like: how come no two caffé lattes are ever the same? And: does Fabrizio ever sleep? He opens up at seven every morning and usually doesn't close until around one the following morning. The man is unstoppable; it makes my head ache just thinking about it. Although that could be due to the thick haze of cigarette smoke that has enveloped the room. Time to head back home and see if the rest of the family has surfaced yet.

There is still some unfinished phone-related business to attend to.

The shiny new mobile phone, which has been acting up ever since I purchased it two months ago from the mega shopping complex down near Valfabbrica, is today going in for another inspection at the local agent for SonyEriccson. This turns out to be a tiny electrical repair shop run by a brooding young fellow who speaks rather too quickly for my liking.

I deposit the phone on the counter and explain how, despite having been 'repaired' once already down in Perugia, the thing still insists on turning itself off and on again at random. Most disconcertingly, I add, for one whose entire business is (or was, until Telecom Italia finally came to the party) predicated on this very device.

Unimpressed by my witty banter, the young lad replies with some rapid muttering that completely eludes me, apart from the unmistakeable words 'that'll be ten Euros' towards the end.

Come again? It's still under warranty.

He motions to the sign behind the counter. Sure enough: all goods deposited for repair officially attract a handling charge of ten Euros. Outrageous, but cheaper than a trip to Perugia in the HGV, so ten Euros it is. Except that I've only got five Euros in my pocket.[14]

14 Well, you wouldn't think to bring along money for a warranty repair would you?

That'll do, says the lad, and promptly pockets the money in his wallet. Hang on a minute: aren't you supposed to issue a receipt? The lad doesn't seem to think so. Come to think of it, he doesn't even have a cash register in his shop. I am staggered by this blatant disregard for the fearsome Guardia di Finanza, widely regarded the bane of every business in the land.

Some years ago, in an attempt to put a lid on the cash economy and extract more tax from honest and dishonest businesses alike, the government enacted new legislation compelling retailers to issue a receipt for absolutely every single transaction conducted in the country, right down to every last gelato and every pair of socks at the street market. This belated and heavy-handed response after years of inaction is typical of the modern Italian bureaucracy, which seems hell-bent on devising new and ever more draconian measures with which to torment its citizens.

Such as the outrageous new road rules, just recently introduced, whereby the police are now actively encouraged to issue fines and demerit points for speeding, dangerous overtaking, bad parking, holding a phone while driving, and failing to wear a seat belt or a helmet—all the cherished staples of Italian driving culture. For heaven's sake: next they'll be making everyone stop at pedestrian crossings! Not to mention the incessant police roadside checks of registration and insurance papers. And a threatened ban on smoking in bars and other public places—the poor high-school girls from Bar Gerasmo will be forced to smoke their pre-school ciggies in the piazza after all.

What is the country coming to? So much for all the theories about traditional Italian culture being eroded by EU regulations and British immigrants; the government is doing a fine job of it already.

Of course, the Italians have always responded admirably to ridiculous government restrictions on their daily lives, especially those pertaining to taxation.

Nobody in their right mind, for instance, would ever declare the actual selling price of their home when it comes to paying stamp duty to the tax office; the usual practice is for both sides to agree that the house sold for half as much, with the remainder to be handed over in a brown paper bag at a later date.

However, the issuing of receipts for cash purchases seems to be unavoidable; indeed, many shops will press the receipt on the customer. This is because the evil Guardia di Finanza (Finance Police) have been known to lurk outside shops and bars checking each and every customer on the way out.[15] If a purchase cannot be proven—even a quick coffee at the bar—both the customer and the shopkeeper may be fined. Some shopkeepers get testy if you leave the receipt in the money tray or try to jettison it in the rubbish bin on the way out. For the love of God take that thing out the door, they implore, and with good reason too.

All of which makes the behaviour of the lad in the electrical repair shop seem downright foolhardy. Now I think of it, he's not the only one.

Last month Eleni was required to obtain a doctor's certificate in order to join a nearby gym, in a valiant bid to address the waistline issue. Our friendly local doctor cheerfully obliged but told her it would cost 15 Euros. And where did the 15 Euros go? Straight into the pocket of Dr. Rossi thank you very much. Not that we would ever complain; Dr. Rossi cheerfully provides us with free health care despite the fact that the official bilateral reciprocal medical agreement thingy between Italy and Australia expired months ago.

And I recall that on another occasion, the ravishing dermatologist Sabrina from Arezzo offered to discount my E50 consultation to E30 cash, no questions asked and not a word to the taxman.

So my guess is that the wallet behind closed doors will remain a potent force in the Italian economy until such time as the Finance Police manage to install Big Brother cameras in every last room of every last business in the country.

Though we think we are doing well in our efforts to explore Sansepolcro and all that it has to offer, particularly with respect to

15 Seriously. It's in the guide books.

food, we still have much to learn from our elders. Only the other day Ivana introduced Eleni to a wonderful fresh pasta shop in the neighbouring town of San Giustino, hidden down a back lane with minimal signage—impossible to find unless shown by a local. Apparently there is another fresh pasta shop right here in Sansepolcro, but the San Giustino one is superior because the fresh pasta is made *by hand* as opposed to with a *fresh-pasta-making machine*. Not that we'd be able to tell the difference, but let it pass.

So a few days later we roll up at the San Giustino shop, all by ourselves and bursting with expectation, only to be told that there isn't any ravioli made up right now. Disappointment, however, turns to elation when the woman offers to make some for us if we could just wait ten minutes. She then proceeds to line sheets of newly-minted pasta with neat dobs of filling, cover them with top sheets and cut them into little squares, all before our very eyes. In less than an hour we are back at home tucking into ravioli barely thirty minutes old—definitely a PB for fresh pasta.

We have also been lucky enough to score a couple of bottles of Ivana's pomorola (all-purpose tomato base), which is perfect as a simple pasta sauce. Hand-made pasta with home-made pasta sauce is surely the healthiest fast food ever invented. Ivana has also taken it upon herself to bring down the occasional home-cooked delicacy every now and then for us to try: oven-baked lasagna, risotto, crostata tarts, sweet biscuits.

We are doing our best to return the compliment, albeit in our own limited way—thus far our side of the international culinary exchange program has been mainly limited to hefty slabs of traditional Australian cake (cooked to perfection, incidentally, in our modern and fully functional oven).

Eleni attempted to up the ante last week with a jar of home-made lemon butter, but Ivana swiftly responded with a tray of heart-stoppingly rich tiramisu. The culinary one-upmanship has now reached a new and dangerous level; it will be difficult indeed to top the tiramisu. Although Eleni has suggested a sushi-rolling feast, which I think should be worth a good many jars of pomorola.

The other day Raffaello turned 76, to our great surprise—we had him down as early sixties. Relations with the landlords are now so warm and friendly that we are deemed to have reached the gift-giving stage, and we have decided to buy him a nice bottle of wine with a handwritten number on it, as well as bake him a cake, naturally.

We arrange to hand over the goods at three in the afternoon after Raffaello has emerged from his nap. The present delivery turns into an extended afternoon coffee session, as we sit around nattering away for hours about nothing in particular like old friends. Or family, more like: Ivana and Raffaello dote on Ruby and Felix like their own grandchildren, while treating us like distant foreign relatives in need of an intensive catch-up course in Italian culture, which we are only too happy to lap up.

The conversation inevitably turns to cooking, and we mention that we are keen to learn the basic techniques for gnocchi, risotto and the all-purpose pomorola. Eleni and I are hoping to be able to take home some cooking wisdom from our time in Italy. Ivana offers to teach us in her downstairs kitchen during summer; we accept gratefully; smiles all round.

And I realise how lucky we are to be here, in this wonderful town, with these wonderful people. Our own little piece of paradise.

7

Stained Milk

Snow is great. Snow is fun. Snow is a novelty that we can't get enough of at this stage. There's only one problem: there's not too much of it down here in Sansepolcro. But a chance conversation with Laura from the real estate agency yields exciting news: there is a ski resort located less than an hour away from Sansepolcro in a place called Monte Fumiaolo.[1]

So off we head one fine Sunday morning on the basis that even if there isn't much snow we should at least be able to get a coffee up there.

On the way up we once again inadvertently attempt to destroy the HGV. This is what happens: halfway up the mountain the road starts to become icy and dangerous, so we sensibly pull over on a nice level plateau in order to fit the chains. But guess what… it isn't level at all, or not as far as our hulking great vehicle is concerned.

No sooner have Eleni and I stepped out of the car than we feel it gently sliding backwards over the ice. Eleni plants her foot on the brake but to no avail; the HGV continues gracefully and inexorably on its way—bearing our two children entombed in their child seats—before finally, mercifully ploughing into a snow bank at the far end of the plateau.

Just beyond the snow bank is a sharp drop down the mountain and… it doesn't bear thinking about. The HGV—and more importantly our children—live to ride another day.

1 Italy Fact: Mt Fumiaolo is the source of the River Tiber.

Now all we have to do is dig our enormous beast of a car out of the snow bank, creating a further delay which is not received at all well in the back seat. Ruby wants to know what we've done to the car *this* time and Felix is shouting for boredom's sake and Ruby is trying to clamp her hand over his mouth which makes Felix shout all the more; meanwhile Daddy's fingers are turning numb with the cold and the chains are hopelessly tangled and… this is shaping up as the original happy family outing.

Eventually, with the blessings of the Patron Saint of Road Safety, the chains are somehow secured and we are free to depart. And what do we notice as we are leaving but another car parked happily in the same spot, waiting patiently as its chains are fitted. Why does the HGV keep doing these things to us?

In the end there is plenty of snow up at Mt. Fumiaolo, the scenery is beautiful, the snow is tasty and we all have a great time. The child-friendly tobogganing slope is great fun, even more so after some young parents take pity on us and lend us a sled. After the obligatory coffee at the nearby chalet-type arrangement, during which we swap telephone numbers with the kindly sled-lenders and agree to get in touch over summer, it is time to check out the ski resort itself, which is just over the other side of the crest.

The *Biancaneve* (Snow White) ski resort may well be the smallest facility of its kind in Italy, if not the world. Actually 'resort' may not be the correct term for something which turns out to consist solely of an aging pommer and three short trails, one of which is already out of contention as far as I am concerned because it has a short uphill section where you have to walk.

Nevertheless, it is perfect for our requirements. The slope(s) are not crowded, which means that the four of us should be able to engage in snow play without getting in the way of any serious skiers. Tragically there is no more time today to explore it further, but it is agreed that we should all come back soon for a day trip, and further that Daddy should return as early as possible on his own to conduct a full reconnaissance, purely for research purposes, of course.

Thus it comes to pass that the following Friday I am dropping Ruby off at kindergarten dressed in garish ski pants (courtesy once again of the post-Befana sales) and heading off to Mt. Fumiaolo for a spot of skiing. Within three-quarters of an hour (including professional-speed chain-fitting in just five minutes!) I am at the base of the track that leads right to the door of the Snow White ski lodge. No need to trek across the top of the mountain from the tobogganing slope like the other day. How clever I was to come this way! The first section of the track looks dauntingly steep, though I have just seen another car disappear up there so it must be easier than it looks.

It isn't.

About a third of the way up the HGV starts to slip and slither, and before long its wheels are spinning uselessly, and shortly afterwards it begins to slither backwards, and soon after that it's starting to skew to one side because the front end's heavier than the back, and finally it ends up stuck fast across the track, with its front and rear bumpers wedged in the snow and its driver fuming in the front seat.

Aaaarrghhh! Why does this car have such a problem with snow? Has it not been designed and built in Sweden, a country that is blanketed with the stuff for half the year?[2] At least this latest snow episode poses no danger to life and limb; it's just that the HGV is comprehensively blocking access in and out of the resort and I'm going to have to trudge up the hill and ask for help. How embarrassing.

The proprietor of Snow White, a cheerful fellow called Franco, is not, incredibly, at all put out at having his resort entrance blocked by a stupid tourist who by now should by now have learned the limitations of his ridiculously large vehicle. Franco and I spend the next hour patiently digging the HGV out of the snow banks and turning it to face downhill, in the process destroying the front number plate. (Fancy tearing metal with water, albeit in an altered state.)

After thanking him profusely I slink sheepishly down the hill and deposit the car in the small parking area where, if I'd had any sense about me, I would have left it earlier.

2 Presumably.

My triumphant arrival at Snow White ski resort is thus severely delayed, and by the time I finally hit the slopes there is only 15 minutes until the pommer closes for lunch. Snow White is very much a family business, and all activity stops between twelve and one o'clock for lunch with the family: Franco, who runs the place and takes care of the machinery; his large jolly wife, who churns out excellent home-made meals in the kitchen; his son, or possibly son-in-law, who operates the pommer and gets to zoom around on the snowmobile; and various surly daughters, one of whom has already ticked me off for using the back door.

After a sumptuous lunch I head back out right on the dot of one o'clock, keen to make up for lost time, only to find the pommer still motionless: Franco et al have not finished eating yet, thank you very much. Eventually someone saunters out at around 1.30 pm and presses the button and the Mt. Fumiaolo skiing fraternity is back in action, all five or six of us. At 2.30 pm I have to finish up in order to make it back in time to collect Ruby from kindergarten, but by this stage I am already so stiff and sore in places that I didn't even know I had places that it is possibly just as well.

It has been such a fun day that before leaving I decide to book the entire family in for an overnight stay the following week (Snow White even has a couple of rooms to rent). This time the HGV will remain down in the car park and we will cheerfully carry our bags up the hill.

Later that evening Eleni reports that the phone is not working. I pick up the receiver. Sure enough: dead silence.

Here we go again then. Back outside in the freezing night to speak with everyone's favourite call centre. At least it isn't raining tonight. Why are you doing this to us, Telecom Italia? Are you trying to tell us something? Do you not want us here? I suspect that one of the lads down at the exchange has spotted my name on the application and called his mate over:

Hey Giovanni, check this one out—there's no 'e' on the end of Simon. Must be another one of those bloody English. Let's hit him with a few line faults and then see what he thinks of la bella Italia. Ehi!

Well, we won't be intimidated by your pranks, Telecom Italia.[3] We're enjoying ourselves here tremendously, goddamit, and we're staying for the whole bloody year no matter what you try on. So there.

Meanwhile, it's back to rugging up for outside phone calls and carting the computer out to the garden shed. Throughout the evening and the next day I pepper the call centre with squeaky-wheel-gets-the-grease complaints while picking up the receiver at regular intervals and listening forlornly for the return of the dial tone. (Just like old times.) At around lunchtime on the second day, one such routine complaint call yields the unexpected news that Telecom Italia are under the impression that the line is working again.

Er, guys, no it's not. Can you fix it please. Soon. And properly.

Just to add to the confusion, a nice chap from Telecom Italia rings shortly thereafter to arrange a date for the new phone connection. What on earth is he on about? After the initial excitement wears off I realise that he is from the Umbrian section of the behemoth and he is following up on the final application we made to connect the phone to the lonely farmhouse, back in early November just prior to the audacious escape.

A huge grin spreads over my face. This is indeed a moment to savour. It's impossible not to feel enormously smug as I tell him thank you but no, we're no longer interested.

But as soon as the nice chap rings off I am assailed by doubts: what if I misunderstood him completely[4] and he was actually ringing about the line fault here in Sansepolcro, and now I've gone and told him not to bother? So much for trying to master Italian via the immersion technique.

While I ponder this exciting new development in the ongoing saga, the mobile phone rings yet again. This time it's none other than

3 Though we will be driven close to tears by the frustration of it all.
4 Always a possibility.

Sandro, calling in from the armpit of Umbria with an update on the Morelli situation. It seems that the ex-landlord has formally replied through his lawyer to our stiff letter of demand. Naturally he refuses to reimburse us a Eurocent. The avvocato however is of the opinion that if we went to court we would have a good chance of winning the case.

This is most encouraging news. The thought of taking Morelli to the cleaners is most tempting—but then again, do we really want a protracted court case interfering with the Italian Odyssey? Common sense says no, but then common sense would never have agreed to uprooting the family for a year to live on the other side of the world on a whim. On this occasion however we may just have to give the points to common sense after all. Though it hurts to think of the Miser King appropriating several hundred Euros worth of free gasolio, it will be much better to put the whole sorry affair behind us.

Then I start worrying that this exchange of legal letters may have enraged Morelli, whom I still suspect to be a closet madman. Are we safe up here? Will he try to track us down? Would the women in the post office pass on our forwarding address? Do the normal confidentiality rules apply in a small backward country town?

Hopefully if it ever came to that Raffaello would spring valiantly to our defence, engaging Morelli in a fierce protracted Battle of the 76-Year-Olds to protect his poor, culturally-challenged foreign tenants. Although it could go the other way: the two of them might unexpectedly develop a strong rapport and end up laughing together uproariously over shots of grappa and swapping old tales of the war.

Actually no, Ivana would never allow that. Morelli is a dirty rotten Umbrian after all.

For no particular reason I am reminded of Sandro's young wife who, forced to leave her picturesque home town of Ripa after getting married, was often heard to opine that the only good thing in Valfabbrica was the pizzeria. Eleni and I are inclined to agree. Even now I still occasionally wake in the middle of the night from nightmares in which the entire family is trapped in a locked room in the lonely farmhouse under attack from Morelli and his army of winged mountain beasts. Needless to say, the feeling of unmitigated relief as my eyes slowly adjust to the gloom and register our bedroom here in Sansepolcro is…indescribable. Euphoric. Better than any drugs.[5]

At 4.30 pm that afternoon, a Telecom Italia technician arrives unannounced and, after a short investigation, pronounces the problem to be due to a faulty cable in the street. The cable is duly replaced, the dial tone returns and all fretting and worrying activities are officially suspended until further notice.

The Italian language is a beautiful thing, and Eleni and I are keen to stop savaging it on a daily basis. To this end, we have engaged a tutor called Paula down in Città di Castello to give us classes on Wednesday mornings while Ruby is at kindergarten.

Previously we had a very different tutor, a friendly Italian mamma called Barbara. Although not a teacher as such and unable to speak a word of English, Barbara was endlessly patient with us, repeating everything slowly and clearly until we finally understood. The problem was Barbara's redoubtable culinary skills; when it came Eleni's turn to ask questions the tutoring session inevitably morphed into an extended cooking class. It soon became clear that the classes were too much fun for language study, and Barbara's job description was duly revised to cooking instructor.

Already we have mastered the basics of pizza dough and sauce, with promises of pomorola and risotto lessons to follow. All agree that it's much better this way.

Paula, on the other hand, speaks perfect English and is extremely knowledgeable on the finer points of grammar such as the subjunctive and conjugation of the remote past conditional twice removed. Which is just as well, because neither Eleni or I have the faintest clue what these things mean in our own language, grammar teaching having gone out of fashion at some point in the 1970s.[6]

5 That I've ever had.

6 Or perhaps we just weren't paying attention.

Finally we have someone who can answer all those niggling questions that the dictionary doesn't explain—not to mention the peculiarities of the local Sansepolcro lingo and the subtle nuances of the Umbrian and Tuscan dialects.

Nevertheless, and despite the excellent assistance of Paula, I suspect I'll never quite get the hang of everyday Italian. For instance, the other morning a woman marches into Bar Gerasmo and says, literally: 'Listen, Fabrizio. I want a coffee.' I can't bring myself to speak like that, even though it's clearly quite acceptable (Fabrizio doesn't bat an eyelid and the woman gets her coffee). We English speakers are brought up to use liberal sprinklings of please and thank-you. Italian has *per favore*, as found in all good phrase books, but in my experience one seldom hears this out on the streets. Or perhaps Sansepolcro is a rude town?

There are certainly formal word structures in Italian, as in many other languages, and Paula has pointed out to me that the woman who ordered the coffee was being polite in this sense, as in: 'Fabrizio, I acknowledge that you are higher up the social order than I am; now make me a coffee.' Which doesn't really help matters much. No, entrenched politeness conditioning is not easily undone, and I continue to vacillate between smarmily polite and uncomfortably curt speaking modes, never managing to find the natural middle ground.

I've also noticed that Ivana and Eleni converse with one another using the informal *tu* form. As Ivana hasn't yet told me to address her as *tu*, I continue using the polite *lei* form. But I'm starting to feel a bit left out. Hasn't she noticed that I am still being insufferably polite while the wife is all matey and convivial? Surely she must sense my hurt and betrayal at being excluded from the inner sanctum of *tu* into which Eleni has been invited. Would it be acceptable, I wonder, to simply leap in and start addressing Ivana as *tu*, or should I wait to be told officially? It's a thorny lexicographical problem with no direct equivalent in English—there's nothing along the lines of 'You know, John, seeing as we're on such friendly terms, you can use a familiar pronoun on me if you like.'

And another thing, I've been wondering, lately: how is it that the bar, such an integral part of everyday Italian culture, is named after an imported English word? According to Raffaello, the word *bar* only crept into the language after the war; originally there were the *trattoria* (cheap pub/eatery), the *enoteca* (upmarket wine bar) and the *ristorante* (er, restaurant). If Sansepolcro is any guide, then the *trattoria, enoteca* and *ristorante* fulfil much the same roles today. So how did the *bar* manage to squeeze itself into the mix? And not only that, but establish itself as the bedrock of Italian social life. Because the ubiquitous *bar* is today a one-size-fits-all venue for any and every form of social activity—breakfast before work, coffee with friends, lunch, late-night drinks, soccer matches on the weekends—serving up not just coffees but all known forms of beverages, alcoholic and otherwise, as well as pastries, filled rolls, snack foods and often cooked dishes as well. Not bad going for an import.

The Italian language is full of twists and turns, like any language I suppose, and trying to wrestle them all to the ground and get them in a headlock is definitely a challenge. But it's worth it for the thrill of being able to understand a little of what is happening around you, let alone the exhilaration of being able to carry on a rudimentary conversation.

I remember in the early Valfabbrica days Sandro patiently teaching me my first Italian phrases for the express purpose of dealing with Morelli: useful nuggets such as *The heating system is not working* and *I'll pay you tomorrow*. And the classic *Please trust me, I'm an honest person*, which sounds pathetic now although at the time I was genuinely attempting to be sincere. Little wonder it had no effect on the landlord; he was probably trying to stifle a guffaw.

These days, thanks to Telecom Italia, I can instantly recognise key Italian phrases such as *One of our operators will be with you as soon as possible* and *For technical faults press one*. Also I have become highly accomplished at stock complaints such as *This is the third time I've called this week* and *No it's still not working properly*. The Wednesday tutorials with Paula, meanwhile, are helping to supplement my telecommunications vocabulary with more down-to-earth words and phrases which I trust will come in handy in that happy time, hopefully in the not-too-distant future, when I no longer have to stand outside the door on the phone, shivering in the cold.

In terms of validation of your newly-acquired language skills, there's nothing quite as satisfying as being mistaken for a local and asked directions. This happened to me just recently, and I *think* I passed the test. Not that there's any way of knowing whether the nice young man in the car ever found the petrol station; for all I know he might have just smiled politely then headed further down the road to ask someone else.

However, for the sake of my ego I'm going to assume that my expert instructions did the job. Experiences like this do wonders for your sense of belonging. After all, if you know where the local landmarks are *and* can explain how to get there, why, you're virtually a local!

All appears to be going reasonably smoothly at the scuola materna in Gragnano. The teachers had Ruby standing up the front teaching English to the rest of the bambini on the first few days, which was well received. But after the initial euphoria wore off, Ruby began to get sick of hearing unintelligible Italian all day long, and there was a stage where she put up fierce resistance in the mornings. This required some creative manipulation of the truth: we argued that Mr. Policeman would get annoyed if she didn't go, which is not strictly true as schooling is not compulsory here until six years of age. Nevertheless we managed to relieve our collective conscience by employing the theoretical construct that schooling *would* be compulsory by now *were* we in Australia.

And Ruby may also be getting bored; whereas her kindergarten back in Australia was full of stimulating play objects and largely devoid of formality, scuola materna involves sitting down for most of the day and the activities seem to be mainly drawing and drawing, with a break for three-course lunch and then more drawing.

Nevertheless, there appear to be a couple of potential best friends on the horizon, and judging from the way Ruby zooms out of the car in the morning, the overall experience can't be that unpleasant. So although she would never admit as much under questioning, I think she is actually quite enjoying herself; she has even expressed an interest in catching the school bus with all the others. The acid test will be how many of her new friends score the big invite to her birthday party in June.

The successful settling in is a major relief all round. One of our biggest concerns was how Ruby would cope after having been plonked down in a totally foreign environment (Valfabbrica) for a couple of months, then plucked out again just as she was starting to find her feet and make friends and deposited in a new foreign environment. But it turns out that her supposed friends at the Valfabbrica kindergarten were not always that friendly anyway. Meanwhile, her Italian is improving steadily; she loves to compare her accent to ours and ask which is better, and we dutifully respond *Why yours of course my dear*, just like the Magic Mirror.

Both children have taken the move to Sansepolcro in their stride. We had no difficulty convincing Ruby that Morelli was an unkind person who didn't deserve us as tenants. And if either of the children were feeling at all disoriented with the change, the unbridled adoration of their surrogate grandmother Ivana soon swept that all away. That and her endless supply of chocolate biscuits.

Felix has been outdoing himself with superlative behaviour, meaning fewer of those two-year-old tantrums. Now learning to speak, his vocabulary extends to, as of this weekend, his sister's name. He has been following her around incessantly chanting 'Ruby?, Ruby?, Ruby?', which she puts up with admirably considering how annoying it must be.

Little brother has also learned to get his milk delivered by asking for 'hot bottle' which is all very cute and everything, but it inevitably reminds me of that song *Hot Blooded* by Foreigner, and since he asks for bottles pretty much non-stop, the damned tune is stuck in my head all day long. Although it could be worse I suppose: if *Hot*

Blooded were a Michael Bolton song I might have had to strangle him by now.

We have established that the five kilometres between scuola materna and home is the perfect distance for a brisk morning walk to work off some of our increased food intake. To this end, we have developed a routine of driving in together to drop Ruby off, after which one of us walks back home. It's a lovely walk too, through the farms and the fields, past the pigs and the chickens, agreeably flat with only the gentlest of undulations and, most importantly, finishing up with a promenade through town along the main street, which presents the perfect opportunity for a warm-down coffee.[7]

These days we can generally be found at Bar Gerasmo in the mornings chatting to the indefatigable Fabrizio, who speaks good English (and a brand of German, as it happens) on account of having spent his childhood in Switzerland. In addition to our shared English-language skills we can also share parenting stories, since Fabrizio's son Francesco is around the same age as Felix. Plus Fabrizio is a highly personable and interesting guy, always up for a chat on quiet mornings after the early morning slam-it-down espresso rush hour has finished.

Our conversations inevitably lead to analysis of cross-cultural differences, such as the ridiculous tendency of Australians to drink caffé lattes throughout the day, and even into the evening, *O Dio*!, with no heed to the known[8] deleterious effects of taking milk in coffee beyond ten in the morning. But, while we're at it, why can nobody in Italy agree on how to make a good hot strong milky coffee, Fabrizio?

The man behind the bar gives the matter some thought before delivering his verdict: What you want, he pronounces, is a latte macchiato and not a caffé latte at all.

What is a latte macchiato? It sounds vaguely familiar from cafés back in Australia. It also sounds suspiciously like one of those

7 I hear that the warm-down is an important part of any exercise regime.
8 Known to Italians, that is.

viciously strong black coffees in ridiculously tiny cups that are the sole preserve of showy intellectuals and old-school Italians. Luckily Fabrizio is here to clear the problem up. A *macchia* is a stain, such as the stain on your shirt when you spill coffee on it. A *caffé macchiato* is a coffee stained with a bit of milk—plain old coffee with milk, then. A *latte macchiato*, on the other hand, is a big glass of hot milk stained with a bit of coffee. Which is precisely what we're after. Simple! And not so scary after all.

The Stained Milk as prepared by Fabrizio at Bar Gerasmo turns out to be the caffeine beverage for which (grammar) we have been hankering in vain all this time: hot, strong, huge, delivered in a glass. Wonderful. Coffee nirvana having finally been attained, the Stained Milk is herewith adopted as the Official Drink of the UN Year of the Italian Odyssey.

Subsequent research over the next few months will establish that the Stained Milk tends to be a safer bet in foreign bars than the wildly inconsistent caffé latte. Now we can order our coffees with confidence, and cappuccinos can be relegated to the status of last resort. But Fabrizio still makes the best Stained Milk in town, meaning that we are effectively wedded to Bar Gerasmo. Which is not such a bad thing, since Fabrizio's bar also boasts superior marmalade cornetti, along with an excellent selection of panini and *sandwiches.*[9] No: the problem is that when Bar Gerasmo is closed on Monday, its official government-regulated Day of Closing, we are obliged to make do with either potentially weak tepid Stained Milks or eighties-era cappuccinos for breakfast, which is just not right.

Having established Bar Gerasmo as our preferred coffee vendor, we are settling into a highly convivial morning breakfast routine. With Felix now waking up at more reasonable hours we seldom make it to the bar for the pre-school session these days, preferring to drop in at nine o'clock or thereabouts on our way back from the morning kindergarten run to Gragnano. The perfect hour, as luck would have

9 Rolls, actually, but let it pass.

it, for tucking in to a large breakfast of panino and cornetto washed down with a Stained Milk.

Again, this is a ridiculously foreign habit; your average Italian might have a sweet pastry and a coffee in the morning, maybe a panino in the event of major hunger pangs, but certainly not both. Well, I can only change my eating habits so far. The ban on milky coffees after ten in the morning is manageable I suppose—anyway, it's not worth the raised eyebrows and suppressed chuckles—but the full breakfast I refuse to give up. Besides, it's good for you. I read it somewhere.

Shortly after our arrival, and well after the morning rush hour has cleared out, the bar is taken over by an entirely different demographic. This is the hour at which the retirees of Sansepolcro begin to congregate for their daily session of coffee and animated conversation over the morning papers. The Old Men's Club, as we have called it, has a base quorum of around five members, swelling to ten or more on a busy day. It convenes every morning without fail and remains in session for at least an hour, often two. Most of the members of the Old Men's Club look to be around sixty or seventy, although there are a few amongst them who could hardly be much more than fifty.

How come they get to retire so early and hang around in bars?

The answer, based on months of painstaking oral history research, is as follows. Back in the good old days, when the Italian government was still being nice to the people, retirement pensions in the state sector were so outrageously generous that if you could manage to wangle a job at the railways or the post office you were effectively set for life: you could retire at forty on a handsome stipend and never have to worry about money again. The only problem for the retirees, then, is working out how to fill in their remaining 15,000 odd days of usable life. Which explains why they're all down at Bar Gerasmo of a morning, trying to kill a few hours before lunch and dreaming up activities for the afternoon.

Interesting, observes Eleni, how you never see the wives here with them in the morning. I'll bet they're all at home cleaning and scrubbing and preparing sumptuous lunches. Perhaps there is a corresponding Old Women's Club in the afternoons? Further research required.

Now that we're something approaching regulars ourselves, we are on nodding terms with a few of the Old Men's Club members, and one of them has even developed an ongoing friendship with Felix. Whenever the old gent is in—more or less always, since he's part of the quorum—Felix zooms over and spends five or ten minutes playing happily on his lap while the parents look on warmly. A true win-win situation: the old man gets to enjoy contact with a youngster and we get to sip our coffees undisturbed in the background.

In spite of our new-found affinity for Bar Gerasmo, though, we've been careful not to abandon our roots: we still pop into Bar Appennini across the road for breakfast every now and then. And it's not only for the burning sense of nostalgia; Appennini boasts the finest doughnuts in town, although you have to be early. Plus we get to feast our eyes on the ravishing Ester-in-the-mornings with the gorgeous long black hair, current favourite for the Best Looking Girl in Sansepolcro award. Appennini is therefore the natural choice on Bar Gerasmo's official closing day. And here we are clearly in sync with the wisdom of the elders, because the Old Men's Club also relocates en masse to Appennini every Monday.

Now all I have to do is train Ester to make the perfect Stained Milk. Since we're already on friendly terms this will need to be done with great tact and subtlety so as not to cause offence. Driving home the key concepts of *hot* and *strong* without compromising our fledgling friendship will be a highly delicate operation requiring skill, tact and careful consideration of cross-cultural sensitivities. Just the job for a newly-arrived Australian immigrant, I reckon.

Today we are off on our first day trip in quite a while. We plan to hit not just one but two towns in the same day: picturesque Urbania, as featured in the Ci Siamo textbook from our Italian language classes in Australia, and magnificent Urbino, described in the Lonely Planet as 'one of the best preserved and most beautiful hillside towns in Italy.' Both of these are located in the neighbouring province of Le Marches, accessed via a terrifying but exhilarating drive over the Appennini mountains past the very spot where we had our inaugural picnic last month. However, the temperature has dropped below freezing overnight and the car windscreen is all iced up. No problem: I'll tip a bucket of hot water over the windscreen to melt it off.

This turns out to be bad science: the hot water instantly freezes onto the windscreen and forms a new and exciting layer of ice crystals which are equally difficult to remove. There ensues a short delay involving frantic scraping and huffing in the background as Daddy once again curses his lack of cultural understanding. Ice on the car is new to me; there must be some special European technique for approaching a frozen car in the morning but I don't know it. Something else to ask Uncle Raffaello about later.

Chosen as a destination purely on the basis of being in the textbook, Urbania turns out to be a beautiful little town with a very lively atmosphere, due no doubt to the many universities and language schools (known to attract Young People) and the higher-than-average quota of cute piazzas. The old section of town is not only raised on a hill but neatly enclosed within the circular bend of a large sunken river, creating a natural fortress complemented by standard-issue castle walls which in turn necessitate a number of suitably picturesque medieval bridge crossings.

After completing the obligatory circuit of the castle walls, including a picnic at one of the aforementioned river crossings, we spend a happy hour or so wandering around the centre of town admiring the general state of disrepair and trying to decide which bar will earn our valuable patronage. It's a tough decision, so eventually we settle for the one on the main street that we recognise from the *At the Bar* chapter of the textbook.

Urbania has a more run-down feel than Sansepolcro, which in my opinion adds immeasurably to its charm. Sansepolcro was hit by the

1997 earthquake—the same one that caused immeasurable Cultural Damage down in Assisi—and has clearly scored some restoration funding, with many of the palazzos around town sporting new rendering and fresh paint. Which is all well and good, but personally I find the ancient crumbling look of Urbania more appealing.[10]

At the other end of the scale, Urbino up the road positively radiates importance and grandeur, as exemplified by the sheer size of buildings such as the Palazzo Ducale. Sadly, due to the combination of our delayed start and the short winter days, we have only a couple of hours of daylight remaining in which to explore Urbino. The first stop on our truncated itinerary is a quick spin through said P. Ducale, which also doubles as a museum. Its enormous rooms feature possibly the world's largest fireplaces, so big that you can sit inside with a fire going, as well as endless artworks hanging on the walls.

On the way out of the museum we spy a presepio in a nearby church. As one would expect in grand Urbino, it is a most impressive presepio, small in terms of floor space but about three or four metres high with multiple levels and studded with twinkling lights throughout.

I think this one is my favourite presepio, says Ruby abruptly.

But surely, darling, not better than our local one in Sansepolcro? It doesn't have any moving parts. Think what you're saying now.

This one *is* better, she replies. See how high it is. It's like a medieval Faraway Tree. And look at all the pretty lights! The Sansepolcro one will have to be my second favourite from now on.

Sigh. No sense of campanalismo that girl.

Stung by Ruby's treason, I declare to all that it is now time to head home. Anyway, it's getting late. Tragically abbreviated by the combined forces of nature and bad planning, our Urbino visit has been short and sweet. We'll just have to come again sometime. [*Of course they never did. Ed.*]

During the return journey we notice that the car is starting to overheat. Actually it has been acting strangely for some time now. The heater inexplicably stopped working in December, and we have been cursing its lamentable sense of timing—cutting out like that just

10 Bloody tourists, never happy.

with winter beginning to bite and all. Also the radiator fan keeps spinning around for a good half hour after the engine is switched off, sometimes causing the battery to go completely flat.

Only a week or so ago I was describing these problems to a gruff chap called Roberto from the Volvo workshop down on the road to Città di Castello. Roberto suggested a complete overhaul of the heating system—a massively expensive job that takes several days as it involves ripping the engine out. I was supposed to bring the car in for him to have a closer look, but I've been paralysed by fear of the truth. This overheating business, however, is serious. No way out of it now.

At the workshop I describe the latest development to Roberto and he nods sagely before asking to take a look under the bonnet, as mechanics do. I hover nearby trying to appear at once knowledgeable and unruffled, although right now I am most decidedly neither of these things.

Suddenly Roberto flashes me a withering look. When did you last top up with coolant? he demands.

Er, I haven't yet actually. Where does it go? *replies Our Hero, instantly robbed of all pretence of coolness.*

Without bothering to answer Roberto ducks off inside and returns with a bottle of strange green liquid which he then proceeds to pour into a dusty old plastic receptacle somewhere over on the right-hand side.

You've been running the engine without coolant, he snorts. Consider yourself lucky you haven't blown it up.

On any other day I might be hurt by these harsh words, or more likely mortified by my own foolishness. But right now I'm overjoyed, ecstatic in fact, at the realisation that all our car problems—defunct heating system, excessive radiator fan action, flat batteries, overheating—have been fixed in one fell swoop for the price of a few litres of coolant.[11]

Roberto hops inside the car and turns on the heater. Warm air! It's a miracle! And a necessity, too, in these freezing times. Eleni and

11 May I just say in my defence that I am very good at checking the oil and water in our old car in Australia. So in the case of the HGV I had applied the reverse logic, assuming that all modern cars can conserve their own liquid unaided. Not much of a defence, I admit, but I'm going to run with it anyway.

I were seriously considering trying to brave the winter without heating rather than fork out to have it repaired, but we now know that this would have been impossible. The car is often colder than the fridge first thing in the morning after being out in subzero temperatures all night.

Seeing as the automobile gods are smiling on me today, I may as well test my luck a bit further. I've seen a few second-hand cars out the front of the workshop with prices on them. Perhaps the HGV could join them.

Do you think you would be interested in selling this car for me? I enquire innocently.

Roberto takes a sidelong glance at the number plate. Nope, he replies bluntly, we wouldn't.

Ah, well. The HGV lives to ride another day.

8

The Joy of Zeds: Pizza, piazza and zizzania[1]

The season of Carnevale is upon us, and we are all too aware of our duty as tourists to investigate this very Italian phenomenon.

I have successfully cashed in some of my brownie points (refer Chapter 6) in order to go on a day trip to Venice on the first Sunday in Carnevale, which has been organised by one of the local travel agencies. Sundays during Carnevale are said to be the most spectacular and the trip promises to be excellent fun apart from one tiny drawback: I have to get out of bed at four-thirty in the morning for the tour bus departure at five o'clock sharp.

Actually there is a second drawback that I didn't realise at the time of booking: this Sunday is also the day after our return, slightly the worse for wear, from the snow trip to Mt. Fumiaolo.

The trip itself was wonderful fun: no snow-related dramas involving the HGV; a picnic in the snow on the first day with the sun shining brightly overhead; plenty of throwing of/playing with/falling over in the snow; and even some amateur sledding and skiing action. During the night, however, the children contrived to wake up several times for no particular reason, once again displaying their special intuition for ruining holidays, so it was a rather tired and sorry bunch that emerged the next day.

1. Zizzania, n. malicious rumour-mongering (worth 35 points in Scrabble).

And an even more sleep-deprived Daddy who hauled himself out of bed at four-thirty the following morning to catch the bus.

But enough of the complaining already.

Venice on a sunny Sunday in Carnevale is like one big fancy dress party, particularly in the enormous Piazza San Marco. The place is positively dripping with exquisitely executed masks and costumes. There are also some low-rent home-made versions in amongst the rabble, making a refreshing change from all the pomp and posturing. After about an hour of this at close range, however, I'm starting to feel a bit Carnevaled out. The camera is already full of mask photos; time to cross this one off the list and move on.

Besides, the piazza is impossibly crowded now. And according to my tourist map, the main island of Venice isn't actually that large; it should be possible to cover most of it in a good day of solid walking. As a lover of solid walking from way back I know a challenge when I see one. World-famous destination; crisp winter day; no children in tow; no cars on the streets, no hills or stairs; a free agent until the return ferry at six o'clock tonight. It doesn't get much better than this. Sleep deprivation be damned, I'm up for it.

The next eight hours see me stomping happily around the island, across bridges, through thoroughfares, along canals, under archways, down laneways, even riding on the odd gondola or two. Without a doubt the highlight of the day is lunchtime. While wandering along a peaceful stretch of canal in the quiet ghetto area to the north I detect the unmistakeable aroma of pizza wafting through the air. Yes, there's the pizzeria just up ahead. And look: a spare table out the front. I ask inside; it's free. Clearly this was meant to be.

Before long the meal arrives and for a short period I attain nirvana: seated in front of a beautifully cooked pizza and a glass of wine, in the sun, by the canal, reading the Sunday paper, completely and gloriously alone. But wait, it gets better: halfway through my meal, the guy at the next table whips out a saxophone and starts serenading the rest of us with an impromptu lunchtime recital, I kid you not. Truly a life-affirming experience. If pizza be a religion, then yea verily I have seen the light.

After lunch, moving along a little more sedately now—the wine and pizza are beginning to take their toll, I'm clearly not the solid walker I once was—my mind wanders to the Venice question. It's a curly one, let's face it.[2] Granted, the island is a veritable feast for the retinas: the ornate buildings, the stately canals, the eye-popping menu prices. And all those who visit must duly admire its grandeur and faded opulence and the rest of it. But the question remains: why go to all that trouble to create a city from scratch on top of some dodgy mud-flats a mile off the coast? Just as cute hillside villages in Umbria and Tuscany were built with natural defence rather than tourism in mind, one assumes that Venice wasn't built as a tourist destination per se—although there must have been a certain element of showing off at the time.

And I understand that Venice was once a formidable marine power, a nuclear superpower of its day. So what I want to know is: how on earth did the Venetians manage to build such an incredible masterpiece of a city on a pile of mud—surely one of mankind's most technically brilliant yet futile projects—and still have the energy left to ferry all their supplies across from the mainland at great expense AND maintain a fearsome navy commanding the respect of the known world? In the words of Foghorn Leghorn: it just don't add up.

The Venice of today is a city perpetually under construction, with the ubiquitous yellow cranes and construction hoardings forming an incongruous addition to the medieval skyline. Not only are the old buildings in need of constant repair and refurbishment, but there are canals to be cleaned and realigned, facades to be washed and repainted, and lanes to be torn up and repaved every time some newfangled technology is invented, requiring yet another set of glossy black cables.

Thus it seems there will always be scaffolding on the streets and cranes on the skyline of Venice, until such time as the mud-flats finally give way and the entire city sinks below the water-line, in which case there will be cranes but no skyline.

My attention is momentarily distracted by a sign on a small dusty shopfront denoting the official premises of the Automobile Club of

2 Not least that S-bend of a canal winding through the middle, ho ho.

Venice. What possible use is an automobile club on an island where all road traffic is banned? What are the good folk of the Club doing in there all day long? Engaging one another in existential discussion perhaps, trying to deduce the reason for their existence. Either that or it's a front for organised crime.

The major excitement of the afternoon session is getting stranded on the wrong side of the canal and nearly missing the ferry home. There I am waiting patiently at the gondola-stop to cross the river when a colourful and highly cultural procession of musical gondolas begins making its way in no particular hurry down the S-bend, and all cross-Canal gondolas are cancelled until further notice. The tension mounts as I consider my options—hijack a spare gondola and make a James Bond-like dash for freedom?—but luckily the procession finishes shortly before six o'clock and I am able to make it back across and pelt over to the ferry terminal just in time for the departure.

From the ferry we all pile back on the bus again, but the bus stays resolutely put in the car park for nearly an hour. Someone explains the reason for the delay: apparently the lady from the travel agency has caught the wrong ferry and is now stuck miles away in a different part of Venice waiting for the return boat. It is decided that we will all repair to one of the legendary Italian expressway service centres for dinner while the bus driver goes back to pick up Mrs. Travel Agency. This little episode sets us back several hours, so that it is well after midnight by the time we finally pull into Sansepolcro. I can't help thinking that my last-minute arrival at the ferry terminal in Venice may have had something to do with the delay. Certainly Mrs. Travel Agency has never quite looked at me the same way again.[3]

Three days later and it's time to do it all again, this time as a family affair in the Hulking Great Volvo. The good old HGV—it may be big, expensive and downright dangerous in the snow, but on long road trips it positively shines. The three and a half hour trip passes in no time at all, and soon we are crossing the bridge into the

3 And several months later I notice that she has gone out of business altogether, to be replaced by a flower shop. Hope it wasn't my fault.

construction zone that is Venice and depositing our trusty chariot in one of the fine car-parking establishments on the perimeter.

Mid-week in Carnevale there is still a good turn out of masks and costumes, and for the next day and a half we enjoy ourselves immensely, and at a nice leisurely pace too. Felix hops obligingly out of his pram at the bridge crossings, Ruby puts in a highly-commendable solid walking effort for a six-year-old, while the Parental Committee takes due care to schedule regular gelato stops for the children and coffee stops for the adults.

Over the course of our stay I've been trying to factor in as many gondola Canal-crossings as possible. This is ostensibly for the benefit of the children; however the real underlying agenda is to nip the wife's gondola cravings in the bud. For months Eleni has maintained that her sole objective in Venice is to enjoy a stately gondola ride down some narrow canals, but the tourist rip-off alarm is clanging furiously in my head. There is no end of luxury gondolas plying the waterways but my preliminary research on Sunday indicates that they are all viciously expensive. Whereas for just 45 centesimi you can cross from one side of the S-bend to the other in an identical gondola, albeit minus the velvet seats with gold trim. Sure, the trip is over in three minutes, but at the end of it you get the warm rosy feeling that comes with still having 100 Euros left in your wallet.

Unfortunately, my cunning strategy backfires spectacularly: having had her appetite whetted, Eleni is now keener than ever to ride on a 'real' gondola with velvet seats and gold trim for a period of no less than 30 minutes. Desperately I try to fob her off, employing obfuscation tactics recently acquired from our good friend Signor Morelli, but she will not be shaken from her mission. The Mexican stand-off eventually leads to the following exchange:

Wife: If you won't take me on a gondola now then I'll just have to come back on my own sometime and do it without you.

Husband: Go on then!

By the way, the children slept wonderfully.

Eleni and I take our touristic duty very seriously. Just as one presepio was not enough at Christmas time, so we are keen to experience as many different types of Carnevale as possible, naturally for research purposes. So when Marius and Christine ring to tell us about the must-see Carnevale celebrations down in Foiano della Chiana we need no further convincing. The Family Day Trip light is flashing, the starter is on his platform, we're racing to go.

If it weren't for its Carnevale celebrations, claimed as the oldest in the world,[4] Foiano della Chiana would probably be a small town in southern Tuscany much like any other, ie perched on top of a hill with stunning views, beautiful old buildings, graceful piazzas, cobbled streets, cute laneways… the usual stuff. For a couple of weeks in February, however, this unassuming hillside settlement moves onto a higher plane altogether.

If Carnevale in Venice is a fancy dress party, then Foiano's version is one big street party where the key concept is *fun*—in stark contrast, it has to be said, to the moneyed posturing up north. The Carnevale parade down the main street of Foiano is an exercise in joyous mayhem, a noisy, colourful, South American-style procession of gargantuan floats and costumed tribes swaying to the thumping music, a pulsating ribbon of colour and movement barely managing to squeeze its way through the narrow canyon of the main street and the pressing throng of spectators.

And whereas Carnevale in Venice revolves around disparate individuals strutting their stuff and waiting for the cameras, the emphasis in Foiano is on massed teams of party-goers in coordinated home-made costumes: here a tribe of Indian natives in grass skirts with bongo drums, there a troupe of fairy dancers in swathes of chiffon and tulle, coming up a choreographed group of go-go dancers in fluorescent red dresses with gold hats and canes, in the distance some sort of crazy flower-inspired types; and many other costumes that defy categorisation altogether.

Meanwhile the enormous floats, towering above the performers and spectators alike as they inch cautiously along the route, feature the most bizarre designs this side of *Mad Max II*, and I strongly

4 I suspect this is an exercise in wishful thinking similar to the 'Beethoven Lived Here' ruse in Austria.

suspect that the good citizens of Foiano della Chiana are heavily into psychedelic drugs. Consider these examples:

- A massive red chicken flanked by effigies of Hitler and Mussolini bursting forth from large cracked eggs on either side;
- A creature that appears to be a cross between a pig and some sort of winged animal, featuring industrial-inspired touches such as a snout made of air duct and bulldozer buckets for claws;
- A crouching techno-beast with gyrating mouth belching forth steam, which is dwarfed by an enormous Godzilla in full Tokyo-havoc-wreaking pose and encircled by a ring of animated dancing monkeys;
- A subdued Madonna teetering forward precariously with arms outstretched as if about to topple at any moment, providing a muted yet physically threatening counterpoint to the animal circus;
- Plus countless other Gothic/fantasy/monster creations that could only be the creative output of severely disturbed minds.

At the end of the day my vote for Best Float goes to the Godzilla entry, not least for the inspirational choice of 'My Sharona' as its theme song, which is belted out at deafening volume all the way down the main street, including the entire guitar solo. Worth an encouragement award for that alone.

Once again there is no evidence of intrusive corporate sponsorship at Carnevale in Venice or Foiano: no signs on the floats, no logos on the costumes, no interference with the artistry on display. Which just goes to prove that such things can be done without the aid of the mighty corporate dollar.

Carnevale sponsorship: now there's a golden opportunity for the multinationals. One can all too easily imagine the Coca-Cola Carnevale in Venice: things go better with a mask on! Not to mention the myriad marketing opportunities offered by the

Christmas break: Befana present delivery brought to you by FedEx, anyone? Your local presepio courtesy of Seiko precision machinery? See how ancient traditional customs are simply brimming with marketing potential.

The local Carnevale celebrations in Sansepolcro, held the following weekend, are a vastly more down-market affair, consisting essentially of a Mexican party band playing out of the side of a delivery truck at one end of the piazza (since persistent drizzle has prevented them from taking to the temporary stage erected at the other end). Younger children have dressed up in costume and are attempting to dance in the wet, but it's a rather dispirited exercise. This year the weather has literally rained on our parades: Christmas Day, New Year's Eve, and now Carnevale.

Meanwhile the Youth of Sansepolcro, completely unperturbed by the rain, are engaged in pitched street battles involving cans of spray foam and string.[5] Before long the piazza is littered with confetti and the detritus of battle. The string is excellent fun—I remember it well from my childhood—so a couple of days later we purchase a can for Ruby. But the problem, as we soon discover, is that you have to go around picking up all the nasty non-biodegradable chemical remains from the garden afterward, a thoroughly unrewarding task. So really, the only time to let loose with the stuff is during Carnevale, when you know the comune street sweeper will be along later to clean it all up. Which is precisely what the uninhibited Youth have been doing all day.

Spring is in the air, and spring means spring cleaning. Up until now I had always thought of spring cleaning as a quaint, outdated concept of little relevance to modern life. Or to my modern life, at any rate: I've never seriously associated the arrival of spring with an urge to clean. Whereas here in our corner of Italy it is one of the immutable laws of nature, like not having milk in your coffee after ten in the morning. Spring means spring cleaning: everyone knows that.

5 At least they're not doing drugs, dear.

The Ivana and Raffaello compound has been transformed into a hive of frenetic activity. Out come all the plants from their little winter hot-house, up go the geranium boxes along the driveway, the garden gets a fresh dose of stinky fertiliser, Vittoria the Home Help is brought in to wipe over all the window shutters, the umbrellas and gazebo in the back garden are opened up, the second kitchen is dusted off and fitted out for the coming summer. Raffaello even presents us with a handsome new umbrella for our own little courtyard area.

At Bar Gerasmo, Fabrizio and Laura are busily cleaning and dusting down the shelves, and the front door now stays open permanently in official acknowledgement of the warmer weather. Most of the bars and restaurants around town have started putting tables and umbrellas out the front. The umbrellas are most impressive, too: monstrous great things big enough for six or eight people, and suspended from industrial-strength horizontal frames bolted to the nearest wall, which neatly circumvents the old pole-in-the-middle-of-the-table problem.

Sometimes the outside area sits up on a raised platform, as at Appennini, while in other cases it is simply a section of the road that has been annexed for the summer season. Fabrizio has chosen the latter option, possibly due to lack of funds, but has nevertheless gone to great pains to encircle his little patch with handsome planter boxes of begonias or some such which creates a most pleasing effect. Like taking tea in the middle of a shrubbery.

Appy Bar, meanwhile, has taken full advantage of its unique status as the sole eatery on the piazza[6] by erecting an enormous gazebo arrangement down in the corner. Something about the sheer size of it makes me think that Appy Bar is cheekily thumbing its nose at all the other local bars around town and their pathetic bolted-umbrella arrangements.

Hardly anyone sits inside Bar Gerasmo any more; it's much nicer out on the street. The Old Men's Club has duly relocated outdoors and we are always stopped for pleasantries on our way in. Felix now has two or three admirers on his roster and shuttles between them

6 In another spectacular failure of town planning, the local authorities have permitted no less than three banks to set up business right on the piazza. Just the thing for that lively bustling feel.

with ease, working the crowd smoothly while we tuck into our Big Breakfast among the Begonias.

However this development has created a new dilemma on those occasions when we feel like having breakfast at Appennini, slightly further up on the right. During winter, it was relatively easy to cruise on past Gerasmo without feeling guilty—eyes straight ahead and keep up the pace—whereas now we are obliged to run the gauntlet of the town elders. Doubtless they are watching us beadily as we head across and disappear into Appennini, nodding sagely among themselves.[7] We wonder nervously what the elders will make of such behaviour and whether they will inform on us to Fabrizio.

Since we are visiting Appennini less often these days, this new problem can't really be said to impact on our quality of life as such. But still, it's the principle of the matter—we feel deprived of our liberty, our freedom of choice, our inalienable right to choose where to go for breakfast. Is this an example of the restrictive small-town atmosphere that the Young People of Sansepolcro often complain about? Where your every move is observed and analysed by others? In which case (more thrillingly), if we sense it too, does this make us genuine locals?

Even assuming that we have managed to embolden ourselves sufficiently to make it past the Old Men's Club and across to Appennini, there is a further difficulty to contend with: the raised platform outside Appennini is diagonally across the road from Gerasmo, with a direct sight line to Fabrizio's position behind the counter. Sitting out the front of Appennini is therefore tantamount to openly taunting Gerasmo where we have been regular customers for months.

This is indeed a cultural conundrum for the newcomers. Should we hide ourselves inside Appennini? *But it's so nice in the sun.* Should we try to divide our time equally between our two favourite bars? *But that would be an unprincipled restriction on our freedom of choice.* What is the correct bar etiquette in this situation? This sort of stuff does your head in.

Much later I am reliably informed by Alessandro, hip groovy

7 Let's face it, they've got nothing else to do.

young proprietor of Bar Appennini, that the two bars in fact get on very well; he himself often pops into Gerasmo for breakfast on Appennini's Official Day of Closing. Furthermore, Appennini doesn't make any money at breakfast time anyway; it exists primarily for the evening session, when it is regularly packed to the rafters with Young People carousing to the strains of Alessandro's eclectic CD collection until three or four in the morning. (Even later on weekends.) All of which means that there is no such thing as competition for the breakfast dollar in this corner of Sansepolcro.

The point is driven home one morning as we are sitting confidently at the tables outside Appennini—having finally managed to reconcile our consciences—when who should stroll past but Fabrizio, enjoying a rare spell away from the counter. Instantly the pangs of guilt and betrayal return. Should we apologise? Play dumb? Help! In the end Eleni manages a feeble 'Sorry, Fabrizio,' but the recipient of our largesse looks nonplussed and continues smiling broadly. Of course he doesn't care in the slightest; what on earth were we thinking?

Shortly before Easter the local priest comes around to bless our flat, or more correctly to bless our section of Ivana and Raffaello's home. The upstairs section has been done already as a matter of course, but if the downstairs weren't seen to as well the evil spirits would simply move in with us, wouldn't they? Which isn't a very nice thing to do to your tenants, obviously, so Ivana has called him in to give our place the once over just in case.

The priest performs a short ceremony which involves sprinkling water around in various directions while his uncomprehending subjects try to maintain a suitably solemn and religious air. We feel a tad rude for not joining him and Ivana in what is clearly the Lord's Prayer in Italian towards the end, but hopefully he has been forewarned about our limited language skills, particularly with respect to religious incantations. At the end, the priest leaves us with a little pamphlet with emergency contact details in the event that an urgent re-blessing is required. And his magic works: the flat appears to have been free of evil spirits ever since (unless one counts bouts of grumpiness first thing in the morning, in which case we may have to dig out that pamphlet).

Felix's contribution to spring, meanwhile, was to start waking up an hour earlier in the morning, but his timing was sadly off; daylight saving kicked in just a couple of days later so he ended up waking us up at the same time anyway, heh-heh-heh. The poor child, thwarted by a global grown-up conspiracy—but no doubt he'll have the last laugh when daylight saving finishes in October and he gets to wake us up two hours earlier than usual.

With the second kitchen now officially open in readiness for the coming summer, Ivana is often down there doing a spot of cooking. Raffaello, too, is frequently to be seen pottering around in the garden, and as a result we are exchanging pleasantries on the garden path almost on a daily basis. Sometime we stop together for a chat over a cup of tea, or a convivial beer in the fading light of the late afternoon.

One day shortly after lunch I emerge from the house to find Eleni and Ivana deep in conversation. I plonk myself down next to Ivana, ready to contribute some idle banter, but it quickly becomes clear that this is no ordinary chat: Ivana's eyes are brimming with tears.

Such a good, kind man, she says. Loved by everyone in Sansepolcro. He would have been such a wonderful doctor. So much promise, such a tragic waste. I can't believe it could happen to him.

Eleni fills me in: Ivana is talking about her beloved brother Giorgio, who is very sick. Giorgio is a full 15 years younger than Ivana. (For some reason, the last child in an Italian family often arrives a decade or so after the rest.) Their mother died when Giorgio was only nine years old, by which time Ivana and Raffaello were already married with their first baby Patrizia, so they took Giorgio in and raised him as their own son. Giorgio was thus always more than a younger brother to Ivana, and more of an older brother to Patrizia and Cristina. And now, at barely 52 years of age, Giorgio is dying of cancer.

Over the following weeks and months we learn more about Giorgio's illness. How the initial attack occurred many years ago, shortly after the birth of his second daughter. How Ivana and Cristina have taken him around a succession of specialists in Arezzo, Florence and Bologna but none of them have been able to stop the spread of cancer. How progressively more and more of his body was amputated until eventually, being a qualified doctor himself, he saw the writing on the wall and cried *Enough*!, resolving to let the wretched disease take its course. And how, as a result, he now has a matter of months to live.

Giorgio spends his remaining days lying in bed, unable to leave the house and dependent on others for his every need, not least food, which explains the daily deliveries from his loving older sister. Recently we'd noticed Ivana climbing into her car at lunchtime with trays of foil-wrapped food parcels and wondered what they were for. An elderly relative? Meals on Wheels perhaps? Now we know: they are all for young Giorgio.

Ivana has spent most of her life caring for relatives in their final years; first Raffaello's parents, then her own parents, and currently Raffaello's older brother Aldo, who has a mental disability and has been incapable of looking after himself for all of his 80 years. The Ivana and Raffaello compound includes a granny flat next to ours downstairs built specifically for palliative care purposes—at the moment Aldo lives there, enjoying home-cooked meals delivered daily. So now Ivana is quietly tending to Giorgio as well. She doesn't mind; she has been doing this for as long as she can remember. And besides, it gives her the chance to visit Giorgio every day, never knowing which will be his last.

With the onset of the warmer weather we have noticed an increasing level of activity in town. Almost overnight, the piazza has been transformed from the silent, grey personal banking precinct of winter into the focal point for a succession of healthy community type events.

Our first inkling that Sansepolcro's main piazza might actually fulfil its proper role as the centre of public life was a children's bicycle gymkhana we discovered by chance one Sunday morning on the way to Gerasmo for breakfast.

This was a well-organised affair staged by the local comune, featuring an obstacle course marked out with white tape, a judges' table and an excessively loud loudspeaker system.

A week or two later the piazza was again pressed into service as the finish line for a marathon, complete with barricades and a podium from which an eager official announced the name of each new arrival at ear-splitting volume.[8]

Then there was some sort of art and craft workshop, which involved students from the local art school laying out floral displays and chalk pictures along the length of the main street. It was just as well that we saw the fruits of their efforts in the morning, for by the afternoon the flowers had been completely destroyed by unscrupulous weekend traffic.

Since then the piazza has hosted a variety of different events, including the current front-runner for Best Piazza Event, the fabulous vintage car rally. There we were, all four of us quietly taking our breakfast among the begonias at Bar Gerasmo, when a commotion of wheezing and creaking announced the arrival of a procession of vintage cars down the main thoroughfare.

Felix was spellbound as one by one the beautifully restored vehicles passed by, the drivers tooting their horns and beaming grandly while local womenfolk dressed up in ancient traditional cultural gear (the official welcoming party, apparently) showered the procession with flower petals.

It turns out that Sansepolcro is one of the official stops on a week-long vintage car rally through Tuscany and beyond. After breakfast we headed back to the piazza to find it had been transformed into a massive vintage car yard packed with the largest crowd ever witnessed[9] in Sansepolcro—a bizarre combination of the vintage car

8 Tip for would-be Italiophiles: avoid buying a home on or near the piazza.
9 By us.

crews dressed in their early twentieth century driving garb, the welcoming party in billowing white dresses, and the rest of us in our modern twenty-first century civvies, all against the medieval backdrop of downtown Sansepolcro.

It's reassuring to find that despite its utilitarian nature by day—encircled by boring banks and used as a parking area by the local proprietors—the piazza is able to serve as a useful public space on the weekends. Being big city types, we find these activities very endearing and community-minded; plus it all adds to the sense of fun and the build-up to summer.

Louise/Louisa, a Sansepolcro local who was brought up in London, says she initially regretted her decision to return to her home town after arriving in the depths of winter to find the place completely dead. But she changed her mind completely after her first summer in Sansepolcro.

You wait until it gets warmer, she said to us, you won't believe the transformation. Everyone concurs: Sansepolcro comes alive, enthuses Laura from the real estate agency. All the big events happen during August and September, says Raffaello. The bar takes twice as much over the summer months, adds Fabrizio.

On the basis of what we've seen already, summer in our adopted home promises to be action-packed. Not to mention September, which sees the week-long *Rinascimento nel Borgo*, a Renaissance festival involving colourful flag-waving, archery competitions and a host of other enticing events. Many of these take place in the piazza, and Raffaello has promised us a ringside seat from the window of the real estate agency. Not to be missed.

There's only one problem: our return tickets expire at the end of August, which means we'd be spending half of the summer packing suitcases instead of enjoying the fun. Moreover, we'd have to completely forgo the festivities in September, the crowning event on the Sansepolcro calendar. Quite apart from the fact that it is still far too early to be contemplating departure from our adopted home, with which we are now thoroughly infatuated—summer, winter or otherwise.

Should we be so cavalier as to abandon our return flights and throw away good money? Er, no, not really. Are we going to do it anyway? You bet. Hardly worth posing the question in the first place.

And so it is that we arrive at the delicious decision to postpone our return, nominally until the following January. Moreover, it doesn't hurt a bit—it is still a good six months until we have to pay for the tickets. Time to sit back and enjoy the festivities.

9

Being John Malcovicci

Having now established ourselves comfortably here in our little patch, we have been eagerly spreading the word among friends and family: come and visit! Friends and family have responded admirably, with the result that April and May have become visitation months. First up are longstanding friends James and Caro and their two daughters, who get on very well with our two; plenty of play potential there. Next we will be hosting my two sisters Liz and Rose for an extended stay, and finally Eleni's brother and his wife, making a brief stop on their last-pitch-at-freedom overseas holiday prior to the arrival of the First Baby.

Our first visitors arrive, as luck would have it, during Sansepolcro's annual Fiera. Who said that the big events only happen during summer? For four days in April, the centre of town is completely given over to an enormous Royal Show type affair that extends down the entire length of the main street from Porta Romana to Porta Fiorentina, then back up lovely old cobbled Via Aggiunti and finally out through the car park, along the front wall and down past the railway station.

Something about street markets gives me a warm rosy feeling inside. I love the regular Tuesday and Saturday market in Sansepolcro: the sight of everyone out and about doing their weekly shopping, picking over the bargains, haggling for discounts. I suspect it's the social role of the market too, the way it acts as a public meeting space—especially the section in the piazza. So the enormous Fiera brings on the same feelings only ten-fold, a veritable deluge of warmth and rosiness bubbling up from within.

There are stalls selling clothing, kitchen things, carpets and hardware items like the regular market (which has been banished to a nearby carpark for the interim, poor thing); stalls hawking E-Z-Cut and Mop-o-matic type products as seen on *la tivu*; vans with electrical goods and appliances, marquees full of handbags, jewellery and shoes, tents showcasing paintings and craft works; and far too many stalls selling identical varieties of roasted nuts and sweet treats. The exhibits outside along the castle walls, meanwhile, feature more serious hardware: pool filters, fireplaces, central heating systems, tractors, agricultural machinery and the all-important outdoor pizza ovens.

And dotted throughout the Fiera are take-away food stalls with outdoor tables and chairs, providing the requisite festival type atmosphere. The weather has even decided to be kind to us this time, with not a hint of rain. I can't think of a more wonderful induction for the visitor: Sansepolcro as a bustling hive of economic activity, if only for four days.

What a delight it is to be able to share Sansepolcro with our friends, not only the busy Fiera but also the more down-to-earth experiences such as massed breakfasts for eight at Gerasmo and Appennini, soccer in the piazza, driving through the countryside to Citerna for doughnuts.

And finally we have an excuse to check out Toto's, the pizzeria on the main street that we have walked past countless times without realising its hallowed status because it has no signage. (Apart from the huge red neon *TOTO* sign hanging in the window. But there's no menu or anything, no mention of pizza as such—how were we to know?)

We arrive at the distinctly un-Italian time of 6.30—although the official opening time on the door says 6.00, the pizza chefs have barely got the oven hot yet. After all, who would go out for a meal before 7.30?[1] But it works perfectly for us because by the time the

1 Foreigners with children perhaps.

crowds arrive, on the dot at 7.30, the steadily rising noise generated by the children running around is drowned out in the general hubbub.

It turns out that Toto's does a nice thin style of pizza, such as we haven't come across since fleeing Valfabbrica. Now we have both thin and thick options at our disposal, as well as whole round pizzas and square pizza slices; meanwhile, should we choose to take the car, the range extends further to include *Ma Mi*, a huge pizza barn on the road to Anghiari recommended by Raffaello, and of course our all-time favourite pizza-by-the-slice place on the piazza at Anghiari.

On Sunday, the last day in Sansepolcro for our visitors, we head up to a nearby mountain village with the rather uninspired name of Montagna,[2] for an Ancient Traditional Cultural Long Lunch. We have booked a table at Vasco's Trattoria, a tiny establishment with room for perhaps twenty diners, which we discovered quite by chance several months back during a bracing family stroll in the mountains. Vasco's serves a wonderful lunch of approximately six courses, although this really depends on your definition of a course; in any case, a steady succession of hearty dishes appears throughout the afternoon, accompanied by endless bottles of wine, and the idea is that you sit around eating and drinking for hours and hours before staggering out dazed and confused into the daylight. You are then offered a fierce shot of grappa to help you negotiate the winding road back down the mountain, a sort of inverted road safety campaign.

During the lunch I was surprised to see a couple of young Italian lads from the next table, aged perhaps ten or twelve, engaging earnestly with young Felix. The cherished stereotype holds that Italians love children, and we've already seen it proven many times over. But this takes it a step further: even the children love children. And teenagers too, if the young waitresses at our favourite pizzeria are any guide. Italy is indeed a great place to be a small child.

It has been wonderful to have the chance to re-appraise our adopted home through the eyes of the first-time visitor, and fall in love with it all over again. Alas, James and Caro and the girls are off

2 Cos that's Italian for mountain, see…oh never mind.

to Florence tomorrow, but we will all be meeting up again within a week, this time at a rented house on the Amalfi Coast. (Another benefit of hosting visitors is that it provides the perfect excuse to organise trips further afield.)

Meanwhile in Sansepolcro the Fiera has drawn to an abrupt close. It took barely a day for all the stalls to be dismantled, the vans driven away and the rubbish cleared off the streets. The centre of town has reverted without fuss to its normal composed state; if it weren't for the occasional roasted nut and torn streamer on the ground one could pretend it was all a grand dream. The peace and quiet is almost eerie after all the commotion. But it is comforting to be able to reclaim the streets once more.

Recently we invested in a no-frills CD player for our apartment, finally pensioning off the tinny old Walkman-with-speakers arrangement that had provided excellent service since the distant lonely farmhouse days. Our snazzy new CD player even has a radio, which enables us at long last to catch up on some Italian pop culture. It turns out that quite a few of the songs on the radio aren't too bad at all—or is it simply the novelty of being able to spot the odd word here and there? Hard to say. Whatever the motivation, we have been sufficiently inspired to purchase a couple of compilation CDs, which Daddy has further condensed into a *Best of Italian Pop Trash* CD, which is currently on high rotation in the lounge-room.

One day while humming happily to one of the soppier ballads on the CD,[3] I am taken aback to hear Ruby singing along to the lyrics. With great excitement I call Eleni over and we get Ruby to go through the lyrics again, like a performing dog. Staggering: she has somehow acquired them by osmosis. The parents are mightily impressed with this effort, as indeed they are meant to be—Ruby beams from ear to ear.

What's more, this latest development has given me a great idea:

3 NB: Included only to make up the numbers. Normally I draw the line at soppy ballads.

pop music as a vehicle for language study! I remember someone telling me once that you can find song lyrics on the internet; might this also apply to Italian songs? Ruby and I rush to the computer to find out.

According to Ruby, the first line of the chorus is '*Dimmi che hai bisogno di me*,' so we try typing that in.

It works! Within an instant, there on the screen are the very words she was singing:

Dimmi che hai bisogno di me
Che mi vuoi conoscere
Dimmi che ci sarai sempre
E che niente é più importante

Which means something along the lines of:

Tell me that you need me
That you want to know me more
Tell me that you'll always be there for me
And that nothing could be more important[4]

We try some of our other favourites from the CD. And yes: there they all are, out there in cyberland, waiting for us to come and get them. IT'S SO EASY. (Any self-respecting Young Person would laugh at this: how come it took you so long to work that out grandad?)

Now a new and exciting phase in the Italian Odyssey begins: the Italian pop singalong. Sure, Italian pop is corny, and every second song is about lerve or the absence thereof—but it cannot be denied that the family singalong is a good wholesome experience. Besides, it's educational.

Furthermore, this new-found internet discovery has provided me with a new and altogether more reliable means of tracking down good songs. The last time I really liked a song on the radio and wanted to buy the CD, I was obliged to hum a few bars of it to my

4 Soppy ballad, remember.

musical advisor Francesco, the young singer/bartender at Bar Appennini. Luckily it was a well-known song and Francesco was able to advise me immediately. Within the hour I had the CD ('Dedicato a Te' by Le Vibrazioni, the definitive hit single of the summer) in my hot little hand, and shortly thereafter it was the feature track on *Best of Italian Pop Trash.*

The next time I bowled up to Francesco with a song request, however, it was a miserable failure: not only was he unable to decipher my humming, but neither were any of the other customers within earshot, who weren't really supposed to be part of the exercise. I never tried it again.

Now, thanks to a number of well-organised Italian websites devoted to song lyrics, I am spared the ignominy of having to sing in crowded bars altogether. Simply work out a line or two of the song in question,[5] then let the internet do the walking. Not only does this make buying CDs easier, it also means we can produce lyric sheets of all our favourite songs. For language practice, of course. There is even a copy which lives in the glove-box of the HGV, ready for those times when we are seized by the urge for a singalong whilst in transit.

Thus it is that the trip down to the Amalfi coast becomes a highly educational family bonding experience, and we arrive in good spirits and with a much improved understanding of the relationship woes of young Italians.

Soon all eight of us are reunited in the front garden of our sumptuous mansion accommodation at Massa Lubrense, marvelling at the uninterrupted views across to the island of Capri. The timing of our trip is perfect: by early April the weather has warmed up nicely, and the mansion has both back and front gardens for playing games (children) and admiring sunsets (grown-ups). The swimming pool, advertised so loudly on the website, has yet to be graced with water, but we turn this to our advantage by inventing the fabulous game of empty-pool soccer, a hit with young and old alike. But best of all, the weekly tariff for the mansion during April is merely outrageous, as opposed to the eye-wateringly exorbitant highway robbery rates they are quoting for high season.

5 Not difficult; we're talking pop songs after all.

Despite having four young children in tow, we manage to see enough of the Amalfi peninsula during our stay to ascertain that it is indeed picturesque, especially the much-vaunted coastal road, a masterful combination of stunning engineering skills and sheer futility[6] on a par with Venice.

Back at the mansion, the three girls spend a great deal of time and energy constructing an elaborate fairy ring in the front garden. The parents spend a great deal of time and energy buying chocolates and treats and sneaking them inside the ring while the girls aren't looking, then feigning surprise when evidence of fairy activity is subsequently discovered. Poor Felix cannot quite see a role for himself in all of this, but laps up his quota of sweets all the same.

All too quickly the week is over and we must part for real this time, with vague promises to catch up again sometime next year back in Australia. If we ever make it back, that is—Sansepolcro presents an increasingly appealing alternative. Clearly we have some serious thinking to do in the months ahead.

Returning to Sansepolcro on Easter Sunday with precious little food in the house, we realise with a rude shock that none of the shops will be open tomorrow. Having finally adjusted to the idea of all shops closing on Sundays, we have completely forgotten about the Easter break. Perhaps we could borrow a few things from Ivana? Our relationship has definitely reached the cup-of-sugar stage by now.

Ivana is horrified at the thought of an under-stocked kitchen—what about the poor children?—and immediately brings down 'leftovers,' which turn out to be a three-course Easter feast with the requisite primo of pasta and secondo of lamb, the designated Easter dish. Delicious. Perhaps we were secretly hoping for this all along.

Imagine our surprise when a couple of days later James rings up to report that the family's return flight has been delayed. Distraught at the prospect of being forced to extend their Italian holiday, they are planning to stay two nights in Orvieto drowning their sorrows. James wonders if we would be interested in coming down for a visit?

6 Why go to all the trouble of building a two-lane road mid-way down a cliff face when you could just run it along the top?

We certainly would: any excuse for a day trip. And Orvieto turns out to be a fine city indeed, with a handsome cathedral, opposite which is an excellent gelato shop serving possibly the best grapefruit gelato in the entire world. Making it another very worthwhile outing.

Next up on the visitor schedule are my two sisters, Liz and Rose, who have managed to successfully coordinate various work and family commitments in order to spend an entire month in la bella Italia.

Our first week together will be spent cruising around Sicily in the HGV. Eleni will be staying at home with the children, this being the quid pro quo payback for a long weekend in London last month, which came about when we caught on to the ridiculously cheap internet fares offered by the British discount airlines. Fully aware that in Italy it is very poor form for the mamma to just take off like that and leave the poor hopeless papà in charge of the offspring, a task for which he is inherently unqualified, I couldn't resist the temptation to milk the situation for personal gain. And it worked: Ivana presented me with an extra large jar of her wonderful home-made pomorola, followed by a hefty slab of lasagne the following day. Wonderful. I must send Eleni away more often, ho ho.

On to Sicily then. A fine and sunny Tuesday early in May sees me barrelling down the highway to Rome, a one-man It-Pop singalong machine shamelessly pushing the boundaries of speed, volume and musical sensibility with the windows wound down for all to see. What would the Polizia Stradale (highway patrol) say to this?[7] I manage to arrive at the designated meeting point without incident, slightly hoarse yet linguistically enriched, to find the sisters waiting outside the station right on schedule. Huge greetings, siblings fling themselves into one another's arms like guided missiles, Australian single kisses all round. Then after a quick bite of pizza it's time to head down to Naples to catch the overnight ferry, like a group of schoolkids off to camp.

On the way to Naples we stop in at a nondescript town called Capua to catch a bit of the family vibe. My sisters and I can claim a modicum

7 'Isn't it pathetic at his age,' probably.

of Italian ancestry; the family name was originally Capuano, having been shortened during the Second World War to avoid persecution or so the story goes. Capuano means 'of Capua,' which means that this dusty impoverished town outside Naples represents our roots.

Are any of our relatives here today? Perhaps if we wander around a bit, we will be recognised and given the key to the city or something. After half an hour of solid wandering, however, nothing of the sort has happened. There is no evidence of family vibe, no powerful sense of homecoming, no mystical spiritual ancestral force of any kind. We stop wandering; we grab a quick coffee and gelato; we hop back in the car and continue on to Naples.

It's never like that in the films.

The Sicily trip is a whirlwind whistle-stop tour of Greek ruins organised by Rose the Cruise Director, with myself, Sister Liz and extra special guest star Susan from America (who has joined us en route) playing the part of the paying passengers. Rose has made it plain that she for one is keen to visit as many Greek ruins as possible, and in the absence of any better suggestions from the passengers, this is what ends up happening.

The Greek ruins are very impressive too, although it does beg the question: what were the ancient Greeks doing in ancient Italy? Methinks they got fed up with ancient taramasalata and fetta cheese and came in search of pizza. Many of the temples are in a remarkable state of preservation, often with all four walls standing and the roofline clearly visible, which gives me a chance to dust off that old chestnut:

The ancient Greeks can't have been that smart, they forgot the roof!

You had to be there I guess.

For the return journey, we will be taking the short ferry hop across from Messina, the northern-most tip of Sicily, to Villa, on the toe of the mainland, then driving up to Salerno for the night.

Tomorrow morning we will do a quick spin around Pompeii[8] before returning triumphantly to Sansepolcro in the evening. A fair distance to cover, but there's nothing like a good road trip with companions, and the HGV is definitely the vehicle for it. I'd hate to drive to Sicily and back in a tiny Fiat.

On the ferry we somehow wind up in the wheelhouse, where the friendly driver/captain/wheelhouse guy insists on showing us all the controls of his massive machine, before recommending a restaurant run by his friend that we simply *must* visit on our way through. After all, we'll need to stop for lunch soon won't we? He checks his watch: look, it's nearly one o'clock. Of course you won't be driving during the luncheon hour, will you? Er, no, we wouldn't dream of doing such a silly thing, certainly not.

Excellent! Wheelhouse Guy whips out his mobile phone and soon all is arranged. Thus it is that half an hour later we find ourselves pulling in to the tiny picturesque seaside resort of Scilla in Reggio di Calabria, which boasts a wide sandy beach tucked into its own private fold of coastline and guarded over by imposing huge rock formations on either side. The weather is hot and the beach is deserted and inviting, but sadly there is no time to spare for a swim—we have a good five or six hours of driving still ahead of us. Never mind; at least Wheelhouse Guy's friend's restaurant's risotto was good.

The journey to Salerno ends up taking even longer than expected, on account of freeway repairs extending for hundreds of kilometres. Luckily for us, Italian eateries are open until late, and the manager of the 'hotel' (not sure what term to give our substandard accommodation, eerily reminiscent of the Bevagna hovel; still, it's only for one night, and it *is* cheap) sends us to his personal favourite[9] pizzeria located just around the corner.

Pizza Più turns out to be no ordinary pizzeria: the pizza-making premises are located on one side of the main road that runs along the Salerno waterfront while the tables are set up in the park opposite, so that the poor waiter is obliged to run back and forth collecting orders and delivering meals while dodging six lanes of trucks and cars

8 Yes, more ruins; but genuine Italian ones this time.
9 Yeah, right. Run by his brother-in-law's cousin, more like.

and Vespas and balancing huge trays of food and drinks.

As we devour our late-night pizza I am struck by an alarming moral and legal dilemma: what if our waiter were bowled over by a truck as he came across with our food? To what extent would we be liable for his death? After all, through the act of ordering a pizza we have entered into a contract with the pizzeria, and the waiter is in the process of fulfilling his contractual obligations, implied or otherwise.

I'm already aware of the dangers of pizza, having burnt the roof of my mouth more times than I care to remember; but who would have thought it could be an outright killer? Thank Gard this isn't America, or we could run the risk of being sued by the dead waiter's family. And probably by the other diners as well, for the stress and trauma associated with seeing their dinner splattered all over the road.[10]

If it's Tuesday, these ruins must be Pompeii. And as far as I am concerned Pompeii deserves all the hype—it is nothing short of incredible to see an entire town from 2000 years ago in such a remarkably complete state of preservation. Apparently the lava flow came hurtling down the hill at about 100 kilometres an hour, so it's a marvel that any of the buildings are still standing. In addition, conservation teams have built roofs back on some of the houses, and the effect is most realistic.

The site is very large—Pompeii was a complete town, after all—and still very much a work in progress; on the map there are several amorphous brown blobs indicating parts of Pompeii that even today are still buried underground. Sure enough, as you walk towards the blob the road suddenly gives way to an enormous mound of dirt (brown, just like on the map) and you have to turn back.

Pompeii also appears to have been a randy town in its day, as evidenced by the number of raunchy wall paintings that have managed to survive. My favourite, located at the entrance to a wealthy merchant's house, depicts a man proudly modelling an

10 Kids: don't worry, the waiter didn't really get run over, it's what's called a hypothetical construct.

enormous bloated … er… sausage, for the benefit of a presumed audience just out of view.[11] Now *that's* my kind of fresco: one with a genuine point to make. While admiring the sophisticated artistry on display, the nuances of light and shade, the colours and texture, the aperture and focus and depth of field, I overhear a guide explaining that the sausage has been calculated as equivalent to 47 centimetres in length. There is no mention of the merchant's wife's feelings on the matter.

Now comes the moment I've been looking forward to all week: our return to Sansepolcro. I can't wait to get back and show the sisters around a *real* Italian town, as opposed to all those tourist haunts we've been shuttling through for the past week.

At the same time, I must admit to feeling a little nervous: how will Sansepolcro rate in comparison to all the breathtaking attractions that Italy has to offer? Because I suspect that ours is an unremarkable little town. Unremarkable in that it is no more than a collection of people going about their daily business of working and playing without fanfare; unremarkable in that there are plenty of other equally if not more enchanting little medieval towns dotted throughout Italy; and unremarkable in that it has no must-see attractions for the tourist. Unless, that is, you are an art scholar, in which case Sansepolcro will be an important stop on your itinerary.

For Sansepolcro is the birthplace of well-known[12] medieval painter and mathematician type Piero della Francesca, the first person ever in the world in space to produce a three-dimensional painting, according to Raffaello. Unless I have misunderstood him completely.[13] One of Piero's original works was painted on the wall of the local museum and remains there to this day. The civic authorities, in an unprecedented display of magnanimity, have replaced the main entrance door with a large glass panel so that the work can be viewed from outside at any time of the day or night (with a torch, presumably), thereby eliminating the need to cough

11 Kids: he's down at the butcher's shop.
12 According to my guide book.
13 Always a possibility.

up the six Euro entrance fee. I myself have seen the work and can confirm that it is indeed Art.

We are not here, however, for the art. And our general lack of interest in things arty makes life in Italy a great deal easier: we are able to sail straight past churches with impunity (except maybe the really big ones), ignore signs for paintings and frescoes and steer well clear of galleries and museums. Which is just as well with two small children in tow.

Thus when friends or family visit Sansepolcro, where we take them is to Bar Gerasmo and Bar Appennini for breakfast, to La Spiga the subterranean bakery, to the gelato shop on the piazza, to the pasticceria down the lane off the piazza and to Toto's pizzeria for dinner. In the evening we might visit one of the wine bars, Enoteca Guidi or Tirar Tardi, or check out the crowds on the main drag on a Friday or Saturday evening, or pop in for the late-night session at Appennini.

Once the food and drink options have been exhausted, we'll show our guests some accredited antiquities, such as Cristina's beautifully renovated real estate agency, the carbon-dated theatre, the former convent at Santa Chiara and any number of stately churches and crumbling palazzos.

For those with more time to spare, the extended itinerary takes in such highlights as the hand-made pasta shop in San Giustino, the legendary pizza-by-the-slice place at Anghiari, Citerna on a Sunday morning for fresh doughnuts and views, and afternoon walks in the mountains. Die-hard art-lovers will also be shown to the front door of the museum.

These are our must-see attractions, and it speaks volumes about our priorities in life that the vast majority of them are food-related.

In accordance with a series of rather convoluted itinerary changes, Sister Rose is now taking off to southern Italy and then the United Kingdom for three weeks, while Sister Liz will be staying on in

Sansepolcro for a week before flying home alone (no, they have not had a falling out).

This then provides an excellent opportunity for yet another trip to Venice (third time for me, second time for Eleni, first time for Liz, children don't count). We find Venice to be in much the same shape as it was during February, although a good deal warmer. Once again Eleni fails to score a ride on a genuine gondola. (Husband: 2, Wife: 0)

On the way back from Venice we make a couple of stops along the Lido[14] area: once to show Liz an Italian beach, with its neat grids of deck-chairs and umbrellas; and again shortly thereafter to be issued with a ticket by our very dear friends the Polizia Stradale for crossing the double white line on a curve. As if they would have bothered with a trifling infringement like that in the good old days!

I clearly remember John, that cowboy who sold us the HGV, assuring me that the police don't book foreign drivers in Italy because of the administrative hassles. ('I even drove through a police roadblock once,' he smirked, obviously fancying himself as some sort of renegade expat Steve McQueen.) Judging from the determined leer of the two officers now dismounting from their vehicle, however, the days of police indifference to foreigners are well and truly over.

In desperation I switch to good old Plan B, pretending not to understand a word of Italian, hoping that they will find me altogether too difficult and simply give up. (After all, it worked back in Valfabbrica.) But the pair are undaunted. The handsome younger one roots around inside the car and produces a special multi-language booklet, then proceeds to read out the English sections with such a beautiful Roberto Benigni accent that I am tempted to kiss him on both cheeks and give him an Oscar.

The older one then joins him for a quick run-through of the classic good-cop-bad-cop routine, in which the embittered Older Cop wants me to pay a much higher fine but the handsome Younger Cop holds him back—for whose benefit I really don't know, since I'm not supposed to understand Italian at this stage. (Perhaps now would be the time to come clean and start arguing my case together

14 Woh, woh, woh-woh … Boz Scaggs, where is he now? Still going strong, unfortunately.

with Younger Cop?) Happily the issue is eventually resolved in my favour without the need for intervention, and soon we are on our way again, 36 Euros the poorer, but wiser for the experience.

And that, as far as I am concerned, is quite enough of Venice for me in this life.

Back in Sansepolcro, we've had an exciting development on the kindergarten front, to wit: Ruby has finally made it onto the scuolabus.[15] She had been keen to ride the scuolabus since fairly early on in her Gragnano kindergarten career, while we were equally keen for her to consolidate new friendships via the time-honoured vehicle[16] of sitting up the back on the school bus. But we hadn't reckoned on the fearsome school bus bureaucracy of Sansepolcro.

First I bowled up to the nice lady who drives the school bus and asked her whether Ruby might be able to join in. She told me to speak directly with the school bus company (*I only drive the thing, I don't run the operation*). The school bus company turns out to be conveniently located a couple of minutes from our house, so that afternoon I went down and asked at the office. The man there told me to speak to the school bus department in town (*we only run the operation, we don't deal with the payments*). A couple of days later I managed to track down the school bus department in an obscure section of a palazzo a short distance away from the primary school at Santa Chiara.

The official behind the desk told me to go back and talk with the school bus company (*I only process full-year payments, none of your two-months-at-the-end-of-the-year caper*).

At this point, the old me might have abandoned the attempt altogether. However, my experience with Telecom Italia has convinced me that every now and then the squeaky wheel really does get the grease.

So a week later I sneak back to the school bus company and find a different person to ask, out of earshot of the first one. And the

15 School bus, magnificently pronounced 'scwolla-boos'.
16 Sorry.

answer is: Why of course; no, don't bother about paying us; you're just over the road aren't you; we'll pick her up first thing on the morning round; see you at 8.15 on Monday then.

And that was that!

In some ways I'll miss the morning run to Gragnano, but I won't miss battling through rush hour in Sansepolcro being subjected to the children's appointed successor to the Barbie Mountain Kidnap tape: the dreaded Babar stories, which were mildly amusing the first couple of times, increasingly irritating thereafter and, by about the 100th listen, unbearable. The roads of Sansepolcro will be that much safer in the mornings without me on them, peering bleary-eyed through the windscreen and trying to remember to stay in the right lane despite the distraction of a herd of French elephants with stupid names like *Poutifour* and *Oleur* and *Hachibombetar.*

Sadly, Sister Liz has now departed, deposited on the bus to Rome early one morning last week with strict instructions to the bus driver to take good care of her (she emails later to say that he was extremely helpful). In the meantime, Rose has returned from her stay in London, which included a weekend hop over to Spain thanks once again to the wonderful discount airlines.

I am keen to show Rose the local theatre, so one night we head out to see a film, any film, which turns out to be *Punch-Drunk Love* with Adam Sandler. It's an unusual and different film at the best of times, let alone dubbed into rapid-fire Italian, but Rose has seen it before and is able to fill me in on the story, such as it is, within the private confines of our box on the first floor.

Halfway through the film there is a toilet break, whereby management simply stop the projector mid-scene and flick on the overhead lights. Rose the film critic is horrified at such cavalier disrespect for the integrity of the film as an artistic statement, such wanton disruption to the natural rhythm and flow of the work as intended by the director. Personally I feel it's a bit rude that the toilet break is only a couple of minutes long, which means that all except the first few to reach the toilets miss out on the start of the second 'half.' Luckily we have been pre-warned by Eleni, so we don't budge from our box.

Afterwards Rose agrees wholeheartedly that the old theatre in Sansepolcro has a wonderful ambience and provides a superior environment for film viewing, toilet break notwithstanding. Such a great place to catch a movie. Such a pity they're all dubbed in Italian, every last one of them.

Soon Sister Rose too will be returning to Australia, but we're not letting her go that easily—not without one more road trip with the family. This time we are headed to Vernazza, one of the five towns in the famed region of Cinqueterre, a beautiful strip of coastline in Liguria.

If Sicily in early May was unusually hot and Venice in mid-May was stifling, then Vernazza at the end of May is, to all intents and purposes, in the midst of high summer. Which allows us the luxury of enjoying a summer beach holiday in Cinqueterre while the place is only reasonably crowded with tourists like ourselves, as opposed to completely overrun.

Vernazza is a beautiful sliver of a town tucked into a fold of the hill, cascading down the steep valley towards a tiny protected bay beach at the bottom in a jumble of impossibly tall narrow buildings painted in the bold primary colours typical of seaside villages. Just above the beach is a spacious piazza encroached on all sides by tables from the surrounding restaurants and bars, creating a perpetual buzz of human activity. At night a jazz band comes and plays to the assembled diners. It is all so convivial that by the end of the afternoon we have decided to extend our stay another night.

The quiet little bay beach at Vernazza is ideal for the children. What's more, a tiny section of the train line which runs along the hilly coastline (mostly through a series of tunnels; another stupendous feat of Italian engineering) is clearly visible from the beach. Felix is thus in his element, surrounded by sand and water with a train roaring past every half hour. Seeing as it's summer, we're swimming every day, as well as catching ferries, going for walks along the picturesque coastal hiking trail, and exploring the labyrinth of steep narrow lanes in the township.

This area of Liguria is famed for the terracing that covers the hills, and it's amazing to see how terraces can transform even the steepest hillside into viable farmland. The farmers ride up and down the hills carrying their olives on dinky little monorail contraptions that snake back and forth across the hillside like mini roller-coaster rides. The monorail engine has a little seat at the front plus a tray for the olives, and I really wish some enterprising farmer would tack on another couple of seats and start offering tourist rides up and down the hill. I would definitely buy a couple of round trips with the children—I'm a sucker for train rides. Besides, it's cultural.

Well that's it for gallivanting around the country. As of last week Sister Rose has departed too, so we have no more visitors left; and anyway, it's too hot now. The temperature has been rising steadily since May and shows no sign of flagging.

We've been spending more time in the garden, often eating dinner on our flash new outdoor table. Raffaello and Ivana have officially switched to summer garden mode and we see them around quite often. Ivana has invited Eleni for a couple of cooking lessons in the downstairs kitchen, passing on culinary wisdom for creamy lasagne, stuffed zucchini flowers and the all-important pasta sauce variants.

This week we have scored our first ever invite for Sunday lunch with the extended family in the gazebo. In addition to Raffaello and Ivana we will be joined by Cristina and Patrizia, Patrizia's husband Sergio, their grown-up children Francesca and Marco, Francesca's boyfriend Gabrielle, and Giorgio's younger daughter Camilla, with Ruby and Felix bringing the total to thirteen.

We're excited but a little bit nervous; it feels like a formal induction, as if we have recently married into the family. After the trepidation of the first few minutes, though, there is nothing to worry about; the atmosphere is festive, the food is plentiful, the wine flows freely and the conversation likewise. Ivana is up and down the whole time serving, prompting everyone for second helpings, clearing plates and setting down new ones. She is rarely seated, in fact—when does she get a chance to eat herself? halfway through the lunch she disappears altogether with a selection of today's dishes carefully wrapped in foil; we all know who these are for, and the group is momentarily plunged into a morose silence until Camilla pipes up and brings us all back to life.

After lunch I manage to cause something of a stir and inadvertently betray my gender by taking my plates to the sink after the meal and even—shock horror—offering to stack them into the dishwasher. As a well-trained Australian husband, I'm finding it difficult to sit back and be waited on hand and foot like this. But judging from the lack of movement around the table, Italian males have no such problem. (Marco the seventeen-year-old grandson helped Ivana make the food, it is true, but he's a trainee chef and doesn't count.) All members of the family—male and female alike—are staggered at the sight of a man willingly handling dirty dishes.

You'd better watch him like a hawk Eleni, warns Cristina, he'll get snapped up if you're not careful. Any woman would love to have a man like that who knows his way around the kitchen.

On one hand Eleni is chuffed by this compliment, which she rightly interprets as vindication of her harsh training regime; at the same time, she is worried that tacit acknowledgement of praise could lead to Complacency in the Male, potentially undoing all those years of hard work. Unable to formulate an appropriate response, she chuckles half-heartedly in agreement.

For the Male in question, however, the situation presents yet another cultural conundrum: while my natural instinct is to continue clearing my own plates and basking in the adulation (easy money, really), there exists the distinct possibility that such eccentric behaviour might alienate me from the other menfolk of the family.

Once or twice might be funny in a cross-cultural sort of way, but traitors to the gender cannot be tolerated on an ongoing basis. I understand this and am keen to blend in. The simple solution, then, would be to cease and desist at once, pretend it was all a joke and remain resolutely seated at the dinner table in future. Although the danger would be if I ever forgot to revert to Australian mode back in our own flat—things could get ugly.

10

Piazza with the Lot

Italians love children. Italians love their food. Italians love arguing about sport and politics. And, we now discover, Italians love respecting the seasons. Just as winter is for presepio-spotting and spring is for spring cleaning, summer is for going on holiday. How many times have we heard—and dismissed as over the top—stories of how all the factories shut down in August and the entire country grinds to a halt? These turn out to be only slightly exaggerated.

It's as if a switch somewhere has been flicked off: summer has officially begun, down come the shutters. The two cinemas have closed their doors for three months. Toto's pizzeria is shut throughout August. Sansepolcro's one and only disco, *Lo Scorpione*, is about to close down for the season. Most of the shops in town have put up signs announcing extended holidays at some point during the summer. Even Fabrizio will be taking a week off during July with the family.

Such behaviour by the town's traders is puzzling—closing down for months at a time sounds like commercial suicide to me. Surely the good citizens of Sansepolcro will want to continue eating pizza during the summer? And what of those who feel like going to see a film or gyrating on the dance floor? It's true that many people have decamped to the seaside, but the town is hardly deserted; there are still plenty of us here, still in need of food and entertainment. We're not all frolicking on the sand you know!

Summer is also for cycling. Bicycles have hitherto been the sole preserve of a few aged stalwarts such as the members of the Old Men's Club, and the lycra-clad triathlon boys who congregate on Sunday mornings for gruelling training runs through the mountains. With summer now officially under way, though, all this has changed: bicycles throughout Sansepolcro are being dusted off and brought out into the streets, and suddenly the whole town is mobile.

Keen not to miss out on the fun, we have fitted a child seat for Felix to the dashing pink second-hand bicycle which Eleni snapped up at the bicycle shop several months back. Meanwhile, Raffaello has kindly lent me his rickety old model, an ancient contraption from the Gulf War days when petrol was rationed in Italy and you weren't allowed to use the car on a Sunday so everyone went out and bought bicycles, or something like that.[1]

Ruby has acquired a hand-me-down bicycle through friends, so the entire family is now fully biked up. Bicycle helmets are largely unheard of in thrill-seeking devil-may-care Italy (except for those head-of-an-alien types favoured by the lycra lads as a means of intimidating other cyclists), which means that hopping on our bikes to go into town for a coffee or gelato is a far simpler exercise than in oppressive nanny-state Australia, with its fascist helmet laws that force law-abiding citizens to spend half an hour fiddling with straps and buckles before putting foot to pedal.

Indeed, cycling in Sansepolcro is a breeze, or at least it would be if only there were a bit of wind about to temper the stifling heat. The best time of day for a ride is after dinner, when we can often be found heading off for a gelato in the piazza followed by a ride through the nearby fields. Nothing can compare with a family cycle through the countryside in the cool of the evening, watching the sun set over the mountains in pink and orange hues. (Except maybe an undisturbed pizza and glass of wine by a canal in Venice, reading the paper and being serenaded by the saxophonist next door—but that was exceptional.) For a while there the fireflies were out in force and the fields were alive with thousands of twinkling lights at dusk. Truly magical.

1 Actually it might have been a different war; he's not sure. Judging from the condition of the thing it was probably World War Two.

The only downside to our new-found love of cycling is that, after congratulating ourselves heartily on the healthy exercise from walking into town, suddenly we're not walking at all. This presents a new moral and ethical dilemma: how are we supposed to work off our increased food intake? We resolve that it's simply too hot for exercise at the moment, and that normal programming will be resumed just as soon as summer is over. Let's see if we can stick to this one.

Luckily, Sansepolcro offers another exercise alternative in the form of a mammoth outdoor pool complex, far more impressive than one might expect for a small country town of barely 15,000 people. It consists of an Olympic sized 50-metre pool; a generous diving pool with three diving boards; a kiddie pool and playground; two huge water slides; a bar serving coffees, cornetti (both croissant and ice-cream type) and panini; and an expansive patch of genuine old-growth forest area sprinkled with picnic tables and chairs. It is without doubt the finest such facility in the region—and much better than the one at Città di Castello down in Umbria, so there.

Unfortunately it is also privately owned, and the entry fee is a whopping five and a half Euros—roughly triple what we are used to paying, and more than enough to discourage the quick-dip-to-cool-off visit (as opposed to the bring-a-picnic-and-stay-all-day experience preferred by the locals). Surely, we reason, the whole point of having a pool nearby is to nick down whenever the mood takes us, especially given that the nearest beach is one and a half hours away and carpeted in matching deckchairs.

Thus the decision is taken to invest in an outrageously expensive season pass for the family. This proves to be an instant success. The sun is roasting every day and with our shiny new pass, the pool is our oyster. According to my calculations we need to visit the pool at least 30 times for the investment to be worthwhile, but if the weather stays this hot that won't be too difficult at all.

Keen as always to fit in with the locals, we too adopt a new seasonal routine revolving one or two swims every day. (An early-swim-and-breakfast routine is also tempting, but I don't trust the pool bar to make a decent Stained Milk.) The Sansepolcro pool complex soon becomes our second home. Felix loves the small kiddie pool, where he spends hours practicing the international language of splashing with the other toddlers. Ruby, equipped with floaties, is at home in the bigger pool, even managing a few dives from the diving boards. Eleni, initially disappointed at the lack of dedicated lanes for lap swimmers, has mastered the art of dodging and weaving among the masses while ploughing through her laps.

And for Daddy there are the towering great waterslides: the curvy but sedate yellow one, and the turbo-charged blue one which is dead straight and goes like a rocket. The local Youth spend their time trying to outdo one another on the blue slide, inventing ever more ingenious tumble-roll moves in a bid to produce ever more spectacular splashes. Occasionally they are joined by a clearly confused middle-aged father of two who makes rather pathetic splashes but seems to be enjoying himself nonetheless.

As with fireworks and bicycle helmets, the official attitude to safety here is considerably more relaxed. Children of all ages are allowed to hurtle down the slides with little more than a perfunctory word of advice from the teenage lifeguard sitting at the top: *Don't forget to hold your nose when you hit the water*, he intones, or *Don't go down in pairs* (they do anyway). Soon Ruby has conquered her fears and is zooming down both yellow and blue slides with the rest of them. Even Felix is permitted to get amongst the action, with me holding onto him tightly. (*Don't forget to lift him up a bit when you hit the water*, I am solemnly advised.)

The Sansepolcro pool complex even comes equipped with an outdoor disco. And I have heard that there are outdoor discos literally on the beach at many of the major resorts. So this is why *Lo Scorpione* has spat the dummy and shut up shop: the Youth of Sansepolcro having transferred their gyrating outdoors for the summer, the poor thing has thrown in the towel.

The mystery of Toto's pizzeria, meanwhile, is solved one Saturday evening when we are invited by friends to an outdoor pizzeria on top of the hill at Anghiari, an establishment which to my mind elevates pizza-eating to new heights.[2] Enclosed within a thicket of tall trees that obscures all signs of the nearby township, we are to all intents and purposes munching on the yeast-based food of the gods in the middle of a national park.

There is no indoor seating at this pizzeria, just picnic tables; the only buildings are a few rough wooden huts in which the chefs toil away working their magic. Thus the outdoor pizzeria is, tragically, a summer-only phenomenon. Moreover, it shuts down strictly at the end of summer, regardless of the weather. No matter if the evenings are still warm and friendly in September; the Seasons must be Respected.

We are told that there are quite a few outdoor pizzerias in this area. This then explains why Toto's has decided to close down during August: given the undeniable allure of the outdoor pizzeria, business at the indoor establishments is naturally going to drop off, so they may as well take a long holiday. Makes perfect sense, really.

So where do the outdoor pizza chefs go at the end of summer? I ask our friends around the picnic table.

Nobody is really sure; it's never occurred to them before.

But this is such great pizza, I bleat; it would be a tragedy for their skills to be wasted for the other nine months.

This observation is met with expressions ranging from incomprehension to pity. Perhaps they are hired by ski resorts during winter, someone offers. Perhaps they find other jobs to do. Who cares? Have another slice why don't you.

The exchange only underscores the yawning cultural gap between us: personally I consider the ability to produce good pizza sacred, something to be treasured, whereas they see it as nothing special. Anyone can make good pizza!

If only it were so.

I am still mystified, though, as to why both cinemas are closed; surely going to a film is a perfectly valid summer activity. As it turns out,

2 Lame wordplay intended.

our favourite eighteenth century/eighth century/medieval/Etruscan/ice-age cinema has not disappeared completely; it has reconfigured itself into a Cinema Under the Stars, held sporadically in the internal courtyard at Santa Chiara primary school. I plan to catch the new *Matrix* film there; I figure I couldn't understand the first one even in English, so I may as well sit back and enjoy the action sequences.

New light is shed on the cinema mystery during a stroll along the main thoroughfare one Saturday evening, when what began as a simple family walk turns into an exercise in tactical manoeuvring of pram and bicycle due to the sheer number of bodies out on the streets. The main street has always been buzzing on Friday and Saturday nights, even back in the depths of winter, but tonight it is positively pulsating, jam-packed with a slow-moving tide that is all but impossible to negotiate.

I remember Ivana telling us some time ago that Sansepolcro is something of a magnet for young people in the immediate region, despite having only the one disco. Now with the disco and cinemas in hibernation, these same young people have nowhere to go but out on the streets, creating a critical mass bolstered by promenaders of all ages—couples, families with children, groups of teenagers, oldies, all streaming up and down the main street until late into the evening. (The real oldies, meanwhile, practise the reverse form of the promenade, sitting quietly outside their homes and observing the passing pedestrian traffic.)

For those of us not away at the beach, then, the idea is obviously to act like we're on holiday anyway by taking to the streets. And in this context, slipping off to the cinema for a film is clearly not the done thing.

Such a collective outpouring of the masses onto the streets during summer is new to us, and it is truly a wonderful thing. We're used to smaller, private gatherings on the beach, at the pub, in the back garden. There's nothing to compare with this very open, public, sea-of-humanity feel. And in my opinion it is something we could all do with a bit more of; after all, is this not what binds a community together?

Although one thing still puzzles me: the seething mass of humanity seems to be confined solely to the short section of the main street between the front gate at Porta Fiorentina and the piazza in the centre of town. Outside the front gate there are crowds of people milling around but no movement as such; beyond the piazza, meanwhile, there is hardly a soul to be seen. Where are they all heading to?

I mention this one day to Francesca, who chuckles and explains the concept of vasca, meaning lap. They're all doing laps of the main street, she tells me. They get as far as the piazza, then they turn around and go straight back to Porta Fiorentina.

Really? It seems so… so aimless, just walking around without a proper destination in mind, *says he, completely missing the point of the evening promenade*. But I'm still not convinced about this vasca thing. So one Saturday evening I resolve to check it out for myself.

I take up position at a semi-concealed vantage point just within the piazza, from where can I spy on the passing traffic. Hopefully this won't look too suspicious. Perhaps I should buy a gelato and pretend to be eating it?[3] Then nobody will ever suspect me as an ethnological researcher.

After a few minutes my first subjects arrive, a group of Young Things. They stop near the ATM up on the corner, look around blankly, and turn tail from whence they came. Now comes another group; same spot, same routine. Then a family, which executes a wide graceful U-turn with the pram, again in the same spot. Next to arrive are two middle-aged couples in the midst of an animated discussion, so engrossed in fact that they get almost halfway into the piazza before realising their mistake and turning back. And then… well, I've seen enough, there's my proof. It shouldn't come as any surprise, really; there are so many people strolling along the main street without going anywhere, the only possible explanation is that they're doing laps. Either that or there's a rent in the fabric of the time-space continuum somewhere in the vicinity of the ATM.

I've half a mind to stay here and see whether they're all back in half an hour after the next lap. Although if the gelato is finished my

3 Better still: I'll really eat it.

cover will be blown. Maybe I could get a stopwatch and measure their lap times, compare them with their compatriots. Organise a competition with an awards ceremony at the end of the night, medals presented from a podium in the piazza and announced at deafening volume:

- Most laps completed
- Fastest lap time
- Fastest turnaround
- Most vacant look upon arrival
- Furthest accidental penetration into the piazza.

Enough of this rubbish. Time now for my other favourite pastime in Sansepolcro, second only to breakfast at the bar: sitting on one of the outside tables at Appennini or Gerasmo and observing the passing parade over a late-night drink or two.

As I sit there sipping thoughtfully it occurs to me that the vasca phenomenon neatly explains yet another enduring mystery: the way the locals always flood into Toto's right on the dot of 7.30 for dinner. How do they manage to be so punctual? Because they're all doing laps of the main street for half an hour beforehand, that's how; they're never any further than three minutes away. When they hear the seven-thirty *bong* from the clock tower they simply execute a swift U-turn and head on in.[4]

Summer means school holidays, and once again the Italians take their school holidays seriously: the break lasts all of three and a half months.

Scuola materna has finished for the year, but the tinge of sadness is more than offset by the exciting news that Ruby's primary school will be none other than Santa Chiara, the majestic ex-convent near the piazza that is currently the home of Cinema under the Stars. At long last, I will be able to realise my dream of dropping Ruby off at

4 An impressive piece of detective work, if I do say so myself. At this rate I'll have Italy fully sorted by the time we go home.

school in the morning and continuing on to the bar for breakfast. I can hardly wait for school to start!

In the meantime, Ruby is about to begin a two-week swimming course at the fabulous Sansepolcro pool together with nine-year-old Camilla, her other great friend at the moment, and Camilla's teenage sister Valentina. Eleni has offered to take the girls every morning while hubby slaves away over a hot computer, and Ivana is so delighted (for some inexplicable reason Camilla has never been to the local pool) that she has promised to repay us with a midday meal in the gazebo every day—possibly the easiest free lunch we'll ever earn.

Thus begins a wondrous new phase in the Italian Odyssey: the regular cooked lunch. Ivana will often say 'I'm just putting out whatever's in the fridge, it's nothing much,' by way of apology for having only five different dishes on the table instead of ten. But for sandwich-eaters like us it's a veritable feast: a hearty primo of pasta (more than sufficient in itself), a secondo of meat and/or vegetables, then an array of fruits and cheeses to fill up any remaining crevices in the stomach lining, and finally a coffee to finish off. Never before has so much been eaten by so few with such relish.

The only problem with the regular cooked lunch is that Raffaello insists we consume several glasses of wine with our meal for digestive purposes,[5] which is wonderful for the conversation flow but tends to reduce translation productivity in the afternoon. We are also expected to take a slug of viciously strong liqueur either with or in the post-luncheon coffee, just in case we haven't sluiced enough alcohol through our systems already.

It must be said that many of the liqueurs brought out at the end of the meal are excellent, Limoncello being our current favourite. Nevertheless, is lunchtime really the best time to be making ourselves tipsy in the name of culinary curiosity? It's all very well for Raffaello; he gets to go off and have a nice nap for a couple of hours. Although I note with interest that Cristina, also a gazebo regular, consistently knocks back wine and liqueur in equal proportions to her father, despite—or perhaps because of—the prospect of a full afternoon of work ahead.

5 He's serious, too.

The Italian constitution is obviously attuned to the needs of daytime drinking, but I suspect this is something that we non-Italians will never quite master, much like our cowardly aversion to letting our children stay up really late in the evenings. I cannot get used to wine at lunchtime: my instincts tell me in no uncertain terms that it is wrong. Although my instincts also tell me in no uncertain terms that a big pasta meal is much better than *sandwiches*, which only goes to show that instinct is relative.

The other upside of the gazebo experience is that Ivana is always out in the second kitchen now, and is only too willing to provide her culturally challenged tenants with cooking lessons. One gets the impression that Ivana never quite had the opportunity to pass on cooking wisdom to her own daughters, what with all the elderly relatives to attend to, and that she is thoroughly enjoying this opportunity for a second shot at motherhood. And since the daily cooked lunch is still very much a bonus and novelty, Eleni and I can't help but fall about in paroxysms of delight as each new and interesting dish arrives on the table. We love the food; Ivana loves the attention. Truly a win-win situation.

In addition to Cristina, we are often joined by extended family members and/or friends who happen to be in the area. In this way, we are steadily being introduced to a broad sweep of the local population: Marco, a retired doctor who spends over half the year in Africa working on aid projects; Gabriella, recently divorced from her husband of over ten years, who is also a Sansepolcro local (which means they keep seeing one another on the main street; now we begin to understand the pitfalls of small-town life); the eternally jovial Piero, Ivana's nephew who lives over the back fence; Marcella, an older, sturdy farming type who hails from way up in the hills and used to make her own bread and pasta and cheese and pomorola and quite possibly re-stumped her house and delivered her own children too. And countless others besides.

Thus the gazebo lunch with Raffaello and Ivana is very much a socially fulfilling experience as well as a physically filling one, providing further evidence, if any were needed, of the immense appeal of summer. Being outdoors somehow makes everybody feel that much more relaxed and sociable, here at home as in town.

In stark contrast to your winter-loving author, Raffaello refuses to be drawn into complaining about the incessant heat, because to criticise the best season in the calendar would be to deny all the wonderful benefits that summer brings. I can see his point, but the fact remains that it's too damned hot—the mercury has been consistently above 30°C for several weeks now.

Luckily, Italian homes are all equipped with sturdy wooden shutters that do a tremendous job of keeping out the heat during the day, so the inside of our flat still provides welcome respite. And there's always the pool.

As promised, summer brings a veritable plethora of events in town. The civic authorities have gone to great lengths to provide an ongoing feast of distractions for the benefit of those poor deprived citizens who have not been able to escape to the beach.

The last few weeks have seen a sketch comedy show in the piazza; an historical play next to the presepio church at Porta Romana; a Moroccan dinner party where a hundred diners ate out on candlelit tables in the piazza; a children's day on nearby Via Aggiunti with sack races, greasy pole contests and a chocolate gelato-eating competition; and a cheap-and-cheerful public dinner event in one of the town parks, whereby you buy tickets and line up for food prepared in makeshift marquees and then all sit down together at big outdoor tables in the time-honoured sea-of-humanity tradition.

Then in late June we are treated to a highly-publicised week of entertainment called *Esplorazioni*. Now the piazza really comes into its own. A huge temporary stage with speakers and light towers is set up at the lower end.[6] The middle area is filled with seating. At the top end there is a mysterious rotunda; this turns out to be an outdoor bar run by none other than our mate Fabrizio, who kindly slips me the odd free beer when nobody is looking. Once again, the Tuesday

6 Our piazza has a gentle slope to it; not as steep as the Arezzo piazza but enough to add a bit of spice to soccer practice.

and Saturday markets are banished to the outskirts of town so that the piazza can fulfil its true role as the hub of town life.

Over the course of the week we traverse the full gamut of modern Italian culture, including of a couple of cabaret shows; a Battle of the Bands competition with a bill of nearly twenty bands, including one fronted by Francesco from Bar Appennini; an evening of ballet, dance and other performances by local youth groups; and an outdoor film screening of Charlie Chaplin in *The Great Dictator*, complete with recalcitrant DVD player for extra added audience camaraderie (indignant shouts of *Not again!* and *What now?* after every breakdown, with knowing smiles all round. *Bloody tecnologia!*).

In addition to all this happening in Sansepolcro, there is no end of posters on the official poster boards around town informing us of festivals, dinners, concerts, fireworks and all manner of other cultural activities in nearby towns that demand to be seen: the scary-sounding Festival of the Wild Boar in Montecoronaro; weekly music recitals in Città di Castello and Monterchi; something that looks like a local horse racing carnival; an outdoor dinner up in the mountains near Monte Fumiaolo. Not to mention the Umbrian Jazz Festival down in Perugia, which this year apparently features a free concert by James Brown; the Spoleto Festival; the famous Palio horse-race down in Siena; and countless other events that you read about in the guidebook by the fireside during winter and think *That sounds interesting; must check it out when summer comes around* but never make it in the end. There's simply too much for the poor struggling tourist to see and do.

To illustrate the extent of our cultural overload: a couple of weeks back we spotted a fun fair set up in one of the car parks next to the city walls. After prevaricating for several days over whether it was deserving of our attention, we finally managed to bundle the children in bed one balmy evening and set off at around nine o'clock. No sooner had we reached the entrance than we were spotted by our neighbours from across the road, who enquired pleasantly as to what the children were up to.[7]

Um, we left them at home.

7 Because surely we could not have put them to bed at this early hour.

What, on their own?

No, no, Ivana and Raffaello are keeping an eye on them from the backyard gazebo.

This being a barefaced lie—Ivana and Raffaello were upstairs watching television—we had no choice but to turn tail and head straight back home to avoid being exposed as deceitful foreigners. So traumatised were we by the experience that we never made it back to the fun fair after all. But in the long run it matters little, because we have already seen and eaten so much.

Today in the gazebo we are joined by Patrizia and husband Sergio, the latter enjoying a rare day off from work. Both of them are mad keen nature walkers, and Sansepolcro is definitely the place for it, the mountains being less than ten minutes away by car. They regale us with stories of the extensive network of marked walking trails, the 2000-year-old Roman roads winding through the hills, the abandoned farmhouses, mountain passes and stunning views. So much yet to discover: Sansepolcro continues to offer up new and enticing surprises. We resolve to go trekking together sometime soon to experience the mountains up close and personal.

Sergio, the most erudite member of the extended family, is highly knowledgeable about everything from Italian history and culture to the finer points of tracking wild animals in the forest from the shape of their droppings. He also has a new twist on the age-old Tuscans versus Umbrians debate, into which (grammar) we are only too keen to tap.

After all, inter-regional rivalry is pure comedy: irrational, unfounded and overlaid with a healthy dose of contempt. And we have good reason to bear a general grudge against Umbria on account of our unhappy time in Valfabbrica. Yes, I know that it's wrong to make sweeping generalisations but it's highly cathartic, all part of the healing process. I'm sure I've read that somewhere.

Tuscans, Sergio pronounces confidently, have a different sense of humour to other Italians.

Really? say I mischievously. So if I were to go two kilometres down the road to San Giustino they would be telling different jokes?

Sergio treats this comment with the contempt it deserves.

Actually I have heard there are people who live in San Giustino and work in Sansepolcro. Do they, I wonder, have to adjust their sense of humour when they get in to the office for fear of being found out as Dirty Rotten Umbrians? Luckily my Italian skills do not extend to such complex sentence structures and Sergio is spared further witticisms.

It is true that the state taxes are much cheaper in Umbria, as are gas and electricity charges, as are a whole host of other things; so it makes perfect sense to live just across the border and make the daily commute into overpriced Tuscany. The Umbrians therefore get to have the last laugh after all: while they might not have the name value of Tuscany, life is a good deal cheaper and they don't have to work so hard to make ends meet. And this might well explain the different sense of humour.

At the mention of Valfabbrica I can't help asking the assembled cast for their opinions regarding legal action against Morelli. The verdict is unanimous: *just put it behind you for heaven's sake*. I might have known.

I see now, with the wisdom of hindsight, that trying to threaten Morelli with the Carabinieri was laughable; I should have invoked the dreaded Finance Police instead. Morelli never provided me with receipts, in flagrant breach of the regulations. He would have been genuinely scared of the Finance Police. Now *that* would have been satisfying.

Actually it still could be. Why don't I ring him up now and threaten him retrospectively with the Finance Police? *Shut up Simon*, the table choruses as one, *leave it will you. Have another Limoncello.*

Monday: Pool, gazebo, work, bed.
Tuesday: Pool, work, gazebo, bed.

Wednesday: Work, pool, gazebo, bed.
Thursday: Pool, gazebo, work, pool, open-air classical music concert in Monterchi.

Yes! Last week I managed to venture beyond the pool, beyond the confines of Sansepolcro even, to *another town altogether.* And I'm feeling rather pleased with myself for this textbook execution of keeping in touch with local events, given our dismal record to date. After carefully monitoring the notice-boards next to the recycling bins I managed to identify an event satisfying the three basic criteria:

1. Free
2. Close by
3. Not too taxing

What's more—and despite the enervating heat of summer—I actually made it there. It was a glorious night out, too: sitting on the grass at the back of the conservatory building with a crowd of a hundred or so, surrounded by a forest of flickering candles, the cicadas chirruping in the background, the roasting heat of daytime subdued now to a gentle glow, the lilting strains of a solo violinist doing his thing carried across on the still night air... heavenly.

And they served drinks and nibblies afterwards.

If only we had the same sort of thing here in Sansepolcro. But I can find no evidence of classical music of any kind. I've enquired at the Tourist Information Centre, I've asked Raffaello and Ivana, I've searched the notice-boards, but there is nothing at all on classical music. Which seems odd in such a hotbed of culture as Sansepolcro, birthplace of Piero della Francesca no less.

Then on Friday night a strange thing happens. An unknown woman turns up at our door to tell us about—would you believe—a classical music concert to be held the following evening at a church right here in town. It seems that the neighbours across the road have told her that we are English (from the number plates presumably—nice work, 99) and therefore likely to be interested in classical music.

Heroically I resist the temptation to say *Actually we're Strine luv, but we still love the Yartz anyway.*

The woman represents a group calling itself Friends of Classical Music in Sansepolcro, which as far as I am concerned technically does not exist, given that nobody knows about it.[8]

Tell me, I ask gently, how is it that nobody has heard of your group? I'm thinking in particular of the Tourist Information office, whose job it is to provide information about such things.

Ah, she replies, we don't publicise ourselves too widely, because otherwise we'd have to pay lots of taxes.

So there you have it: a clandestine underground secret classical music appreciation society operating right under the noses of the dreaded Finance Police, not to mention those evil royalty-grabbing publishing companies. Though in my humble opinion, the Friends of Classical Music in Sansepolcro have done such a good job concealing themselves from the authorities that also they've managed to conceal themselves from everybody else, including the lesser-known People Who Like Classical Music and Happen to Live in Sansepolcro. Or maybe I just don't have the right contacts.

Disappointingly, there are no secret handshakes or passwords on the night, only a smiling usher welcoming us inside a magnificently restored church, rendered in brilliant white throughout. Strange how the insides of the churches around here are so well maintained, even while the flaky exteriors look fit to crumble to the ground at any moment.

The recital itself is a magnificent hour and a half of flute and piano pieces, with all-natural echo effects supplied courtesy of the stark white walls of the church. The flautist[9] does a marvellous job of staying on his feet while blowing into a small tube, in spite of heat so oppressive that most of the audience spend the entire time fanning themselves with their programs.

And they serve drinks and nibblies afterwards.

I have asked the nice lady—and also the neighbours, who are in on this freeloading secret music-listening scam—to keep me

8 See extended discussion of existentialism on p. 348.

9 Who is described in the notes as an American virtuoso—how does an illegal music society raise the money to snare a musician of such calibre? Yet another enduring mystery of Italian culture.

informed of future concerts, via special hand-signals if necessary.

Meanwhile the evening concerts at Monterchi continue right through August, and I hope to be able to catch a few more. Like Citerna, Monterchi is an impossibly picturesque little village drooped lovingly over the top of a hill like medieval icing. Every time I come back from a concert I rave endlessly about how beautiful it is and how we simply must visit.

So one Sunday morning we head off in the HGV to have a closer look. Alas, the heat is so intense that after no more than an hour we are forced to admit defeat and return home to the comfort of the pool/gazebo/bed routine. We'll have to go back and explore Monterchi properly when the weather cools down. [*And do you think they ever did? Hard to believe that in all that time they couldn't manage a return trip to a town barely 15 kilometres away. Unbelievable. Ed.*]

The two-week swimming course finished long ago, but there is no question of us returning to our dismal sandwiches; all parties are enjoying the lunchtime gazebo experience too much for that. Ivana now takes it for granted that we will be seated at the table by 1.30 unless we inform her otherwise in the morning. I suspect that the original lunch-for-swimming offer was nothing more than a devious ploy on her part to get us to the table and inculcate some proper eating habits. And it's worked a treat, too.

There may also be a nostalgia factor at play. Many years ago the family used to live out in the nearby countryside in a grand home with a tennis court and pool, where friends constantly dropped by for lunch during the summer. Ivana says she was often cooking for 10 or 15 people, and one suspects that she still likes to see a full table of guests at lunchtime. Naturally we are more than happy to oblige.

As Eleni pointed out the other day, when we first arrived in Italy we were wistfully observing the long Italian lunch and wondering if we'd ever get to be a part of it; suddenly we're having one every day.

We are being fed so well, in fact, that we do very little food shopping or cooking these days, as per the following equation:

Breakfast at the bar + Massive cooked lunch = No need for dinner

Actually the Italians go one step better:

Breakfast at the bar + Massive cooked lunch = Gelato for dinner

It's true—we have confirmed this one directly with Ivana. On days when you've had a really big lunch and can't manage a proper dinner, you are allowed to have a gelato instead. Forget about nutrition and the five major food groups—it's summer, have an ice-cream for dinner. Heady, liberating stuff.

Meanwhile, I have finally hit on a solution to the alcohol problem: watered down wine. As long as Raffaello can detect a hint of red in the glass he leaves me alone, content in the knowledge that I am getting at least some of the digestive benefits of red wine into my system.

Lunchtime in the gazebo is never a dull affair. Cristina is ever at the ready to engage her father in the kind of rapid-fire, hand-waving, eye-rolling, gesticulation-enriched discourse that so thrilled us on that fateful day long ago when we signed the contract at the real estate agency. (Who would have thought way back then that we would end up being treated to regular performances at close range?) Many times the argument reaches fever pitch and we wonder as we shrink into our seats whether it might be advisable to slink off quietly and do the dishes; however, order is always restored with no evidence of hard feelings on either side. We decide that the theatrics must be all part of the process of handing down the family business from father to daughter.

Our new status as de facto family is confirmed during one such typically heated exchange, with Cristina and her father becoming increasingly stroppy over some real estate issue or other. Ivana gently suggests that the two of them leave it until later, to which Cristina retorts *Come on Mum, they're family for heavens sake* and ploughs right on.

Time to do those dishes perhaps?

Sundays, of course, are always devoted to the extended family lunch, often with extra guests called in to boost the total headcount to the required range of 10 to 15. And although the Sunday lunches fit neatly into our stereotype of the close-knit Italian family unit, it is refreshing to discover genuine tensions lurking underneath, as in any healthy family structure. Ivana grumbles that the girls never help out in the kitchen; Raffaello concurs sagely. The daughters, for their part, are occasionally heard to complain about having to turn up every week when often they'd rather be elsewhere on a Sunday.

Meanwhile, Ivana confides in us one day that Raffaello has taken to occasionally depositing his dishes in the sink after lunch. Is it a token gesture or evidence of a seismic shift in thinking? Either way she is amazed: next he'll be picking up the vacuum cleaner!

In town, the unthinkable has happened: Fabrizio has shut up shop for a week and taken off to the beach. Not only that, but Alessandro from Bar Appennini has decided to take a few days off at the very same time. Eleni and I are shocked to find the various members of the Old Men's Club scattered at random among several different bars in the vicinity. It is a most dispiriting sight—where is their sense of cohesion and purpose? Don't they have emergency procedures in place for this sort of calamity? I must have a look at their Articles of Association when Bar Gerasmo reopens.

Although *Esplorazioni* has finished and the stage and seats have been dismantled, there is still plenty going on in town. Now we start to see a few more events organised by outside organisations, apparently on the premise that the only way to attract attention and get your message across is with a decent festival. One evening, for instance, we stumble across another comedy show; this one has been put on as part of a three-day blood donation festival organised by the Red Cross (not sure of the connection here—does happy blood make for better transfusions?), and is played out against a backdrop of smart red and white donation tents strung across the piazza. I myself am unable to donate, having had the bad luck to spend some time in London many years ago during what the Red Cross considers to be have been a high danger period for Mad Cow Disease, but I certainly got the message.

Meanwhile, anticipation is already starting to build ahead of the week of festivities in September. Posters are going up on the notice-boards and in the bars, and the four flags for the different quarters of the town are starting to appear, dangling from windows and mounted on flagpoles, adding a splash of colour to the streetscape.

At the archery practice area in a fenced-off reservation alongside the castle walls on the south side, local crack archers are busy practicing for the upcoming tournament with arch[10] rival Gubbio. As well as the constant *thud, thud* of arrows plunging into the bullseye (hopefully!), in the evenings we can often make out, wafting across from the school grounds next to the pool, the unmistakeable sound of the drumming teams getting in training for the event, the *rum-tum-tum-tiddle-tum* providing a satisfying rhythmic counterpoint to the incessant drone of the cicadas.

Today is our first gazebo lunch for a week. A whole week! Enough to produce withdrawal symptoms. The reason for our inexcusable absence is that we have just come back from our official summer holiday on the island of Corsica, having finally succumbed to the pressure of cultural expectation and organised a trip to the beach like everyone else. In the end it seemed rude not to, really.

Despite being a French territory, Corsica is only four hours on the ferry from the west coast of Italy, closer in fact than the island of Sardinia, which really *is* part of Italy. At one time Corsica was an Italian territory, and the connection remains strong today, though most Corsicans speak only rudimentary Italian. It turns out that our grasp of Italian is marginally better than theirs, and so—seeing as we're always up for a spot of linguistic larking about—we seize this

10 Sorry.

opportunity to pass ourselves off as Italians. Pretending to be an Italian tourist in France certainly adds a new dimension to the feeling-like-a-local gag. And the ruse works beautifully, although I suspect that sustaining the deception for any longer than a week could generate a profound identity crisis on a number of levels.

Much of our time in Corsica is spent availing ourselves of the excellent brie, baguettes and cakes on offer in the vicinity of our accommodation. And as an extra bonus, the skies of Corsica actually contain ozone, which means that Felix gets to wear his handsome shorty bathers on the beach without running the risk of instant melanoma as in Australia, land of the great wide hole in the ozone layer. At the end of the week it is agreed that the French do better bread and cakes but the Italians do better coffee. Also that the French have cuter accents.

Back in the warm embrace of the gazebo, we recount our holiday stories to the collected gathering, which today includes friends of Ivana and Raffaello who used to live in Gubbio. It transpires that they used to do their shopping at the Collestrada mega-hyper-mart and had to drive through Valfabbrica on a regular basis. We all agree, over several glasses of full-strength wine,[11] that Valfabbrica is a characterless backwater with no redeeming features whatsoever. Spurred on by this positive vindication, I can't resist the temptation to trot out some of the classic Morelli stories. Raffaello and Ivana, who've heard them all before, provide superb backup, complete with the requisite overtones of regional rivalry. Soon the table is in hysterics. Those dirty rotten Umbrians! We all have a wonderful time bagging Valfabbrica in particular and Umbria in general. *So* cathartic.

And to finish with, here's one for the They Said It Would Never Happen file: those generous fagiolo-counters at Telecom Italia, after pondering on the issue for the better part of a year, have decided to refund us the deposit we paid to have the phone connected in Valfabbrica.

11 No work today—with excellent timing, the translation industry in Japan has also decided to take the week off.

This unprecedented act of generosity comes as a bolt from the blue, given that I had long since written off the telephone debt as all part of the experience, along with Morelli's free tank of gasolio and the rest of it. Now that our phone line is on its best behaviour I've had little cause to ring up my good friends at the Telecom Italia call centre, apart from the occasional half-hearted reminder about the refund—for old times' sake, really.

In any case, the response has always been the same: *si, si*, your refund will be out to you very soon. Which I figure is Italian bureaucratese for: in your dreams, mate.

But just when I had officially given up hope, a chance conversation with a fellow Telecom Italia hater[12] convinced me to have one last go. Give up on the call centre and reel off an Angry Letter, was his counsel; they won't take any notice of you otherwise. The letter was duly written, translated into Angry Italian, and delivered, via Angry Registered Post, to the head office of Telecom Italia, every month on the month for good measure. It felt good in a final-parting-shot sort of way, though I certainly wasn't holding my breath.

Three months and three Angry Letters later, a small unmarked envelope arrives in the mailbox.

Inside is a cheque. For 562 Euros. A full refund, in other words.

I can scarcely dare to believe that this scrap of paper is a genuine financial instrument with real cash value. Could it be a practical joke by the lads in Accounts? Better rush the thing down to the bank pronto before it turns into a pumpkin. At the counter, the smiling teller accepts the cheque (happily still in non-vegetable form) from my trembling hand without a second glance; and several days later my account balance goes up by E562.

And now everything is all right, the struggle is finished.

I have won the victory over myself.

I love Telecom Italia.

12 = ordinary Italian person. *Everyone* hates Telecom Italia.

11

Medieval-a-go-go

Finally the long, hot summer is over, and I think I can speak for all of Europe in saying: PHEW. It has been *unbelievably* hot here, particularly August, when the temperature hovered around 35°C for the entire month. The season ticket to the pool turned out to be one of our wiser investment decisions in Italy: by the end of the summer we had been to the pool more than fifty times.

The record heatwave ended in spectacular style with a truly massive storm. Unfortunately we had arranged to have a coffee with friends in the piazza at Città di Castello at the very hour when the storm broke, so we all got drenched. The drive home was a bit hairy, what with massive lakes of rainwater and broken-down cars along the road and the emergency services flying back and forth with their sirens screaming. But the sturdy HGV got us home without incident, and in the true adventuring spirit we all had nice hot showers and ordered take-away for dinner.

The next day Felix and I celebrated by wearing shoes and socks into town for the morning coffee.

Since then, the mercury has been plummeting in a most satisfying manner, although this, combined with the end of daylight saving time and the first decent rain for months, has made life in general feel a bit damp and dark and chilly. In the space of less than a month, we've gone from closing our shutters during the day to keep the heat out to closing the shutters at night to keep the heat in.

The bicycles of Sansepolcro have been returned to their sheds, and the smell of wood smoke is once again in the air, which makes us all nostalgic since wood fires were in full force when we arrived here last November.

In town, the atmosphere has changed almost overnight; all the tables and chairs and umbrellas and pot plants out the front of the bars and restaurants have been packed away until spring and the streets are looking decidedly naked and cheerless. Now we understand why the locals get so worked up about summer. Funny how Sansepolcro didn't seem at all subdued this time last year—but then, everything was new and exciting back then.

These days, while we may be used to the delights of our adopted home and slightly less awestruck by it all, there are still plenty of new discoveries to be made. The major excitement this week, for instance, is the beginning of primary school at Santa Chiara. We enrolled Ruby in the traditional six-day, 8.30 am to 1 pm class—out of necessity rather than choice, since the new-fangled five-day 8.30 am to 4 pm classes (brought in to cater for the increasing number of families with two working parents) were already full. School on Saturdays seemed at first like a terrible burden, until we discovered how civilised it is to have her back with us for lunch every day, and realised that she actually spends less hours at school overall.

I am pleased to report that the morning routine is everything that I imagined. Shortly after eight o'clock Ruby and I set off for the walk to school, stopping off on the way to buy a snack for her morning break—usually a slice of delicious salty foccacia known as *cia-cia*[1] from La Spiga the Tardis bakery or, if we're rushed for time, a simple ham roll from one of the bars on the way through.

At the convent, we wait in the open-air quadrangle with the other children and the teachers until the bell rings at 8.30 precisely. This is the signal for the bambini to head up to the classrooms and Daddy to head off to Bar Gerasmo for a hard-earned breakfast. By nine o'clock I am back home and seated at my desk, fully satiated, lightly exercised and with a lungful of good country air, raring to tackle a new working day. Just like in the cereal commercials.

1. Pronounced cha-cha. Kind of like the guy from *Appy Days*.

A few short hours later, it's back to join the crowd of waiting parents in the courtyard out the front of the school. At the designated time of 1.05 pm, the bell rings again and the teachers escort the children to the front door, from where they scan the courtyard and release each child individually following positive identification of a matching parent.

But why the big deal on security? This is, after all, a town where children regularly wander in and out of the piazza unattended by adults, playing soccer, eating gelati or just hanging out. Where youngsters of all ages are allowed to go down the blue slide. Where groups of youths congregate freely along the main street on Friday and Saturday nights. A nation, indeed, where seat belts are rarely fastened, fireworks are unregulated and young children are allowed to stay up dangerously late in the evening. Personally I cannot see the logic in releasing a child safely into the arms of a parent who will then allow him to roam freely around the piazza, and probably equally freely around the inside of the car on the trip home.

In preparation for the upcoming *Rinascimento nel Borgo* celebrations, we have decided to brush up our medieval credentials by taking in an ancient traditional cultural joust in nearby Arezzo. Like the archery contest in Sansepolcro, this involves the four quarters of the city competing against one another, and we are reliably informed that it is very keenly followed by the citizens of Arezzo, even the disillusioned Youth who manage to put away their Gameboys for the evening to get involved.

Unfortunately we won't be around for the joust itself—in the sense of actually witnessing men in tights lunging at one another on horseback with spears—since it doesn't get underway until 7.30 pm[2] and is said to be unbearably crowded. The consolation prize of the parade and blessing ceremony during the afternoon, however, is more than enough compensation for our cowardly aversion to keeping the children up late in the evening.

2 The teeth-cleaning hour in Australian Standard Parenting Time.

If the costumes are anything to go by—and I think one can safely assume that they are—then the Arezzo joust is a highly-organised and well-funded event (once again, with no sign of corporate sponsorship). There must be well over a hundred participants, all of them decked out in colourful, exquisitely made and perfectly coordinated sets of tunics, kilts, capes, boots, leggings, headgear, the lot. Two of the quarters have gone for motifs with bold primary colours—one based on a rich red, another featuring brilliant blues and yellows—while the other two have opted for more sombre combinations of black, white and grey. The costumes are complemented by lots of terribly authentic-looking medieval accessories such as crossbows, spears, shields, helmets, flags, banners and poles, plus acres and acres of chain-mail. Even the horses are draped from head to hoof with coats, headgear and tail accessories in matching colours.

I wonder what happens to all the costumes and stuff during the rest of the year—do they get hired out for fancy dress parties perhaps?

Meanwhile there's excitement aplenty back in Sansepolcro. In an important new development on the coffee front, I've successfully trained Ester-in-the-mornings at Bar Appennini to make a decent Stained Milk. The training operation was completed without incident, leaving our friendship intact and, more importantly, providing the family with a reliable new breakfast option. Because Ester's early-morning doughnuts are just too good to let pass by.

Also we have been introduced by Alfredo and Sandra, parents of Ruby's official best friend Giulia, to a new coffee purveyor hidden down a narrow cobbled side-street, which turns out to be one of those places that roasts and grinds its own coffee beans while providing fresh coffees almost as an afterthought. Eleni claims that the cappuccino here is the best in Sansepolcro, although for my money Fabrizio's Stained Milk still takes the points.

Not least because the morning coffee experience at Gerasmo just got even better: in another stunning breakthrough in coffee technology, we have discovered the DIY version of the Stained Milk: a big glass of hot milk served with a tiny jug of fresh coffee.

The DIY approach has been hailed as milestone in consumer empowerment which affords extra peace of mind at breakfast time, since even Fabrizio has been known to slip up occasionally with a viciously strong or disappointingly weak beverage. It also adds a new element of visual stimulation: watching the milk turn brown as you tip in the coffee. Breakfast has never been so fascinating.

Finally, I have identified another promising new bar which serves excellent apricot danishes and could potentially be Trained. Though in truth this particular bar (name unknown) is unlikely to ever make it beyond last resort status because it's located in an uninteresting new bit of Sansepolcro and, let's face it, when you travel halfway across the globe you want a bit of medieval action with your coffee, not concrete and aluminium. Nevertheless, it does provide us with a potential Third Way in the event of a coffee crisis such as both Gerasmo and Appennini being closed at the same time.

On the culture front, the love affair with Italian pop continues unabated. For years I have had no interest whatsoever in mainstream radio; yet now, all of a sudden, the floodgates have opened, unleashing a wellspring of pent-up demand for pop music[3] that quite frankly I never knew I had in me.

Alessandro at the music shop (not to be confused with Alessandro from Bar Appennini) has assumed the mantle of musical advisor and offered to guide me carefully through the minefield of the local music industry. My modest but growing CD collection constitutes an excellent primer in late twentieth century/early twenty-first century Italian popular music, a sort of Italian Pop 101. So if my translating career ever falls in a heap I figure I can always be a lecturer at the Europop Faculty of the University of Rock.

Although I must admit to feeling slightly unsettled about the seismic shift in my musical sensibilities. Can it be healthy for the bar to have been lowered so far? Is too much pop music bad for your health? More to the point, is this what a year in Italy does to you? Perhaps we should have gone to Greece after all.[4]

After much soul-searching I have eventually resolved in my own mind that singing along to bubblegum pop songs is all part of

3 Including—I cannot tell a lie—the odd soppy ballad.
4 Actually no, not if the Eurovision Song Contest is any guide.

growing old gracefully. Surely there can be no better way to hone one's language skills while simultaneously bonding with one's children.

Our official status as rank outsiders in this country was underscored—nay, rammed home—last week during the annual application for renewal of our Permission to Stay forms. Happily, Sansepolcro is just large enough to have its own tiny outpost of the Questura. None of this waiting in line from six in the morning with hundreds of other hopefuls like at Perugia; one simply sails in and lodges the forms at the local office, from where they are forwarded on to the bureau at Arezzo. How civilized!

Except that the nice Questura policeman has decided that this time we will need to have our fingerprints taken.

But, I protest, there was no fingerprinting required last year when we lodged our applications in Perugia.

Really? How odd. He could have sworn that foreigners have to be fingerprinted.

He rings his boss to confirm, while I drum my fingers beadily on the desk. Fingerprinting indeed! Like common criminals. My only other fingerprinting experience was in Japan, where all foreigners[5] are obliged to undergo the ignominy of fingerprinting so they can be issued with a—wait for it—Alien Registration Card. You can just about hear the Robot shouting *WARNING, WARNING, ARIEN OBJECT APPLOACHING* as you pass through airport customs.

Five minutes later, Mr. Questura puts down the phone and looks up apologetically. No two ways about it; he will have to fingerprint me. So be it, then.

But this is no ordinary fingerprinting process: first he takes imprints of all five fingertips, twice, on separate pieces of paper; then the whole length of my fingers; and finally my complete hand—palm, fingers, fingertips and all. Then he repeats the entire process for the other hand.

5 Including, outrageously, a small but significant population of Koreans born and raised in Japan who are treated as outcasts in their own country.

At this stage it wouldn't surprise me if he ordered me to strip naked then lathered my whole body in ink and laid me out on an enormous roll of printer's paper. Front *and* back please.

Signor Questura is highly apologetic about this scandalous treatment of foreigners over which he himself naturally has no control. By way of justification he explains that within a few years even ordinary decent God-fearing Italians will also be having their civil liberties infringed in the same way. Which strikes me as even more ludicrous: what sort of country fingerprints every last one of its citizens? And imagine the environmental scandal over the mountains of paper that would be needed to collect 60 million sets of fingertip, finger and palm prints. Hang on: *both* hands—make that 120 million.

Eleni is required to present herself to the Questura a couple of days later to be similarly infringed. The children are mercifully spared the fingerprinting treatment although—as in Perugia last year—we are required to trot them down to the office in the flesh, presumably to prove that we are not child-stealing gypsies. Or that we have not stolen them from gypsies. Or whatever.

They say, rather irritatingly, that all good things must come to an end. So it was inevitable that the exhilarating, chest-bursting culinary adventure that was summer in the gazebo would eventually run its course. With the onset of the colder weather, Ivana has spirited away her supplies to the regular kitchen upstairs, Raffaello has lashed vinyl curtains to the gazebo walls for protection over the winter, and the large table is now covered with an array of flowers and pot-plants deemed too sensitive to survive in the open air.

And so we mourn the end of an era. It has been a wonderful summer of laughter and stories, of cooking lessons in the kitchen and history and culture lessons around the table, of games with the children in the backyard, and most of all of being steadily drawn into the embrace of the extended family. Lunchtime had become an institution. Even Felix knew the routine: after waking from his midday nap he would come straight down into the back garden for some reheated pasta and grandparental doting.

One of the unexpected highlights of the gazebo season was the chance to hear Ruby speaking Italian, initially while playing with young Camilla when she thought we weren't listening, and later, as she became more confident, with the adults too. We are immensely proud of how she has handled herself in Italy: accepting, adapting to, and now actively embracing the foreign environment into which she was so rudely thrust one year ago.

I recall asking Ruby one morning long ago on the way to Gragnano what she thought of scuola materna.

I don't like it that much, she replied matter-of-factly, but I know I have to go so I do: a typically stoic response which caused considerable consternation to her parents at the time. We were, after all, being slightly disingenuous—kindergarten is by no means compulsory in Italy.

But we kept sending her there all the same, and our intransigence seems to have finally borne fruit. For she is now enjoying primary school immensely, cosseted within a select coterie of friends and provided at last with a genuine learning challenge as opposed to endless drawing.

Every night there is homework to be done, and quite a bit of it too. The bambini of Grade 1C are currently working their way through the Italian alphabet and the sounds produced by the various phonetic groupings—the hard *ghe* from *spaghetti*, the chewier *gn* from *gnocchi*, the wonderful trilled R's, the sexy double-Z combinations, and the impossible *gli* and *gle* sounds.[6] Year 1 at primary school, in fact, provides an excellent primer in the basics of the Italian language.

Homework in the afternoons has become a family affair, as we grill Ruby on the wisdom she has acquired during the morning session. Unlike the English language, with its endless spelling exceptions, pitfalls and disappointments, Italian is written just how it sounds. Which means that once you've mastered the basic rules, it makes for far more satisfying writing practice, for adults and children alike.

6 Happily, these turn out to be equally difficult for Italian bambini as they are for foreign adults.

Even Felix, after three months of concentrated playing with Ivana and Co., has acquired a few key words and phrases. His current favourite (which was definitely not taught to him by his grandmother) is *Qui è Sansepoppo*—'This is Sansepoppo'—which he finds hysterically funny because *poppo* is the local term for poo.

Food shopping. Meal planning. Cooking. Eating alone (well, just the four of us). We have been reflecting on the cold harsh reality of post-gazebo life over the past few days, and it's not a cheery prospect. Will we be able to cope with the transition?

It turns out that we won't have to. Ivana announces that we shall simply follow the family upstairs for the winter. No doubt she can't bear to think of us sitting downstairs miserably hunched over our nutritionally-challenged bread snacks. And neither can we.

Well that's that sorted, then. No need to start shopping again just yet.

Weekday lunches upstairs are distinctly more subdued. Outlying members of the extended family are less likely to pop in and invited friends are rarely sighted. The contrast with the gazebo experience only serves to illustrate the different mindset that applies during the warmer months. Out in the gazebo the sun is shining, the birds are singing, there's plenty of space, come and join us, the more the merrier. Upstairs, by way of contrast, lunch is reduced to its base form: a meal eaten in the middle of the day without fanfare. Not that the meal itself has been compromised in the slightest—we can still look forward to a pasta primo, meat secondo, crusty unsalted bread, wine, cheeses, sweets and coffee. Sure beats the hell out of sandwiches.

The end of the gazebo season may actually be a blessing in disguise, for Eleni and I occasionally wonder whether some of the extended family might not be starting to tire a little of those Johnny-come-lately Australians. Who would have thought that the new tenants downstairs would suddenly ingratiate themselves into the family unit before anyone knew what was happening? Now look at them: forever the centre of attention, prattling on with their supposedly insightful cross-cultural observations and peppering everyone with endless questions about Italian language and culture. Carrying on as if Sansepolcro were paradise on earth and ordinary decent Italian lunches were manna from heaven.[7] And as for those atrocious accents…

My suspicions are confirmed one day during a family stroll along the main street, when we happen to come across young Marco with a group of friends. As he walks towards us, I decide to hide behind a pillar and then—oh the shame, I can hardly bear to recount the details—jump out merrily at the last minute, feigning surprise and astonishment. Marco is mortified. And in that instant, several important neural synapses are formed in the deepest recesses of my brain:

- That sort of stuff works well with young children.
- Marco is a teenager.
- He is out with his mates.
- You have just embarrassed him comprehensively.
- You idiot.

Isn't it insidious the way the generation gap creeps up on young parents, even as we're all valiantly trying to pretend that we're still back in our late twenties and still nominally in touch with Youth.

The next time we spot Marco in the street, he keeps his head down and his cap pulled low in a concerted effort to remain unnoticed. Initially I am stung by this none-too-subtle rebuff, until I realise that the incident only serves to cement my position within the family—as the Embarrassing Uncle Figure. I suppose there has to be one in every family.

While I might have preferred Groovy Ex-Rock-Star Uncle or Fascinating Japanese-Speaking Uncle or even plain old Normal Uncle, if this is not to be then I shall accept my lot with good grace. But I tell you what—the next time I see that lad in town he'd bloody

7 God knows what they must eat down there in Australia.

better keep his head up or he'll cop a clip over the ear, the cheeky monkey.

This latest development only serves to accentuate a gnawing sensation that has been niggling away at us recently, reminding us that maybe, just maybe, the time has finally come to think about leaving. Despite all the fun. Despite all the food. Despite the bars, the theatre, the pool, the school, the piazza, the pizza restaurants, and everything else that we love about being here.

Why the change of heart?

It isn't really a change of heart, though. In the back of our minds, we always envisaged the Odyssey as being a year long. (Remember the return tickets?) Back in July, we had no problem making the decision to extend our stay and prolong the fun—after all, flexibility is the key to survival in this ever-changing world in which we live in.[8] Now, however, having spent well over a year in country, we sense a vague, unexpressed feeling about moving on. And as Pooh Bear and Lady MacBeth will attest, you just can't argue with a vague, unexpressed feeling about something.

Perhaps it is because we have, in a sense, already achieved our unstated aim of fitting in. Over the last few months we have been virtually inducted into the family upstairs. Further, we now boast a good working knowledge of the local area. Just the other day we managed to surprise Raffaello and Ivana by introducing them to a new outdoor pizzeria up on the hill at San Giustino, as well as a new bar tucked in a corner of a small palazzo in Anghiari. And if having all the bills arrive in your name means you're a local, well, we're there already.

To take this thing any further, then, would mean giving ourselves over completely to this country, adopting the Italian lifestyle wholesale, abandoning our status as tourists. Life in Italy would gradually cease to be new, different and exciting. There'd be less to discover; the magic that underscores our very existence here would start to disappear.

We'd have to start complaining endlessly about the government, shouting at the soccer on the telly and drinking small bolts of viciously strong black coffee.

8 Poor grammar courtesy of *Live and Let Die*, first verse.

We'd have to start spoiling the children rotten, feeding them Nutella for breakfast and keeping them up really late in the evenings.

We'd have to start churning out delicious three-course meals on a daily basis.

More worryingly, we might find ourselves ensnared in the tentacles of the British community in this section of Tuscany[9]. Before we knew it we'd be whinging endlessly about how the Italians don't queue properly and how frightfully difficult it is to find a decent builder.

(Over the past year we have met a staggering number of Brits who have renovated/are renovating/would like to renovate old farmhouses in the countryside. Local builders are apparently flat out pandering to the needs of Italiophiles desperate to convert crumbling old barns that should by rights have come down in the last earthquake into sparkling new residences with stainless steel wardrobes and granite toilets and internet fridges and heating in the floors and walls and ceilings and a massive pool out the back and a spa for the dog and high perimeter fencing to keep out the natives. I blame it all on Sting. That, and the introduction of feeble warbling oboe solos into pop music.)

Well, if we're serious about leaving, we'll need to make a start on all those interesting-sounding places that we never got to during summer. Such as San Gimignano, described enthusiastically by a friend of a friend as the loveliest village in all of Italy. Better check it out then.

Ahem. The less said about San Gimignano the better.

Having said that, let me say this: San Gimignano is overrated and overrun. Certainly it is a handsome and beautifully preserved town, but Italy is already littered with handsome and beautifully preserved towns. What San Gimignano does have by way of product differentiation is the spectacle of 17 tall towers a-towering over the cobbled streets (down from an all-time record of 42[10] back in the middle

9 Also known as Chiantishire, the British Empire's newest colonial outpost.
10 Or 72, or 90, depending on which guidebook you believe.

ages). And while the medieval towers are indeed magnificent, they present much the same dilemma as ancient traditional cultural temples in Japan—after about the third or fourth one they all start to look the same. You can always buy a postcard. Stay at home, wash the car, I gave it a three.

A quick side trip to Siena on the return journey from San Gimignano, however, provides the highlight of the weekend. For a start, Siena boasts an excellent central piazza, Piazza del Campo, which is absolutely enormous, fan-shaped rather than square and gently sloping to boot. This is the venue for the brutal Palio horse-race, with the slope adding an extra element of danger as the horses slip over on the inclined turns. I am positively overcome with piazza envy. At the base of the fan shape is a single, very tall tower that provides Piazza del Campo with an important focal point in architectural and cultural terms, while also pointing the finger triumphantly at nearby San Gimignano. Which I think adds a nice touch.

Wandering through the piazza, we come across some young Japanese students who claim to be enjoying themselves immensely in Italy, unlike some girls we overheard complaining bitterly in Perugia one time.[11] The students chat away to Ruby in Japanese while the parents look on warmly. We swap phone numbers and invite them to come and visit us in Sansepolcro. Although somehow I don't think we'll be seeing them up our way: how could a small country town with a tiny piazza possibly compare with this?

Describing a wide curve around the back of the piazza is a bustling pedestrian thoroughfare lined with bars and shops, a veritable delight for promenading. And this, tragically, is the sum total of the Siena experience for today because it is time to head back to the car and start the long journey home. We'll definitely have to come again another weekend and do it properly.

[*Of course they never did. I can't believe they only managed a paltry couple of hours in Siena, one of the must-see attractions of Tuscany. According to my guidebook anyway. Ed*]

11 And thus nature balances itself.

The four of us are standing on a sturdy aluminium platform at the window of the real estate agency, together with Ivana, Raffaello and Cristina, looking out over the central piazza of Sansepolcro. Temporary tiered seating has been erected along three sides, turning it into a mini stadium. Already the seating is nearly half full, and spectators continue filing through in a steady stream.

Today is Sunday, the last day of the *Rinascimento nel Borgo* festivities, the day reserved for the grand performance of the colourful sbandieratori, the ancient traditional cultural formation flag-waving performers of Sansepolcro. Actually a number of other towns also have sbandieratori (Siena, Gubbio, San Marino and Lucca, to name a few), but the glossy brochure in my hand insists that Sansepolcro was the first to start waving flags in formation and therefore boasts the oldest continuously operating sbandieratori festival in Italy.[12] (Notwithstanding a brief interlude during the war, of course. Wars are futile and unnecessary and they play havoc with the continuity of sporting and cultural records and should be banned.)

The show we are about to witness is the culmination of a full week's worth of Renaissance-inspired activities. Every night there has been something different: a medieval banquet in the courtyard at Santa Chiara, complete with traditional dancing and singing (prohibitively expensive, sadly); a grand Renaissance parade through town with a cast of hundreds; a children's pantomime show (with a start time of 7.30 pm—vetoed immediately by the Parental Committee); and a variety of musical recitals and theatre performances.

The highlight thus far was the parade. There were the drumming teams a-drumming, fresh from their earnest practicing over summer; there were horn and bugle players blasting their way enthusiastically along; there were horses with riders and horses hitched to buggies; there were town officials carrying flags on poles and scrolls of parchment; there were archers with bows and arrows; and then there was about half the local population dressed up in medieval garb for the event. (Later we found out that the costumes are available for hire on the day. If only we'd known—we could have had Renaissance Ruby and Medieval Felix among them!)

12 Sounds a bit Beethoven-Lived-Here to me but let it pass.

The route down the main thoroughfare and back up via Aggiunti was lined with Renaissance-style flaming torches[13] and decorated with streamers, banners and tree branches. There were tables with craftsmen making bows and arrows, blacksmiths beating iron and potters potting. There were tables decorated with cloths and branches and laden with medieval wares, set up by local vendors along the route.

And there were stalls devoted to arts and crafts and displays of textiles and ceramics and food and wine and all manner of things including, bizarrely, an enormous pig's head—can't quite see the Renaissance connection but there it was anyway, staring dully up at us from the table.

Then there were the costumes: the townspeople in their long dresses, capes and thick rolled headgear, the men in their tunics, vests, leggings and chunky pendants, and the maidens in their billowing white dresses and garlands of flowers. The parade also featured children of all ages, even some Renaissance babies.

And above all, there was much laughter and gaiety. I was struck by the contrast with the much more serious parade at Arezzo, where the joust lads were no doubt quaking in their chain-mail boots at the thought of the spears and rushing horses to come in the evening. Here in Sansepolcro, where anyone can hire a costume and join in the fun, the parade through town is an altogether more inclusive affair, since even those who aren't dressed up are sure to spot friends and neighbours in Renaissance drag at some point.

The other main event of the *Rinascimento nel Borgo* week was yesterday's balestra (archery) competition. It turns out that the competition is not held between the four quarters of the city as previously reported.[14] Sansepolcro is not large enough to have quarters; instead it is divided into two halves corresponding to the main gates to the city, Porta Fiorentina at the front and Porta Romana out the back.

The Porta Romana cheer squad came well-equipped with buckets and tins and sticks to beat them with, and had an excellent time up on the top tier of seats chanting well-rehearsed slogans at their foes-

13 Looking suspiciously like cheap wickerwork mosquito lamps from K-Mart.

14 Refer disclaimer page 2.

for-an-evening over the far side of the piazza. The Porta Fiorentina squad weren't so well organised in the noise-making department, but they made up for it by spending most of the time jeering loudly at their counterparts and applauding wildly every time their archers hit the target. And in the end they had the last laugh because victory went to Porta Fiorentina, although the result is largely immaterial because next week is the big one, Sansepolcro vs. Gubbio, and any lingering intra-city rivalry will be quickly put aside in the interests of inter-city rivalry.

As the piazza starts to fill, Cristina makes us all some industrial-strength sump-oil coffees in tiny Barbie-sized plastic cups from the espresso machine in the corner, then announces that she will not be staying for the festivities today.

But surely it's fun to share in the excitement of Sansepolcro's big day?

Not when you've already seen it twenty times, she replies. I'm off home to wash the dog.

Pity Ivana and Raffaello, then—born and bred in Sansepolcro, they must have seen the sbandieratori performance a hundred times already between them; now they're going to do it all again for our benefit. But I think they enjoy the experience vicariously through their guests. And we are certainly not the first: the viewing platform was commissioned by Raffaello many years ago, specifically for this purpose. Corporate entertainment, small-Italian-town style.

From our ringside seat at the real estate agency window we can see a handsome medieval tower on the opposite side of the piazza, perhaps five or six stories high. The tower has been incorporated into a palazzo, and now forms a centrepiece sticking up in the middle like an oversized chimney. There are many more such towers dotted around Sansepolcro and we have heard that they all used to be far higher until some nasty bloke from Florence, probably with penis envy, came along in the fourteenth[15] century and ordered them all shortened. The official explanation is that this was necessary for safety reasons following a major earthquake but I have my doubts.

15 Might have been sixteenth.

By the time our Florentine friend with low self-esteem had finished, only the Torre di Berta in the middle of the piazza was left standing at its full majestic height. Poor old Torre di Berta was then comprehensively bombed by the Germans during the war, leaving Sansepolcro with a collection of cruelly truncated towers and a wide open piazza. Although in hindsight this unfortunate series of events was probably a good thing: San Gimignano, as we have seen, has seventeen tall towers still standing and is horribly overrun with tourists as a result.

As we finish our coffees an announcement can be heard over the ubiquitous loudspeaker system: the performance is about to get underway. From our vantage point we can just make out the procession filing slowly along in the direction of the piazza: first the drummers, making a thunderous rum-tum-a-tum sound that echoes down the narrow canyon of the main street; next the buglers, a good ten or fifteen of them, with colour-coordinated flags hanging from their bugles: then the archers, who have turned up for the occasion although they aren't performing today; and finally a straggle of Renaissance spectators, a watered-down version of the grand parade, who get to sit in the prime spots at ground level in front of the tiered seating, lucky things.

Now the drummers, still a-drumming, form themselves into a wide semi-circle together with the buglers. The spectators are all seated. All movement has ceased. An air of expectation hangs over the piazza. The crowd noise dies down slightly, although the drumming continues apace. *Drums must never stop.*

Suddenly the drumming gets louder; and here they are, streaming into the piazza in a long line, the handsome brave fearless young sbandieratori running full pelt with their enormous flags flapping wildly behind them as they complete a preliminary lap of the arena to tumultuous cheers.

If the piazza during winter is a dull, grey space, now we see it at the other end of the spectrum: a seething mass of colour and medievalry, packed to the rafters with an enthusiastic and vocal crowd. The eyes are entertained by the intricate, multi-layered sbandieratori costumes, once again with a strong emphasis on primary colours; the huge flags, featuring vivid designs of red, yellow and orange; the drummers and buglers, with their coordinated attire and accessories such as the furry hats and bugle-flags; and the Renaissance spectators, providing a nice counterpoint in their sombre browns and rich reds and sporting the familiar rolled headgear for the townsfolk as well as garlands of flowers for the maidens.

Without further ado the performance begins.

First we see all twenty-eight sbandieratori showing us some of the basic semaphore moves: flags left, flags right, up, down, twirl, swap hands and so on. The sight of twenty-eight flags moving in perfect unison is engrossing—think synchronised swimming with more colour and movement and less water.

The original twenty-eight all run out and a new group of about ten enters. Their act is more adventurous and features new moves such as swooshing the flags round in a wide arc, flicking them deftly to the left and right, furling them tightly and shooting them up into the air, exchanging flags via daring aerial throws, and pirouetting on the spot with flags twirling. The drumming accompaniment has also gone up a notch, and now features special drum-rolls for all the difficult moves so we know when to clap. *Drums must never stop.*

Next on is a smaller group of five who are more keen on the furling and throwing side of things. The aerial flag exchanges become increasingly complex, but are executed without so much as a fumble. Before long the five are replaced by an energetic duo who engage in a highly choreographed and brilliantly executed flag swordfight packed with jumping and lunging.

Finally, the Grand Master comes on and performs a solo act juggling first two and then three flags, passing them over and under through his legs—no mean feat considering that each flag measures over one metre square. Every now and then it seems one of the flags has dropped on the ground, but it is actually resting on the Grand Master's foot. A moment later, he flicks the flag back up deftly off his toes and catches it while throwing another into the air and juggling the third without missing a beat. Amazing.

The drummers, meanwhile, have been going solid throughout the performance, pausing only to let the bugles have a run once in a while, and even then for barely a minute. If I were a drummer, my arms would be fit to drop off by now. How do they keep going? I guess they're all young and bursting with energy.

Which they very much are. There is a large youth component in today's performance. Even Cool Groovy Alessandro from Bar Appennini used to be a performer a few years back. It's nice to know that these sorts of activities are still held in high regard by the embittered Youth of the twenty-first century. (Or perhaps Italian youths are not embittered and disillusioned after all? Is this the generation gap speaking?) *Drums must never stop.*

To finish off, all the sbandieratori stream back into the piazza and do a lap of honour and are cheered mightily for their efforts.

And then, finally, incredibly, the drums stop! No bass solo, just blissful silence. Performance over, time to go home. Even the loudspeaker system has fallen silent.

But nobody is in a hurry to leave. Particularly not those in costume; the piazza is now filled with a genial crowd milling around, laughing and chatting and making the most of their annual opportunity to hang out and look medieval.

Thinking back over the course of the year—the *Esplorazioni* festival, the vintage car rally, the sporting events, the bicycle gymkhana and so on—I realise that today is by no means the only big event on the calendar. Life in Sansepolcro is one long ongoing cycle of activities, which only underscores the community feel of the town.

The sbandieratori performance, for instance, is touted as a tourist attraction, but is it really? Judging from the scene below, I would have described it as a special occasion for the locals, a chance to get dressed up and have a bit of fun. So for us up here in our corporate box at the window—we feel as if have been let in on something very special.

At times like this it's difficult not to think of Sansepolcro as a huge holiday resort offering a range of exciting holiday programs for both adults and children: medieval, modern, traditional, historical, artistic, exercise-related, food-oriented, sporting, religious, what have you. Which only shows that, however much we might like to pretend otherwise, our world view of Sansepolcro is still very much through the eyes of the tourist. And this is not such a bad thing, since every new discovery is still fascinating, every promenade down the main street and every slice of pizza still endlessly enjoyable.

A week later sees us enjoying possibly the smallest Sunday lunch ever: today's cast consists of the four of us and the grandparents plus Cristina, Patrizia and Marco—and that's it! The more intimate setting is actually quite nice for a change. Less people means less cooking and a more relaxed Ivana, who has been known to grumble at times about the effort involved in cooking for ten guests and appears visibly relieved on the odd occasion when numbers are down.

Halfway through the meal, the phone rings and Ivana answers. Her face falls. She mutters something to Cristina and Patrizia, who drop their forks in their bowls—literally—and head straight for the door. Within thirty seconds the three of them are gone.

Silence descends. Even the children fall mute.

What happened? I eventually enquire of Raffaello.

Giorgio, comes the response. No further explanation is forthcoming, nor is it necessary.

There will be no more conversation today. We clear the dishes together with Marco then take our leave.

A few hours later the women return, visibly shaken but with no sign of tears. Relief: Giorgio is still with us. But it is clear to all that he could just as easily have left us this afternoon. And if not today then maybe tomorrow, maybe next week, maybe next month.

Any day now.

Eleni is away tonight, down in Rome. But she's not shopping; she is down there to pick up our next guests in Sansepolcro. Eku and Shige, a kindly Japanese couple who were virtually our surrogate parents during the years we spent in Tokyo, are coming to visit us here in the land of the rising pizza. But Eku has read in her guidebook that Japanese tourists are routinely targeted by petty thieves in Italy (unfortunately quite true) and is too terrified to catch the train up to Sansepolcro without an escort. So Eleni has agreed to go down to Rome to fetch the two of them from the airport, an excellent excuse indeed for a quick trip to the centre of the ancient world.

Our guests arrive the next day, wallets and handbags intact, and are immediately escorted upstairs for a welcoming cup of tea, where Eleni and I grapple with the convoluted construct of trying to facilitate conversation across the kitchen table between two sets of surrogate parents from different times and places. It's not easy to translate between Japanese, a language with which we are reasonably familiar, and Italian, a language with which we are still grappling, without accidentally slipping into English, a language which is of no use to anyone here.

In particular the emphatic *so!* in Japanese performs a similar function to the Italian *sì!*, and after an hour of increasingly muddled translation I hardly know whether I'm *sì*ing or *so*ing…it's messing with my brian. *Si* what I mean?[16]

A couple of days later Eleni is off again, taking Eku and Shige on a Japanese-style three-day whirlwind tour of Florence and Venice, where she finally succeeds in experiencing the real-deal gondola ride for which (grammar) she has been hankering all year. Meanwhile back in Sansepolcro, Daddy is afforded no special treatment this time during mamma's absence—no jars of pomorola, no hefty slabs of lasagne. Ivana has clearly decided that a man who can wash the dishes does not need any help looking after his children. Another major tactical error on my part.

As a consolation prize, though, Daddy scores the escort role on the return trip to Rome. For a lark I decide that we shall stop for the night at the same hotel near the Colosseum where the family stayed

16 Sorry.

four years ago on the way back from Greece, where the whole they-said-we-were-crazy-they-said-it-would-never-work Italian Odyssey plan was hatched.

Funny how the Colosseum looks just the same.

After delivering Eku and Shige to the airport I wander the streets of Rome for the rest of the day, aimlessly, and with an increasing sense of guilt: I ought to be taking this rare opportunity to check out the ancient capital at my leisure, but I'm just not interested. And it's hard to shake the uncomfortable feeling of being a fish out of water, a country hillbilly down in the big smoke—especially when at one point a snappy young thing on a motorbike zooms up and tries to sell me a stolen mobile phone. That sort of thing would *never* happen in Sansepolcro.[17]

By the end of the day it is a relief to be back at Rome Termini station, safe in the knowledge that I will soon be on the fast train, speeding away from all the lawlessness and cacophony towards the reassuring confines of a small walled town in the country.

At the station cafeteria I order a chicken focaccia and cappuccino, and notice the lad chuckling behind the counter. Why, I wonder idly; then I think *bugger it, I'm going to ask.* After all, I haven't spent the whole year learning Italian for nothing.

Ah well, he ventures cheerfully, it's just that… we wouldn't normally combine a milk-based drink with a chicken dish, that's all.

Ah well, I reply breezily, that's what we foreigners are here for, to give you guys a good laugh every now and then.

And I realise how much I'm going to miss these sorts of exchanges. Sure, life will be easier back in Australia—our English pronunciation is better, we're familiar with the local culture, we won't be making such silly mistakes, we won't be chuckled at. Easier maybe; but nowhere near as fun and interesting.

Why the hell are we going home?

17 Motorbikes aren't allowed on the main street for a start.

12

De-Sansepolcrisation

It's official: we're having too much of a good time. The fun will have to stop. Eleni and I have seen the writing on the wall, and though we may not be able to decipher the writing as such, its meaning is clear. This week I have been down to the travel agency to book a set of return tickets, and before long we will be back in comfortable suburban Melbourne living the quiet sedentary life that is our true and proper destiny.

But why? Why indeed. Many people have asked us recently, as well they might, and our response inevitably sounds vague and shifty because we can't even articulate the reasons to ourselves. Much less to others. Let alone in Italian. How to explain the inexplicable? As my mother always said: sort out your thoughts in a list. So here goes:

1 Homesickness

Ruby says she misses life at home. Fair enough. Although it has to be said that she is also having a great time at school with her new friends. The longer we stay, the less she will remember Australia and the less she will miss it. Eleni and I, needless to say, are not at all homesick at this stage and Felix, bless his heart, doesn't count.

2 Education

The plan was always to get back in time for the new school year in Australia to minimise the disruption to Ruby's schooling. Yet there can be no doubt that she is already receiving an excellent education courtesy of the Italian state school system. As would Felix in his turn.

3 Accommodation

Our little apartment has been great for the year, but its limitations are becoming increasingly apparent. For one thing, it's not easy to run a mighty global translation empire from a corner of the bedroom. Then there's the tiny kitchen with its back-breakingly low sink, and the bizarrely-designed bathroom with the world's smallest shower cubicle crammed in opposite the toilet. But more to the point: if we lived elsewhere, would summers ever be the same without the gazebo?

4 Transport

The HGV's insurance runs out in February and cannot be renewed with English number plates. We would need to either re-register the HGV in Italy (expensive, complex, impossible) or buy a new car.

5 Timing is everything

I remember as a boy my father telling me that Kevin Bartlett should have quit football right after the 1980 Grand Final *while he was still ahead, son.* And in a classic example of life imitating sport, I am determined not to repeat KB's mistake. *Get out while you're still ahead, son.* OK OK, I heard you the first time.

6 Motherhood on the wane

After six years of concentrated child-rearing, Eleni is keen to launch into a high-powered shoulder-pads glass-ceiling-busting career of her own. Italy presents visa problems.

7 The 'longer you stay, the harder it is to leave' factor

Self-explanatory really, but particularly heart-rending when it comes to breaking up childhood friendships.

But none of the above constitutes a truly compelling reason for returning home. Even all of them taken together don't amount to much. So what is it then? We're having the time of our lives. Our stay here in Sansepolcro has been a life-defining experience, the most fun we've ever had. Though we've been in Italy little more than a year, it feels more like five, which shows how settled we have become.

Devo were right: there *is* such a thing as too much freedom of choice. It would all be so much easier if I had a proper job and the HR division of my evil multinational conglomerate employer were ordering the family to return to Australia against our collective will. Or if Morelli's deportation orders were to come through, depriving us of our liberty altogether.

Perhaps the real source of our gut feeling about moving on, more than any of the limp excuses in the list, is the realisation that ultimately this is not our land, that we can only ever be visitors. I think I shall term this Cultural Honesty. So at least we can console ourselves that we are trying to be honest to our cultural heritage.[1]

Anyway, enough of the whinging and introspection; we've got some serious travelling to do over the last few months. Due to the immobilising heat of summer we now have an unfeasibly large backlog of places on the travel wish list. All those destinations we'd been saving up until sometime later in the year—well, later-in-the-year has arrived. It's now or never.

Last week we succeeded in reducing the backlog slightly by removing Ruby from school for a quick road trip to the north-west corner of Italy with the blessing of her kind teacher, Laura.

'Normally we would say no to such a request,' she smiled, 'but seeing as you're off to discover more of la bella Italia, well...'

Before she had time to finish the sentence we were off home to pack our bags and in the car heading for Diano San Pietro, a tiny and otherwise nondescript olive-farming village up in the western

1 Try explaining *that* in Italian without sounding vague and shifty.

reaches of Liguria. This particular village has long held semi-mythical status for us because it is the real-life setting for *Extra Virgin*, the best book ever written about foreigners in Italy and one of the primary inspirations for the Italian Odyssey.

The author still lives there, although tragically she was not in residence during our visit, so we amused ourselves instead by trying to identify the various landmarks featured in the story, in a case of real life imitating art written about real life. Thus we managed to track down Stefano, the owner of the local bar that plays a pivotal role in the narrative, who confirmed that we were but the latest in a steady stream of intrigued readers making the pilgrimage to his village.

As an added bonus, Diano San Pietro turns out to be barely an hour away from the border with France, and we toyed momentarily with the idea of popping over to Monte Carlo for lunch one day just so we could brag about it later. However, in the end it was just as well that we spent the weekend in Italy; the Italian Riviera and surrounding hinterland is wonderfully laid-back and ultimately more enchanting than many of the more obvious holiday destinations. None of your pretentious city-on-the-water or road-halfway-down-a-cliff-face malarky here; just a series of graceful if slightly dilapidated seaside resort towns framed by steep terraced mountains soaring away quietly in the background. And plenty of good pesto to be eaten, too.

No sooner have we arrived back from Liguria than planning begins for the first trans-European HGV road trip, destination Salzburg. But we will not be in Salzburg to investigate the birthplace of Mozart, nor to admire the castles and scenery, nor even to gorge ourselves on Austrian cakes and pastries;[2] no, our primary objective is to go on the Official Sound of Music Tour, thus enabling Eleni to fulfil another of her lifelong ambitions.

After arriving in Salzburg it only takes a few hours of wandering

2 Though this may occur from time to time.

around town for us to conclude, with the aid of sweeping generalisation skills, that the buildings in Austria are rather more neat and well-kept than those in Italy. Almost too much so, in my opinion—the overall impression is like some sort of Disney Europe-land exhibit, all pristine and glistening. I guess I've become accustomed to crumbling masonry and peeling paintwork as part of the fabric of life.

The Sound of Music tour is everything we expected but not much more. On the bus we run through a quick How-Sound-of-Music-Are-You quiz, before shuttling through some of the key locations from the film: the gazebo where Captain von Trapp kissed Maria, the church where the marriage scene was filmed, the lake where everyone fell out of the boat. Towards the end of the tour we are rudely turfed out at a cheap souvenir store complex, cunningly located in a far-flung spot well out of reach of alternative forms of return transport, and ordered to spend 40 minutes emptying our wallets in accordance with an ancient traditional contra deal between the tour operators and local retailers.

The *Sound of Music* tour is notable in my mind for the number of locations that we *aren't* allowed to visit, suggesting that not everyone in Salzburg shares our love of all things von Trapp. Apparently the locals have little knowledge of or interest in *The Sound of Music*; they consider it no more than a cheesy American film which happens to be set in Salzburg and which has generated a slightly embarrassing tourist industry that refuses to die off and leave the city free to concentrate on its core business of flogging Mozart paraphernalia.[3]

Despite professing to be a genuine card-carrying aficionado of the *Sound of Music*, Ruby is singularly unimpressed with the tour and spends most of her time in Salzburg working on her Italian R pronunciation—*rrrRRRrrr, rrrRRRrrr, rrrRRRrrr*—eventually developing an authentic trill that sounds like a recalcitrant Vespa engine. Hopefully the teachers will be pleased with her efforts.

Back at home in Sansepolcro, we tally up the number of destinations still left on the wish list and compare this with the time remaining, factoring in the six-day school weeks and the limitations

3 Such as the deliciously risqué Mozart Balls.

of teacher Laura's largesse, and taking into consideration the Christmas break, not forgetting the potential for travel fatigue… and swiftly conclude that there's absolutely no way we can fit them all in.

Something has to give, and we are obliged to institute a cultural culling process involving the basest of tourist criteria. For instance, we're not going to deny ourselves the opportunity to say we've been up the Leaning Tower of Pisa, a measly two hours away. And I am very keen to visit Verona to see the Arena, a fully intact and functional (if slightly smaller) version of that decrepit old ruin of a Colosseum down in Rome.

So most of the other destinations are unceremoniously dumped: the return visit to Siena, the expensive ceramics shops at Deruta,[4] beautiful Lake Como up north, Mt. Fumiaolo for more skiing, Naples, Pompeii (Eleni's turn), Sardinia (for an Italian island experience). Not to mention Prague, Dubrovnik, France, Spain, Holland, Finland, Switzerland, Legoland and all the other lands in Europe that we initially imagined—with the blind optimism that has characterised the entire Odyssey experience—that we would be able to get to within the year. [*What is it with these people? Most tourists cover more territory in four weeks than they've managed in 14 months. Somebody buy me a return ticket to Italy for God's sake and I'll write the rest of it for them. Ed.*]

Closer to home, we have promised the children a trip to Gubbio to see the Christmas-tree-on-the-hillside display that we didn't make it to last year. This time we take the scenic back road from Sansepolcro so as to avoid passing through the Town-That-Must-Not-Be-Named. Gubbio looks much the same as it did a year ago, including the buses, which reminds me that I have forgotten once again to check the guidebook and find out what all the tourists are here for. Probably something cultural or artistic anyway.

The rickety bird-cage cable-car contraption is open today, so we travel right up to the top of the tree and discover a church containing, of all things, a full-size model of a person in a glass coffin plonked on top of the altar. As it happens, Ruby has been recently been working her way through the story of Snow White, and has been enquiring

4 Possibly just as well, but don't tell Eleni.

about glass coffins and the like, and I have assured her that nobody makes them in real life any more these days, and—bloody hell, there's a glass coffin up there. Another blow to Daddy's credibility.

A couple of days later Eleni and I take Felix for a quick spin over to Urbania, keen to reacquaint ourselves with one of Italy's most charming towns before we take our leave of the country and our senses. We plan to spend the morning pottering around until midday, then head back to pick Ruby up from school. But we hadn't reckoned on market day in Urbania. The lure of the street market is too great to resist, and we find ourselves spending more time perusing underpants and fresh vegetables than exploring the myriad laneways of Urbania.

We're having so much fun at the markets that before we know it, midday has come and gone and we will be too late to pick Ruby up at the designated time of 1.05. So we ring Raffaello and ask if he wouldn't mind doing us a small favour…

Why of course, no problem, he'd be happy to fetch her after class. After all, that's what family's for, isn't it?

Downtown Sansepolcro is looking rather festive at the moment. This year the comune has sensibly done away with the hugely unpopular Christmas-time replica of Torre di Berta in the middle of the piazza, presumably in an effort to demonstrate to its detractors that the birthplace of Piero della Francesca and all-round home of high culture still occupies the aesthetic high ground when it comes to Christmas decorations.

The presepio at the disused church near Sale e Pepe is back again, but somehow it doesn't seem as good as last year. Perhaps the novelty has worn off? But no, there are definitely fewer moving parts. Nevertheless, we pop a gold coin in the donation box out of a lingering sense of campanalismo. For a town that will soon be no longer ours.

Though the end may be near, we're still making important and exciting discoveries. For instance, the recently redeveloped SMA supermarket over the road now features an even wider range of pizza slices.

Also we have identified a major damp problem in our flat. Ah, the human capacity for taking things for granted. The very same thing happened last winter—I clearly remember seeing drops of water along the bottom of the wall behind our bed—but we hardly gave it any thought, we were just so glad to be here. This year, however, it is definitely annoying, so we approach Ivana for advice. It turns out that Italian houses don't have ventilation holes in the walls, which means that our habit of drying the washing inside the house during winter has created instant rising damp. The solution, according to Ivana, is simple: keep a fire burning all day long.

Silly us, clinging desperately to the misguided fantasy that heating systems are for keeping the house warm and fires for creating a cosy atmosphere in the evening. Were we not told by Sandro on day one about the importance of fire-powered heating? Have we not gazed in awe at Raffaello's enormous woodpile in the basement? And surely by now we must have cottoned on to the cost of mains gas in resource-poor Italy.[5] Take a tip from the locals: Ivana and Raffaello have a snazzy enclosed fireplace with tubes running through it and fans that pipe the hot air around the house. They barely use their gas heating system at all. They go through an awful lot of wood though.

And as any fool knows, you have to order your wood for the winter well ahead of time—in the middle of summer, in fact, when it's still nice and dry. Naturally, we foreign types have done no such thing, and as a result are now struggling to make do with poor quality December wood that hisses and fizzles and refuses to catch. Half my time these days seems to be spent in front of the tiny fireplace blowing madly through the traditional cultural medieval fire-blower thingy[6] that we bought from the hardware man at the market, hyperventilating madly in the process. Bring on the Melbourne summer…

And so the long and drawn-out process of de-Sansepolcrisation begins in earnest. With our remaining in-country time now down to

5 How could we forget: the shock of the first winter gas bill will remain one of our lasting memories of the Odyssey year.

6 A black metal tube with curly spikes on the end.

a matter of weeks rather than months, Eleni and I are having considerable trouble getting our heads around the concept of leaving. No more buying things for the house, no point looking for clothes; we are now going through the five stages of grief as we prepare to depart for good. It really hurts to see posters and flyers around town advertising festivals and concerts that we won't be around to see.

For a while there I thought I should try to experience the daily minutiae of life in Sansepolcro in an extra-hard and meaningful way in order to create lasting memories to take home. A complete waste of time, of course. In any case, we already have plenty of wonderful memories, not to mention a hard-disk full of photos.

So then I figured that it might be easier to disengage from Sansepolcro by convincing myself that we don't really fit in here or don't really like it that much.

There are times, I will admit—such as when it's cold and dark and rainy outside, or when I'm trying to wash myself in the world's smallest shower cubicle, or when I'm bent double over the hissing fire—there are times when this is theoretically achievable. But on a fine morning as I wander into town with Ruby, through the lanes and under the arches, stopping at La Spiga or Appy Bar to buy a morning snack, heading down through the piazza to deliver her to the ex-convent, then following up with a quiet coffee and panino and a half-hour brisk walk through the olive fields back to the desk… it's well-nigh impossible.

Early one morning there is a knock at the front door while the children are eating their customary breakfast of Very Nice[7] cornflakes and bananas. I open the door to see Ivana in her dressing gown, and her ashen face says it all: the end has come. Giorgio has finally left us.

Quickly I envelop her in my biggest, strongest embrace. (Presumably this is what the man is supposed to do.) Eleni appears from behind.

7 Very Nice is a brand of breakfast cereal manufactured in Bergamo. I kid you not.

'Is there anything we can do, Ivana?' she asks tentatively.

'No, no, it's enough that you're here for me,' she sobs.

And I think: how bizarre that we, who have known Ivana for barely a year, could be of comfort to her at a time like this. Surely such recent blow-ins can't provide the same emotional support as genuine family?

That we can only goes to demonstrate the depth of friendship that has developed between Ivana and Eleni over the year. For it is Eleni who has heard most of the stories about Giorgio, often after lunch in the gazebo when everyone else has gone, and Eleni who has provided a sensitive ear for Ivana during what has clearly been an agonising time. In fact the entire extended family thing is essentially driven by the Ivana-Eleni bond, with the rest of us all caught up in a big swirling milky whirlpool of love and pasta radiating out from this pulsating core.

Thus Ivana is much comforted to have Eleni here by her side at this moment.

For me this is all new territory; I haven't experienced a death in the family since I was a child. Hang on: I've never even met Giorgio—who am I to call it a death in the family? How is it that somebody I don't know feels like family? It's all mightily confusing.

Yet although I never knew Giorgio—and even Eleni has met him only once—we've heard so much about him from his adoring older sister. Ivana has talked us through all the photos on the mantelpiece: Giorgio with Cristina and Patrizia as a boy; Giorgio at University accepting his medical degree; Giorgio holding Camilla as a baby; Giorgio out in the back garden with the extended family. And Eleni has heard even more stories in the gazebo. So we feel as if we do know him, at least in some small way.

That Giorgio would succumb to the cancer was inevitable, a matter of counting the months. And it was generally accepted that the sooner he was relieved of his suffering the better. But none of that lessens the shock of having to let go of a beloved son and brother when the moment eventually arrives. Especially since he remained lucid and candid and even spirited right to the end—to all intents and purposes the Giorgio of old, except for being confined to his bed and amputated beyond belief.

The funeral takes place at a church out near the Coop supermarket. Half the township is here to pay their respects; there are more people waiting outside the church than inside listening to the service. In amongst the family contingent we are surprised to see an instantly recognisable face: that of Felix's admirer from the Old Men's Club at Bar Gerasmo. This turns out to be Piero, father of Michela, newly bereaved wife of Giorgio. Small world, isn't it! Small town, more like.

The long procession to the cemetery makes its way down the main road, oblivious to the traffic, then turns left at the Coop and files into the cemetery grounds. Although cremation is popular in Italy, Giorgio is to receive a full burial in the traditional manner.

So here we are standing on the rough earth in front of the hole. In goes the coffin, that most confronting of objects, taunting us, daring us to face up to the reality of death. It's even worse when the bobcat machine starts casually flinging dirt down on top. That's his *body* in there. And he was only fifty-two.

I have never even met the man, yet I am moved to tears. I look up to see Camilla's face buried in her mother's long winter coat and realise that there is a chilling parallel between Camilla and Giorgio, both of whom lost a parent at just nine years of age.

How I wish I could have met him. How I wish today were just another episode in the long-running daytime soapie *Sansepolcro Families*, with Giorgio being written out of the series in order to pursue a career in film.

When is the right time to die? Not when you've still got a nine-year-old daughter, that's for sure. In the back of my mind is the inevitable thought: there but for the grace of God… it doesn't bear thinking about.

Afterward, Patrizia takes a moment to thank us for being such a comfort to la mamma, and I realise for the first time that having the Australians downstairs might have had significant benefits for the family during the emotional upheaval.

Friendships aside, there can be no doubt that we have provided Ivana with a welcome distraction from the issue of Giorgio's declining health, thereby alleviating the burden on her immediate family. Although by extension this means that our decision to up sticks and leave while Giorgio was still very much alive could have appeared a little callous. We never thought of that.

I am seated at the desk opposite the impossibly handsome young travel agent (early Alec Baldwin?), pen poised in readiness to sign the credit card authorisation slip for the purchase of four one-way tickets to Australia.

The enormity of the moment presses down upon me. For it is this act, more than anything else, that finally, formally signifies the end of the Odyssey as we know it. Thus far we have been comforting ourselves with the notion that we have not yet paid for the tickets, that there is still time to change our minds. We could stay on indefinitely, find another house and car, forget about Australia, go Italian, learn how to drink black coffee and eat stale bread and buy firewood in summer and all the rest of it.

Yet although we could undoubtedly manage all these things, the real question is: do we want our children to grow up as Italians? What if Ruby turned into a Bar Gerasmo schoolgirl, smoking before school and plastering herself with make-up in her early teens? What if Felix turned into a classic Italian mummy's boy, great at soccer but hopeless in the kitchen? Could Australian parents cope with Italianised offspring?

Something is not quite right about all of this: surely we should not have to be grappling with such momentous ethical and moral dilemmas at this point. The Odyssey year was only ever meant to be a working holiday. We weren't meant to enjoy ourselves *this* much, goddamit. Where did it all go wrong?

Too much freedom of choice, too many big decisions. It's like confrontation time with the Telecom Italia Cable Guy on the hill at

Valfabbrica, magnified ten-fold. (And why, by the way, am I always left to make the tough decisions alone?) Mind you, instinct was right on that occasion. Let us place our faith in instinct once again today. And remember: Cultural Honesty.

The pen hits the paper. The ink flows. We're going home.

13

Denial

The last remaining matter to be sorted out before we depart is the good old HGV. Enormous hulking great petrol-guzzling beast though it is, the HGV has nevertheless been a faithful companion to us throughout the Odyssey, whisking the family to and fro across the Continent in comfort and safety. It has even developed a sense of humour—on long road trips the tape player occasionally overheats and refuses to turn off, subjecting us all to the same music at the same volume again and again.[1] And who could forget those legendary tangles with the snow up at Mt. Fumiaolo? How we laughed!

But now the end is near, and so the HGV faces its final curtain.

Over the last few months I have been making general enquiries around town but to no avail. Our car is simply too large, too strange and too foreign (for administrative purposes) to be of any interest to anybody here. I am routinely advised that our best bet would be to offload it to expatriate Brits in Italy, who are unlikely to be fazed by the English number plates. Having remained resolutely aloof from the expat network over the year, however, we don't have the necessary contacts.

Several months ago some friends in London suggested listing the HGV on a couple of British used car sites, but the response has been less than overwhelming, and the few emails that do trickle in are from people who make such ridiculously low offers or live in such remote parts of Europe that it is hardly worth the effort.

1 Ruby and Felix think this is wonderful—children love repetition.

Meanwhile, in the back of my mind there lurks a deliciously fiendish solution for the worst-case scenario where the HGV ultimately proves unsaleable. It is extremely naughty but highly tempting. It goes like this.

The HGV is still registered in John the cowboy's name. I never bothered to send the change of details form over to the UK, reasoning that it would only be one more thing to sort out at the end of our stay. We thus have no official connection to the car. We could leave it by the side of the road and flee the country and the authorities would be none the wiser.

Better still, we could drive it down to Morelli's place and dump it on the front lawn outside the lonely farmhouse with the doors locked and throw away the keys. Morelli would immediately recognise the car and identify the culprits—who would by then be winging their way across the globe. He would be forced to part with some of his beloved money[2] to have the vehicle towed away and properly disposed of. Take that you miserly old sod! My heart pounds with excitement just thinking about it.

Alas, the worst-case-scenario solution is summarily abandoned when I discover that the HGV is genuinely worth something to a second-hand dealer in the UK who specialises in left-hand-drive vehicles. This entails driving across Europe and catching the ferry over to the motherland, depositing the car with said dealer, then taking a flight to Milan, followed by various trains and buses back to the bosom of Sansepolcro.

A European road trip sounds like a great adventure, but there is the small matter of the registration papers; I'm not too keen on the idea of driving into and then through the UK in a car that isn't in my name and hasn't had its road tax or roadworthy paid in years. Should the British authorities choose to check the HGV over, things could get unpleasant.

Not to mention expensive. Then there are the French road police, said to be fearsome in the extreme, and the possibility of intense official scrutiny at the ferry crossing. The Morelli option looks increasingly appealing.

2 How about the money saved from the free tank of gasolio?

Nevertheless, arrangements are made, schedules drawn up and tickets purchased. The plan is to set off on Boxing Day and arrive in the UK three days later, then spend the weekend with friends in London before heading back home to Sansepolcro. Before heading back home to Australia.[3]

Having a concrete date for the demise of the HGV certainly focuses the mind regarding road trips. After further ruthless culling we manage to reduce to the list to just two: Verona, to check out the North's answer to the Colosseum, and Pisa, to climb the tower. After all, it's our duty as tourists.

And what an impressive medieval amphitheatre the Arena at Verona is, mainly on account of its remarkable state of preservation. The seating and stairways are all perfectly intact, and it's still used regularly for opera and concerts. The only concession to two thousand odd years of aging, weathering and earthquakes is that the outermost ring of seating has been completely destroyed, save for a forlorn fragment that hangs in space over at one end, providing a tantalising reminder of the original size of the thing. Apparently it used to hold over 20,000 spectators.

All the usual amphitheatre rules apply—excellent acoustics, superb sight-lines from every seat, a vast network of underground tunnels for transporting lions and hapless prisoners. As well as rock stars and roadies; this is, after all, the venue of the legendary summer Festivalbar pop concerts that we saw on the television. Such a pity that we never got to see one. Another regret to add to the list.

The rest of Verona—or what we manage to see of it in 24 hours, this being no more than a weekend dash—is instantly appealing, every bit a grand old European city of the large coffee table book variety. I give four and a half stars to the enormous oval-shaped central piazza, lined with shops and cafés, graced with fountains and boasting a suitably tall tower to one side. And Eleni is particularly excited by the discovery of an 87-centesimi shop lurking down a side-street off the piazza.

All in all, we are so taken with Verona that we award it the coveted title of Place We'd Most Like to Live After Sansepolcro.

3 Note the inherent contradiction.

Verona feels somehow cosy, like a big medieval dressing-gown and slippers: comfortable, well-worn, reassuring, familiar. Even the flagstones on the streets are nicely rounded from centuries of use. No nasty sharp corners in this town.

Raffaello informs us later that Verona gets horribly foggy in the winter, but I suspect this is campanalismo speaking. We will not be shaken from our conviction: Verona is fantastic. We'd live there.

A week later, it is time for the next in a succession of last-ever experiences in Italy: the final family HGV road trip.

This time we're off to fulfil our duty at Pisa. On the way we will be stopping at Lucca, which we visited briefly on the way home from Corsica in summer. Had it not been recommended to us by Ivana we might never have known about this wonderful city, surely one of the best-kept secrets on the tourist trail.

Lucca may not be a drawcard in the same league as nearby Pisa and Florence, but it ought to be: a stunningly beautiful and well-proportioned city crammed with fine churches and palazzos, long thoroughfares and huge tree-lined piazzas. And boasting the best castle walls in the world in space—a stupendous set of massive and perfectly preserved ramparts topped with a stately tree-lined boulevard that forms a complete four-kilometre circuit around the entire old quarter. On Sunday afternoons the Lucca walls are a mass of promenading and cycling humanity, a joyous celebration of life in the slow lane.

So we are very much looking forward to our return visit. Then along the way, something unexpected happens that increases our enjoyment of the trip tenfold. An English fellow living in St. Raphael on the French Riviera rings to ask whether we might by any remote chance still have that Volvo advertised for sale on the internet a few months back.

Why yes, as a matter of fact we still do.

I'd happily take it off your hands, he says, if you could deliver it to St. Raphael for me.

He wants to buy it! He wants to buy the HGV! And with a road trip to France into the bargain! (I'll be able to pop over to France for lunch after all.) It's too good to be true; I am ecstatic. It is only now, unburdened at last, that I appreciate how heavily the impending road trip to the UK has been weighing on my mind.

And the timing couldn't be better.[4] We will keep the HGV right up until Christmas, after which I will drive it over to France, then catch the overnight train back to Italy. For the last two weeks in Sansepolcro we will be without a car, but this is no problem since everything is within walking distance.

The last HGV road trip now has extra added resonance. Lucca is once again a joy to explore, not least because this time we have had the foresight to pack Ruby's bicycle into the back of the HGV. With Ruby on two wheels and Felix in the pram we manage to get more than half way around the city walls before coffee and gelato withdrawals set in. A special side trip is made to the famed round piazza, where Daddy insists on trying to set up a photo of the family eating square pizza slices in a round piazza. (Get it?) Alas, there is no pizza-by-the-slice place to be found. Truly a tragedy of thwarted comic talent.

Wandering through town after an early dinner, we spy an ice-skating rink set up in one of the magnificent sweeping piazzas and finally, albeit inadvertently, make good on our promise to take Ruby ice-skating. Though it is officially dinnertime now and the promenading hour is well past, there are still plenty of people strolling through the piazza. As with Verona, the atmosphere in town is relaxed and welcoming. In fact today has been so agreeable that it's now a toss-up between Lucca and Verona for the Town We'd Most Like to Live in After Sansepolcro award.

Verona is a fair way north. Raffaello might be right about the fog. Better give it to Lucca instead.

Here we are then, and there it is: the tower of a thousand postcards, butt of a million jokes, tourist drawcard of the ages. (After all, it's brought us here.)

4 Well actually, if he'd rung last week it would have saved me the cost of the return flight from London. But let's not split hairs.

The Leaning Tower of Pisa has only recently been reopened after years of painstaking straightening work,[5] so we consider ourselves lucky indeed to have made it inside. We desperately want Ruby to share in the experience, which means we have to lie and say she is eight in order to satisfy the regulations. The tour guides don't look entirely convinced, but they don't seem to care too much either.

Up we go, slowly round the spiral staircase, doing the Pisa shuffle. At the top the lean really is quite unnerving. So they didn't straighten it out too much, then. Meanwhile the wind is bloody freezing. And there's only a makeshift fence between us and a hundred-metre drop. My hands go clammy just from looking at it.

Can we go back down now?

Afterward we go for a wander around the streets of Pisa because it seems to be the right thing to do—it is after all a town, not just a tower. The streets of Pisa are pleasant enough, but nothing can possibly compete with award-winning Lucca. On the way back to the car we are obliged to run the gauntlet of souvenir shops and Ruby buys a tiny model of the tower.

And with that, we can finally rest easy in the knowledge that we've climbed the thing *and* contributed to the local economy. We came, we saw, we leaned. Bye-bye, Pisa!

The pre-Christmas salutations this year are tinged with sadness; another last-ever experience to add to the list. Moreover we seem to have lost the presepio-spotting urge, which blunts the focus of the Christmas season somewhat. Everything, it seems, is a bit more cold and dark and miserable this time around. Or maybe it's just us.

Those pathetic hissing fires don't help matters much either. Last year we had roaring beauties courtesy of the nice dry Valfabbrica wood, purchased in early October at the urging of the Signora Who Gets Things Done. Come to think of it, I vaguely recall Raffaello telling us to order in the wood months ago, back during summer. Why oh why did we not listen to him?

5 Not too much one would hope. No attraction in the Vertical Tower of Pisa.

A couple of nights before Christmas Ivana takes Eleni, Ruby and Felix to see a live presepio at a village down near San Giustino, featuring all the presepio standards such as banging anvils, threshing wheat, working in the fields and admiring the baby Jesus, except performed by real live people in medieval costumes. They are even baking bread, which is distributed to visitors. The children are most impressed.

Then on Christmas Eve Ivana escorts Eleni to midnight mass. Neither Eleni nor I would call ourselves religious, but as Eleni points out there is an undeniable allure to the church-going experience—the serenity, the ritual, the sense of togetherness. Not to mention the distinct possibility that it might provide answers to some of life's leading questions, if only we understood Italian a bit better.

Christmas day dawns bright and sunny, in stark contrast to the dismal drizzle of last year. The day begins with—what else?—breakfast at Bar Gerasmo. But only a light Italian-style breakfast this time, because soon we will be heading home for a massive festive lunch upstairs with a cast of thousands. This year there was no question that we would be dining together with the extended family. Ivana even went so far as to apologise for failing to extend the same hospitality last year.

Come on now, Ivana, we hardly knew each other then!

Wandering back from breakfast, we come across a sign saying that Sansepolcro's main bell tower (the campanile, the thing that generates feelings of campanalismo) will be open from 1.30 pm onwards. Wonderful: there's nothing like a good tower climb, especially when it's your very own. And it provides the ideal excuse for a walk after lunch, without which we might be tempted to just sit around and be excessively lazy.

Despite the recent trauma of Giorgio's passing, lunch is as lively as ever. The headcount today is an entirely respectable thirteen, including Camilla, Valentina and Michela. There is much talk of Giorgio, but in a positive way. One gets the sense that the family as a whole is finally able to move forward.

After lunch we go back into town to climb the vertical tower of Sansepolcro. It turns out that the campanile is administered by a volunteer group calling itself the Friends of the Sansepolcro Campanile—presumably motivated by a strong sense of campanalismo—who open it up to the public on only a handful of days during the year. How clever of Daddy to spot the sign! (Why did I never see it before?)

We arrive just in time to see men ringing bells, a special treat indeed given that Sansepolcro and Gubbio are said to be the only places where the bells are still rung manually.[6] They make an almighty racket when you're standing next to them and the force of the movement causes the tower to wobble noticeably, but it's worth it for the sensational view over the rooftops of the town in the darkening afternoon, with the Christmas lights twinkling down the main street and the mountains looming away in the distance.

On Boxing Day we take advantage of the continuing sunshine to go for a walk through the snow in the nearby mountains with veteran trekkers Patrizia and Sergio and their friend Marco (no relation), the grandparents having kindly offered to mind the children for the afternoon. Our trek takes us along a 2000-year-old Roman road which, to be brutally honest, looks like any old dirt track these days, but the sense of history is nice all the same.

Along the way, Patrizia and Sergo point out the remains of medieval watchtowers erected by the Romans to provide a chain of defence through the hills. As it happens, we can lay claim to intimate inside knowledge of Roman watchtowers: several months ago we had lunch with a family who lives in one. They showed us the little seats built into the walls under the windows where the Roman lackeys used to sit for hours on end, watching and waiting and rubbing their eyes and trying to stave off boredom. Imagine the job satisfaction in staring at a mountain all day long—not too far removed, when one thinks about it, to staring at a computer screen all day long.[7]

The scenery flashes past the window as the HGV speeds hungrily along the expressway, chewing up the white lines and hurtling

6 Warning, warning: Beethoven-Lived-Here alert.
7 Not that translation is at all boring.

inexorably towards its new home. For once the car is silent: I am too scared to listen to music lest the tape player decide to trot out its hilarious not-turning-off joke one last time for posterity, in which case I won't be able to park in Nice tonight. Imagine how the local gendarmes would react to a locked stationary English Volvo blasting out Italian pop music into the quiet of the evening.

Due to the enforced silence I now have several long hours at my disposal during the Last Great HGV Journey to reflect, once again, at great length, as if further reflection were necessary, which it isn't, on the exhilarating ride that has been the Italian Odyssey.

First things first, then. Why did we do it? On a purely superficial level that's easy: because it looked like fun.

But there must have been deeper, unexpressed motivations at work. What prompts a mild-mannered suburban family to take such a plunge into the unknown? What made us willingly put ourselves in a situation with such potential for disaster? Was it purely for the thrill and the challenge—a sort of married-couple-with-kids equivalent of bungy jumping? And if one accepts that every journey can be considered an expression of desires known and unknown, as the physical embodiment of a spiritual quest to understand one's deepest needs, then what were ours?[8]

Perhaps it is that today, in the comfortable and liberated twenty-first century, deliberately venturing outside the comfort zone is the only means we have of defining ourselves, of differentiating ourselves from the crowd. Perhaps deep down we all yearn to abandon the security of home and family every now and then in order to rediscover a sense of belonging somewhere else, and in the process to reaffirm how much we need to love and be loved.

Sometimes I even wonder whether at some deeper primordial level we secretly wanted Valfabbrica to be a disaster so we could emerge triumphantly at the other end, spiritually stronger for the experience and mentally toughened in a team-bonding motivational exercise kind of way.

Who would have thought that a simple year overseas would turn into such an intensive exercise in navel-gazing? During the course of

8 Pizza and coffee, obviously. Next question.

the year we have often asked ourselves what it is we were looking for in Italy. To fit in? To belong? To make friends? To be accepted amongst the locals?

In the end we can proudly claim to have achieved all of these things. And in a broader context, we can also claim to have honed our skills at adaptation to different environments and different cultures. And if this is what it means to be a good global citizen in the twenty-first century, then young Ruby in particular must be a model citizen.

So yes, it has been a fantastic experience in all the obvious ways: rural Italian lifestyle, small country town, extended family, uninterrupted supply of high-quality pizza. But if we are to be honest we must also acknowledge that the experience has been sugar-coated, in the sense that the Odyssey has essentially been an extended holiday.

During a normal holiday over a few weeks or months, it is understood that the reality of day-to-day life is put on hold. You forget about your everyday existence; you pretend that you don't have a job to get back to; you lose touch with the daily news and the sports results. These things are not important for the moment because you are living a different and infinitely more exciting life, aware all the while that it can only ever be a short-lived experience. This ability to suspend reality is precisely what makes a holiday feel like a holiday.

Most people can successfully keep reality at bay for a brief period, until either the holiday ends or reality intrudes.[9] Whereas we managed to stretch it out to sixteen months!

And what a fantastic sixteen months it has been. But is it realistic to expect that it would always be this good? No. Life cannot remain sugar-coated for ever. I think instinctively we knew this all along; hence the decision to return to Australia, however agonising, was inevitable.

The theory of suspended reality is directly relevant to the behaviour of expatriates in Italy. Too many expats, it seems to me, want to enjoy the freedoms of being far from home but without making any commensurate connection with their new surroundings.

9 Mobile phones are good for this.

They remain resolutely aloof from their adopted country, instead inhabiting a fantasy world consisting solely of medieval artworks, hilltop views and intriguing local dishes.

Sixteen months of suspended reality is already pushing it; any longer, one suspects, is downright unhealthy. Too many years spent in the fantasy world breeds a certain type of arrogance and contempt, a distorted mindset that allows people to behave in ways they wouldn't dream of back home. Like driving through roadblocks.

This phenomenon is already occurring out in Chiantishire, generating a growing sense of resentment among the locals. The British are said to be unfriendly; they stick to themselves too much; they shop at the big supermarkets that open during siesta hours so they don't have to mingle with ordinary Italians. There are entire towns, it is whispered, that have been taken over by the British. Even discounting for exaggeration, the underlying sentiment is genuine.

Here in Sansepolcro, Cristina complains of Brits who occasionally march into the real estate agency and start barking loudly at her in English, as if expecting to trigger some sort of spontaneous improvement in her foreign language skills.

I wouldn't go over to England and start shouting at them in Italian, she sighs in exasperation. What gives them the right to behave like that here?

To which one can only reply: better that we leave right now before it starts happening to us. Cultural Honesty and all that.

The coastal road from Nice to St. Raphael winds along one of the most picturesque sections of the French Riviera, providing an unexpected bonus on the final leg of the Last Great HGV Journey. I am in no mind to admire the scenery, however; imagine running off the road at this stage in proceedings. Luckily there are regular lookout stops on the way for the benefit of single drivers. Today's route even passes through world-famous Cannes which, devoid of the film festival and Our Nicole and other starlets, comes across as an uninspired collection of tarted up designer shops.

Within the hour the HGV is parked outside the designated meeting place at St. Raphael station. The setting—waiting in a foreign environment to sell a car to a complete stranger—prompts an involuntary flashback to the time we trooped down the main street of Valfabbrica with the children to collect our new car, trusting only in blind faith and human nature. I recall the wave of panic on that day, and the same fear grips me now: what if the guy simply fails to show up? How embarrassing! Although then I could go back and dump the car at Morelli's place I suppose.

Happily, the inherent goodness of human nature prevails once again. Chris the potential purchaser duly appears, and suggests that we repair to a nearby car park for the official handover. He leads me down to a marina on the edge of town, under a boom gate and around the back out of view. If this were a film, the music would be swelling ominously: it's a sting operation you fool! As soon as you arrive twenty federal agents will spring out and surround the HGV and demand the registration papers!

I guess if I want to be rid of the thing, I'm just going to have to take that risk.

At the marina Chris dismounts, looks over the HGV and declares it satisfactory. The transaction itself is short and sweet and wonderfully shady: I hand over the registration form, and he produces an envelope stuffed with cash.

Go on, count it, he says.

What, here? In full view of government spies?

And that's it. The sale has been concluded with alarming speed. Can it really be this easy to sell a car in this day and age? If we were in Italy there would be all manner of official documentation to be exchanged—receipts, transfer of insurance, proof of sale, authorisation from a notary. Presumably the same applies elsewhere in Europe. Yet when an Australian sells a car to an Englishman in the south of France, cash in an envelope is the order of the day. How can this be?

The lawlessness of it all sheds new light on the expat issue. Here we both are, carrying on as if we were somehow exempt from the normal laws and procedures of the land. (Whatever they might be: the HGV is registered in the UK, insured in Italy and being sold in France, and I have no knowledge of due process in this country. Chris may know, but he's not letting on.) But I really don't care; I'm just so relieved to have it taken off my hands.

Chris kindly drops me back in the centre of town. After a few hours touring the bakeries and assembling a selection of provisions for the return journey, I pop back into the station to wait out the last few hours. And discover to my horror that the overnight train through to Pisa has been cancelled on account of repair work in the tunnel under Monte Carlo, to be replaced by a convoluted arrangement of trains and buses.

The anticipated relaxing cake-filled journey back to Sansepolcro is thus transformed into an all-night marathon involving several hours waiting for transfers at deserted freezing railway stations with nary a coffee to tide me over. The only compensation is catching a glimpse of the twinkling lights of the luxury yachts bobbing away serenely in Monte Carlo harbour as we all trudge resignedly along beside the railway line in the semi-darkness near the tunnel entrance.

When the train finally pulls into Pisa at some ungodly hour of the morning for yet another transfer, the station bar has opened for the day, heaven be praised.

It is massively comforting to be back on Italian soil, and in particular at the counter of a real Italian bar. Why I cannot say; this is not my homeland, this is not my language, these are not my people, yet it feels much more warm and friendly here. Perhaps it is just a relative thing, in that Italy is more familiar to me than France. Or maybe it's because they've got the heaters on.

Five trains and two buses later I am finally back in civilisation. Eleni and I agree that it is actually rather nice to be without the car. The expanded SMA supermarket now provides everything we could possibly need right on our doorstep, so for the last couple of weeks we will just potter about in town. It is a bit weird to step out the front door and not see the HGV parked in the street as usual. But then, everything is a bit weird at the moment.

Our last New Year's Day in Sansepolcro is memorable chiefly for the fact I am unable to locate a single trusted bar open for breakfast and am obliged to turn tail and eat toast at home for the first time in so long I can't even remember the last time.

Over the last year both Eleni and I, but particularly I, have become addicted to the morning routine of breakfast at the bar. For one thing, it's actually quite cheap. While many things in Italy may be costly—gas and electricity come to mind, as well as anything at all to do with the car—breakfast is not one of them. My preferred menu of a panino and a cornetto washed down with a Stained Milk costs less than three Euros. At this price, one can have breakfast at the bar every day. And one does.

The upshot, however, is that one is now constitutionally incapable of eating breakfast at home. The Simultaneous Bar Closure Fiasco thus comes as a tremendous shock to the system, a veritable effrontery. Never mind, we shall nobly rise above it. For very soon, we will be in a place where there are no decent bars at all.

On the morning itself we wake at five, heave the luggage into the hire car and head upstairs for the Last Ever Meal at the home of our two favourite people in all of Italy.

Today we are treated to a traditional cultural Italian breakfast[10] of cornetti with jam for us and tinder-dry biscottate slathered with Nutella for the children. Plus Ivana has made up her very own version of the Stained Milk, using the frother jug she bought down at the market especially for the occasion. Ivana confesses that she has recently developed a taste for milky coffee of a morning, which makes us very proud. If we can leave this country with Raffaello clearing the dishes

10 Sort of. A really genuine traditional Italian breakfast, as eaten by people such as Morelli, consists of a large cup of coffee with biscuits dissolved in it to produce a thick milky sludge. Enough said.

and Ivana drinking Stained Milks then surely we will have made an important contribution to cross-cultural understanding.

The conversation is a trifle stilted; it isn't easy at this hour of the morning. Anyway, how can we possibly start to say goodbye to all of this? How can we even begin to thank them for a year of friendship and fun, of kindly advice and patient tuition, of endless pasta and unconditional love?

The solution is to avoid the goodbyes altogether. Yes, we're going back to Australia, but this is by no means the end. We'll be back to visit someday. Ivana promises to keep a room ready for whenever someday comes. If only Australia weren't so bloody far away we'd be back every few months, like those lucky Brits with their cut-price airfares, popping across to the Continent for the weekend whenever they feel like it.

Strangely, as we climb into the car (Last Ever Car Trip) and prepare to head off, there are no tears. But as we wind our way out the back of Sansepolcro and through the familiar olive fields (Last Ever Glimpse of Vines), I feel hollow to the pit of my stomach. It's exciting to be going home and yet… which home? *Home is where your family is.* Which family? We've got family on both sides of the globe now.

Flying down the freeway with my head feeling numb. In the passenger seat Eleni has dissolved into floods of tears. Suspended in our own separate bubbles of misery, we're incapable of comforting one another. Leaving Italy isn't easy, you know, but we had to go. Knowing me knowing you, it's the best we can do.

Not even the Abba tape can cheer us up.

On the outskirts of Rome we fill up with petrol (Last Ever Petrol Stop). It costs next to nothing. Of course; non-hulking diesel cars are exceptionally fuel-efficient. Think how many pizzas we were cheated out of by the HGV! More regrets.

At the airport we chat with one of the baggage check-in staff about the fun we've had. I suspect it still hasn't dawned on us that we are in the process of slamming the door shut on the most entertaining and fulfilling chapter in our lives. Deliberately. Irrationally. Stupidly.

Every moment now is a last-ever experience. Last ever proper Italian coffee. Last ever over-the-counter purchase in Italy. Last ever conversation in Italian. Is this how it all ends—in a series of lists?

Twenty-four hours later we're stepping out of the airport into a balmy Melbourne evening, with the smell of jet fuel and the family welcome and the suitcase trolleys and the yellow taxis and the rush of familiarity.

And half an hour after that I'm sitting out on the back deck of our house in the gloom, sulking.

I recognise this place all right, but is it mine?

Epilogue

The place looks just the same. I can see it all laid out below me from up here on the balcony of the bell tower. Or is it the window of the plane? Hard to say. There's the familiar grid of straight streets: the palazzos, the piazza, Appy Bar, the gelato shop, the school at Santa Chiara, the underground bakery, the bank. The scaffolding's still up on the front of that shop across from the theatre, and they're still doing up the back of Sale e Pepe. But look—work has finally finished in the laneway opposite the cathedral! Will wonders never cease.

Down the main street now, heading to Bar Gerasmo. People floating past, everything's a bit quiet. Shoes softly scuffing on the paving stones, hardly any sound, no voices. Was it always like this? Plenty of them recognise us and stop for a chat. They're all pleased to see us, like renewing old acquaintances should be. Double kisses all round. I've dreamt this already a hundred times, rehearsed it in my head over and over again. How excited will I be? How pleased will they be? How will I react?

Through the door of Bar Gerasmo now, steeling myself for an explosive round of greetings with Fabrizio and the gang. I've been dreading this moment in a way—what to say, how to sound pleased but without overdoing it. The old Italian's a bit rusty, should have practiced more. We've bought presents for everyone, little gifts to say… to say what? Here, take this; now make a fuss of us.

And they do, for a minute. Before resuming their normal routines once more. Because life goes on, whereas we were only ever passing through, and now we're just another group of visitors who came, and stayed, and fell in love with the place, but ultimately left. Real locals don't leave, do they? Tourists do. Even ones who know the way to the nearest petrol station. That's the difference.

Eleni cried bitterly when we got back. I want to go back to Sansepolcro, she sobbed. I would have cried too, but for social conditioning. We heard later that Ivana cried for an entire day after we left. How can so much pain and heartache be right?

My heart remained firmly trapped within the walls of a small township in Tuscany. There were too many reminders. Every day the computer flashed up a new photo from the Odyssey. Every day the Radio Italia website provided me with another fix of Italian pop. Every day I wrote some more of this book. The sugar-coated memories were never far away. Listening to Radio Italia was particularly upsetting on account of their habit of promoting outdoor summer concerts starring my favourite singers. Probably at the Arena in Verona, too.

And it wasn't easy readjusting to life in Melbourne.

Wooden floorboards are too noisy. Italian stone floors may be hard and unforgiving, and downright cold in winter, but at least they don't squeak.

The children were no longer any good on long car trips. The 'are we there yet?' questions from the back seat started after only half an hour. How did we ever manage to get them to Salzburg and back?

The local fruiterer turned out to be Greek instead of Italian. So much for regular language practice.

During our absence the cost of eating out had risen substantially—coffees, breakfast, pizza, wine, everything seemed cheaper back in Italy.

Daily exercise wasn't the same. Traipsing along the streets of suburban Melbourne hardly compares with a stroll through the olive groves.

And there was no central piazza for soccer, no main thoroughfare for perambulating. Where were we supposed to congregate? In front of the television, presumably.

But *Who Wants to be a Millionaire* was too boring in English.

It was all wrong. The children didn't understand what we were carrying on about. Ruby told us to get over it—that's easy when you're seven, when there's no such thing as nostalgia or regret.

Frequent calls were made to Ivana and Raffaello, but international phone conversations never feel natural. Poor line quality stifles linguistic creativity. And anyway, how many different ways are there to say 'wish we were still there' with a limited vocabulary?

After several months of tears and denial, we gave in to our deepest desires and took advantage of some cheap tickets via Japan to make a return trip to Sansepolcro, in an attempt bring some closure to the Italian Odyssey.

Of course it was a ridiculous, impulsive, spur-of-the-moment decision of the heart, neither sensible nor financially prudent. Of course we were out of our minds. Again. We were well aware of that. But it felt good, really good. We were going home!

Everything is exactly as it was. But of course; it's been like this for half a millennium, why would a mere nine months make any difference?

So strangely familiar… actually no, not strange at all. This is normal, utterly normal. This was our life for a year. This was our town, our place. We belonged here. This could be our place again, you know, says a little voice in my head. Why not come back and do it all over again?

More confusion: the return trip was supposed to bring closure, but it's only stirred things up again.

Cursed by the tyranny of distance! Then again, if we hadn't been so far from home in the first place it might not have been such a grand adventure. [*Oh yes it would have. Ed.*]

At Bar Gerasmo we give Fabrizio a little plastic sushi on a plate, brought all the way from Japan. He looks at it in bewilderment; he has no idea what it is. I thought sushi was pretty much a worldwide phenomenon by now, but this corner of Italy is safely cosseted away from much of the world. Which is precisely its appeal: unchanging, non-threatening, protected. Untouched by sushi. If sushi is a metaphor for change and globalisation, then it is surely better that Fabrizio has never heard of it.

Next we pop over to Appennini to exchange greetings. Ester looks somehow different this morning, not quite as ravishing. Perhaps she had a late night last night; or maybe she is no longer the same Ester? People do change, after all; you think you know them but you don't really. What right do we have to expect Sansepolcro to remain frozen in time like it was when we lived here?

Once again I find myself wandering the streets trying to imprint the sights and sounds and smells of the town in my memory, for in barely a week it will be cruelly wrenched away from me. And once again it is absolutely futile.

The return trip has proved at once comforting and unsettling. We've spent nine months dreaming of this moment and here we are at last, yet there is no excitement. It is an anticlimax. This not a special holiday; this is life as usual, at home in Sansepolcro.

So many questions remain unanswered.

When do they put their children to bed? Is the letter Z worth less in Italian Scrabble? Is the ability to make pizza learned or genetically inherited? How do they make the Very Nice cornflakes very nice? What will happen to the high-school girls from Bar Gerasmo? Is Telecom Italia really any worse than Telecoms in other countries?

And is life in Italy really that much better, or are we all under the spell of some sort of collective delusion?

I wonder sometimes if there isn't some terrible dark side to Italy that makes life hell for ordinary Italians but is hidden from happy-go-lucky outsiders. Crippling taxes perhaps? Stifling bureaucracy? Government meddling? Evil gypsies? Whatever it is, we didn't see it.

What we did see was people going about their daily business, wandering along the main street to the shops and stopping to chat and going out for pizza with friends, and people riding bikes and splashing about at the pool and meeting up for gelatos in the piazza with friends, and people finishing school and looking for jobs and going out for drinks at the bar with friends and THEY THINK IT'S NORMAL,

THEY DON'T REALISE THEY'RE LIVING IN PARADISE.

Or do they? I recall Raffaello regaling us constantly with the comment, '*See how wonderful life is in la bella Italia*!' Although that was often delivered with a heavy dose of irony, like the day the first gas bill arrived.

At least we managed to solve one of the major burning issues of the Odyssey year. Our absurdly cramped bathroom, with its two mammoth sinks down one end and the toilet squished in next to the shower down the other, turns out to have been designed—if that is the word—by Raffaello, without consulting Ivana. Truly a boy's bathroom.

But as for the rest of it, I just don't know any more, I don't know what to think, I don't know how I'm supposed to feel. What I do know is that I'd love to go back and do it all again.[1]

After all, we got ourselves where we wanted to be. Sansepolcro feels like home. We could fly over tomorrow, find a house and car, send the children to school, take breakfast daily at Bar Gerasmo, shop at the market, learn more of the language, eat more of the food, ask more piercing questions, solve more cultural conundrums. (And deliver another full report. Stay tuned for the sequel.)

But can a soufflé rise twice? Now *that's* the real question.

1 Minus the Valfabbrica bit.

Available from New Holland Publishers (Australia)

ISBN: 9781741103533

Available from New Holland Publishers (Australia)

ISBN: 9781741100594

Available from New Holland Publishers (Australia)

ISBN: 9781741103960

Available from New Holland Publishers (Australia)

ISBN: 9781741101522